DRAWING & PAINTING BOTANICALS FOR ARTISTS

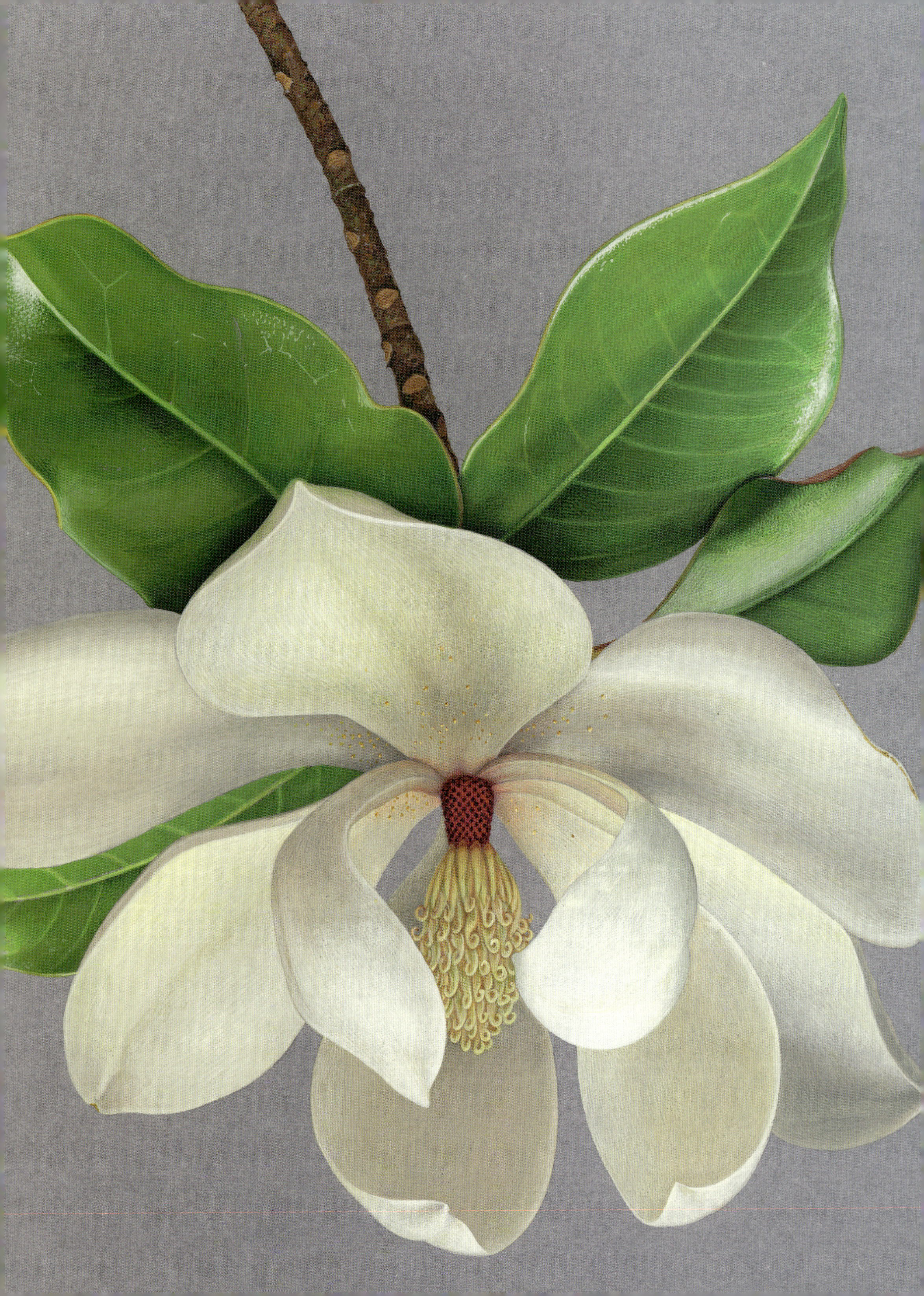

DRAWING & PAINTING BOTANICALS FOR ARTISTS

How to Create Beautifully Detailed Plant and Flower Illustrations

KAREN KLUGLEIN

ROCKPORT

First published in 2020 by Rockport Publishers, an imprint of The Quarto Group,
100 Cummings Center, Suite 265-D, Beverly, MA 01915, USA.
T (978) 282-9590 F (978) 283-2742 QuartoKnows.com

10 9 8 7 6 5 4 3

ISBN: 978-1-63159-857-9

Digital edition published in 2020
eISBN: 978-1-63159-858-6

Library of Congress Cataloging-in-Publication Data

Names: Kluglein, Karen, author.
Title: Drawing and painting botanicals for artists : how to create beautifully detailed plant and flower illustrations / Karen Kluglein.
Description: Beverly, MA, USA : Rockport Publishers, 2020. | Includes bibliographical references and index. | Summary: "Drawing and Painting Botanicals for Artists offers artists at all skill levels a comprehensive survey of drawing and painting mediums and techniques, along with guidance for creating accurate, detailed, and beautiful botanical artworks"-- Provided by publisher.
Identifiers: LCCN 2020002537 | ISBN 9781631598579 | ISBN 9781631598586 (eISBN)
Subjects: LCSH: Botanical illustration--Technique.
Classification: LCC QK98.24 K59 2020 | DDC 581--dc23
LC record available at https://lccn.loc.gov/2020002537

Design: Samantha J. Bednarek
Cover Image: Karen Kluglein
Page Layout: Samantha J. Bednarek
Photography: Karen Kluglein and Shutterstock on page 72 and 124
Illustration: Karen Kluglein

Printed in China

Dedication

*To my two artistic parents
who were always an inspiration
and forever encouraging.*

Contents

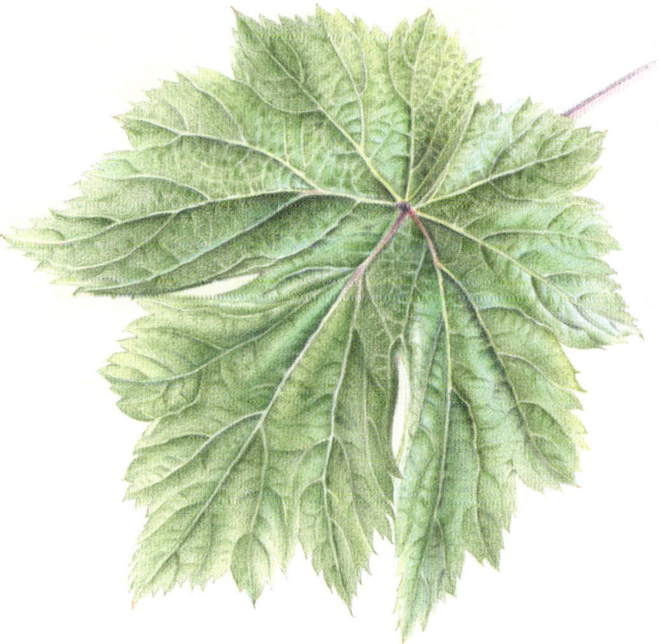

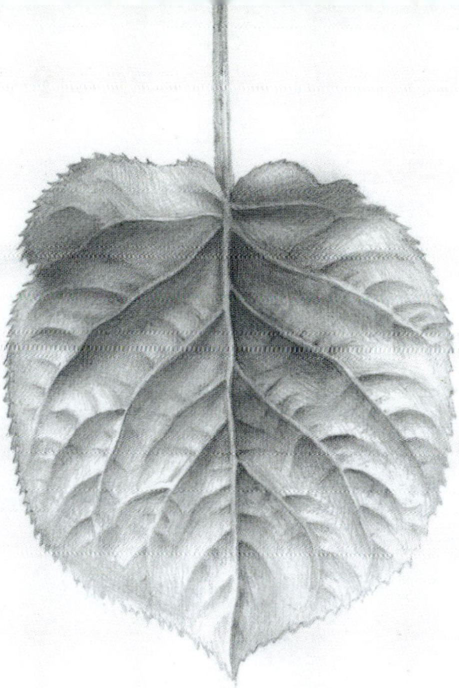

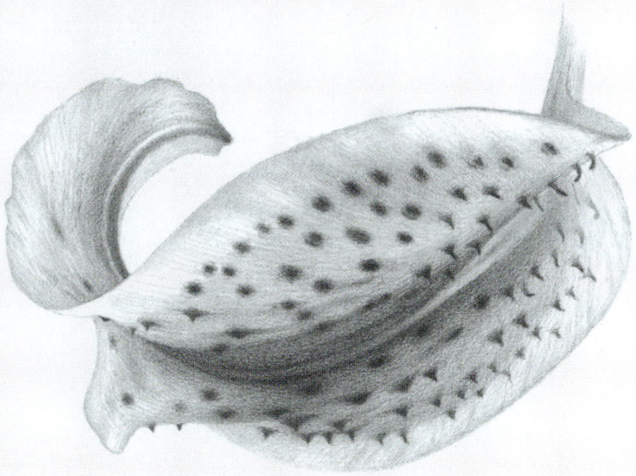

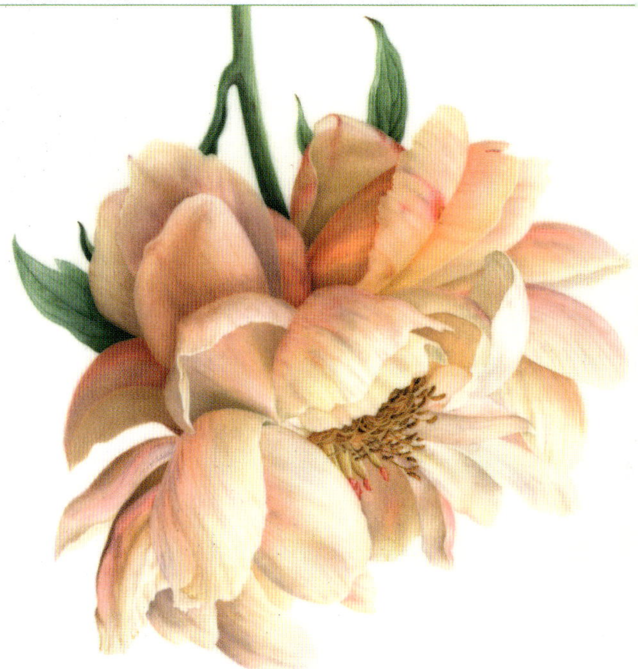

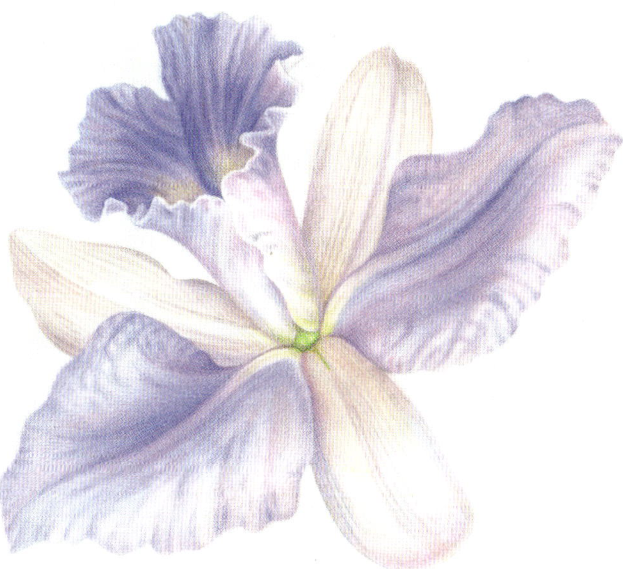

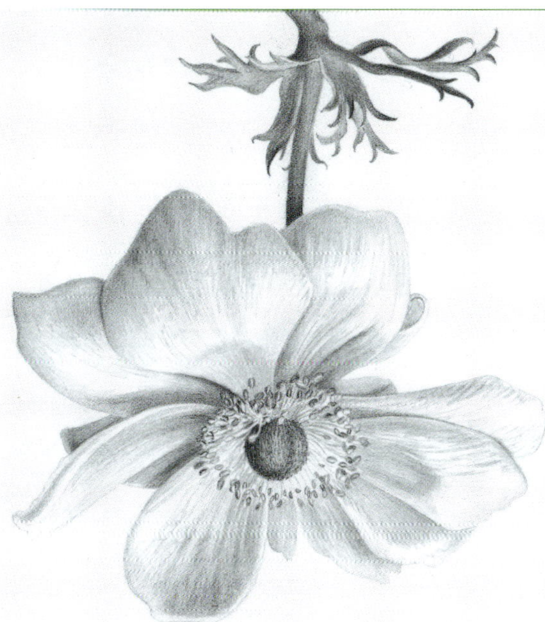

Introduction

In botanical art, we're enhancing what we see in the specimen before us. The bend of a stem or curve of a leaf can be changed to artfully portray our subject. We begin with scientific accuracy, being mindful of extracting details in every possible way. But then the artistic part comes in and we can take some liberties to make the image our own.

There are no shortcuts with this style of botanical art. Botanical drawings show minute detail and bring out form and textures in much the same way as painting; the only difference is the medium used.

It can be labor-intensive, especially with the watercolor finishing work of details and drybrush. Watercolor, though known to be a difficult medium to work with—after all, we're trying to control water!—is also quite adaptable. There's no one correct way or rule to approach this. Whatever works for you and gives you the results you want is fine. But here, I show what works for me. I've tried to provide the information, tips, and tricks that I know, and I hope you find something to take away from this book.

The slow process used can be meditative and relaxing, so enjoy it as you go and remember that practice makes perfect!

LEARNING TO SEE, LEARNING TO DRAW

What helped me most when I was a young student were the many hours I spent drawing.

My high school had an experimental program that gave students free time during the day to use as they wished. The hope was that the time would be used constructively in something that interested them. It enabled me to spend many hours drawing in sketchbooks and exploring numerous mediums in the art room.

Drawing for hours on end trains your eye and develops hand-eye coordination. You're able to look at something in front of you and immediately know how you'd go about representing it. You'll know the angle of a line needed or how to mimic a curve. You'll know how dark or light something should be and how to make correct proportions and perspective. Little by little, your work will improve. This ability just takes practice and time, and eventually, it will come naturally.

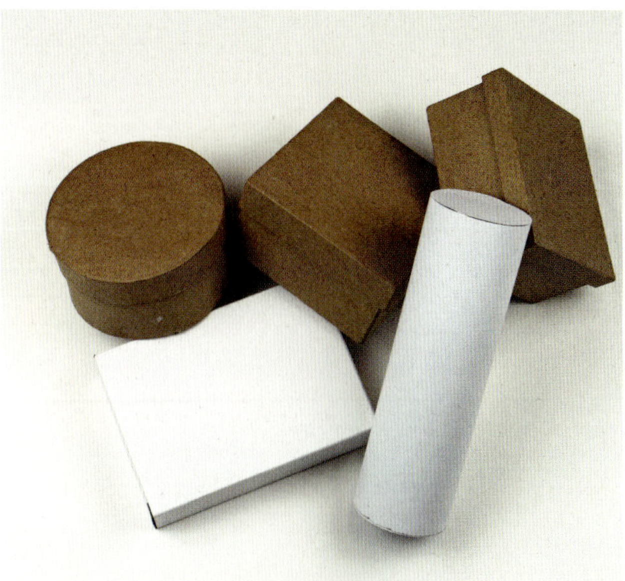

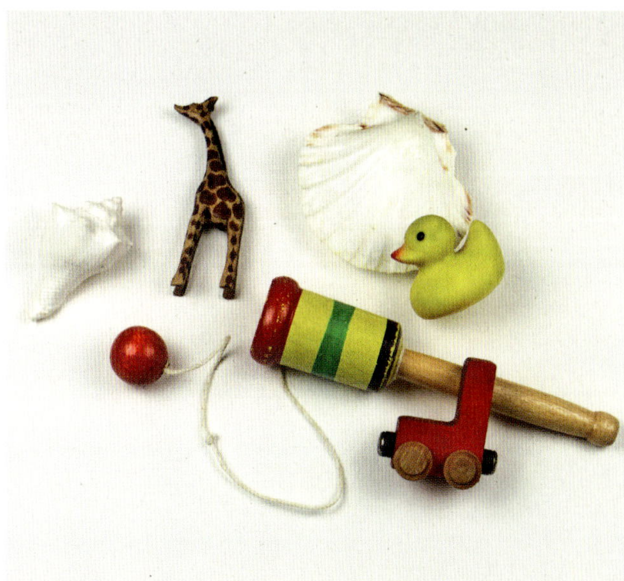

Train your eye with simple shapes and then gradually try drawing more complicated objects.

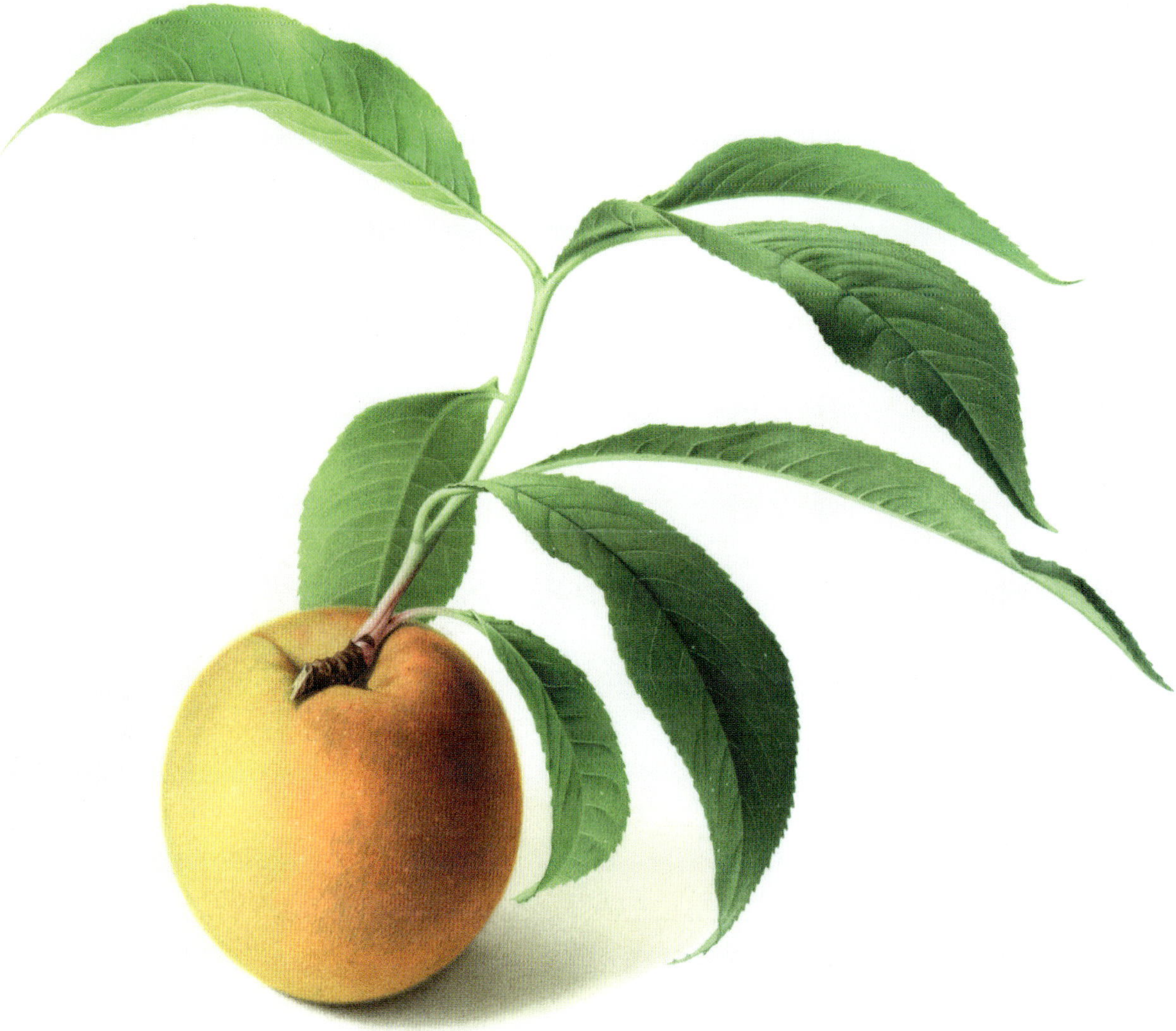

"August Peach" watercolor on paper 8" x 10" (20.3 cm x 25.4 cm)

CONSIDER THE SUBJECT

Choose something with an attractive shape, maybe a lyrical curved stem or petal or the delicate filigree of a dried autumn leaf. It makes the task easier when you find a personal connection to your subject and feel strongly about portraying it. Working with a real specimen, as opposed to a photo, is of paramount importance to convey the accuracy needed in botanical drawing. Photos may be taken and used as reference when the blossom has faded, but they aren't a reliable substitute for seeing the real thing in front of you and taking detailed notes. These notes can be in the form of written words as well as small graphite or colored pencil sketches that explain what you see before you. They're for your eyes only, just to remind you of your observations.

For more on working from a live specimen versus a photo, see pages 26-27.

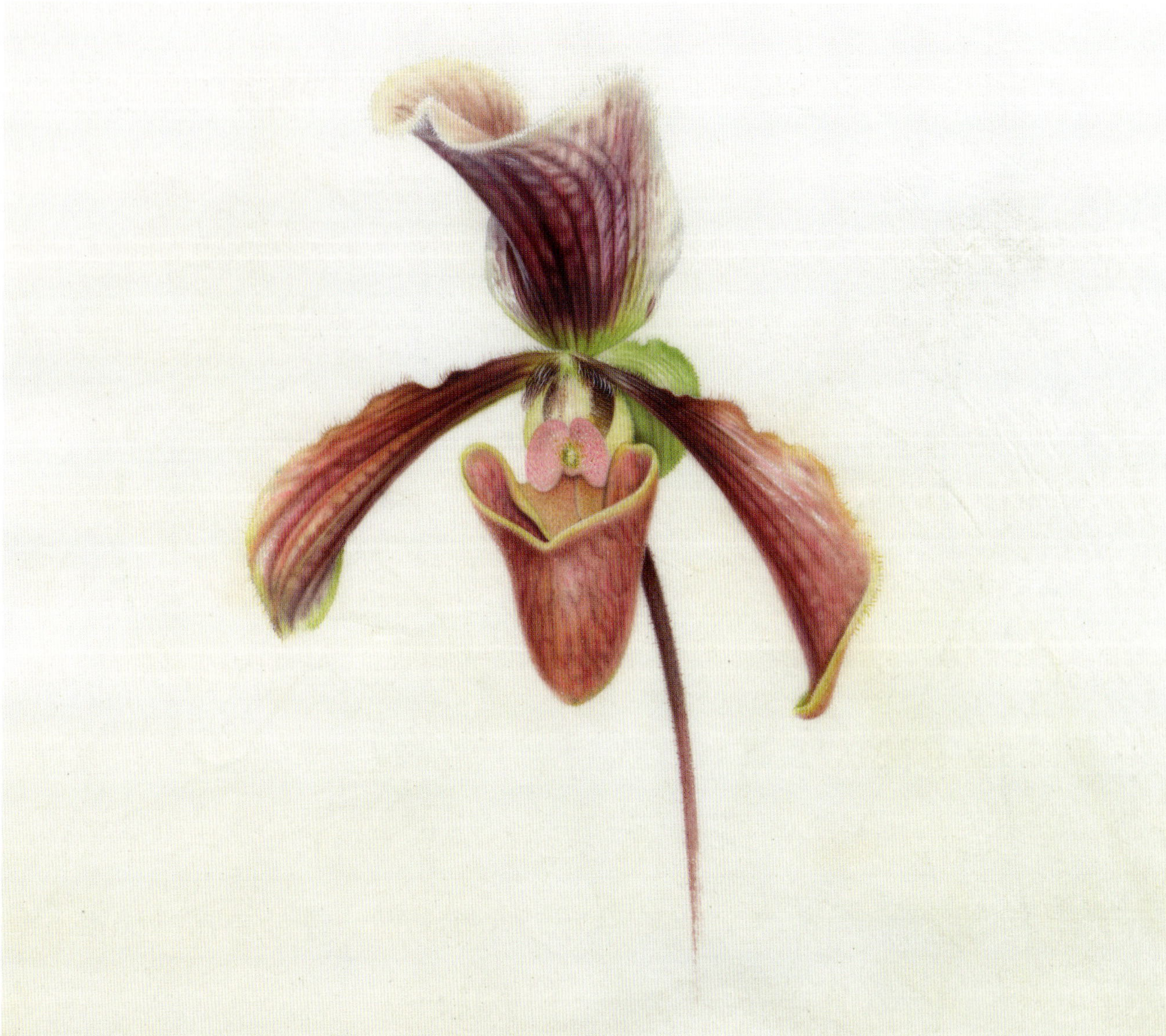

"Slipper Orchid" *Cypripedium reginae* watercolor on vellum 7" x 7" (17.8 cm x 17.8 cm)

KEY TERMS

I've included these brief definitions of botanical subjects and the art materials and techniques featured in this book so you can familiarize yourself with the terminology used throughout.

- **Ambient color:** The reflected color from what surrounds the subject.
- **Archival:** A material that's especially permanent and acid-free so it will withstand time.
- **Atmospheric perspective:** A method of creating the illusion of depth in artwork. As objects recede into the distance, they may become less clear and have less contrast and color.
- **Background:** The part of the artwork that appears to be farthest from the viewer (opposite of foreground).
- **Bloom:** A natural waxy, dusky blue protective coating on the surface of some fruit.
- **Blotting:** The process of removing pigment with an absorbent material from the painting's surface.
- **Botanical art:** Artwork that's botanically and scientifically accurate but that emphasizes aesthetic.
- **Botanical art:** Artwork that's botanically and scientifically accurate but emphasizes aesthetic value and doesn't include all the information needed by a botanist for identification. *See also* **Botanical illustration** and **Floral painting**.

- **Botanical illustration:** Artwork that emphasizes scientific accuracy and includes all the important aspects of a plant for identification. It may also include the plant's life cycle and dissections. *See also* **Botanical art** and **Floral painting**.
- **Burnishing:** A technique of blending with a colorless or light pencil (after a colored pencil drawing is complete), until none of the paper's tooth, or texture, shows through.
- **Cold-pressed paper:** Paper manufactured with a bumpy textured surface.
- **Color mapping:** The technique of placing different colors in different areas of your drawing or painting.
- **Complementary color:** Two colors on opposite sides of the color wheel (for example, red and green or orange and blue).
- **Composition:** The placement or arrangement of visual elements in an artwork.
- **Contour:** The outline that defines a form, figure, or body.
- **Contrast:** The placement of opposites (light and dark, rough and smooth, large and small) in a piece of art to create visual interest and drama.
- **Crosshatching:** The application of layers of lines with pencil or paint going in different directions.
- **Daylight bulb:** A full-spectrum lightbulb that emulates the quality of natural daylight.
- **Depth:** The apparent distance from near to far in artwork.
- **Dimension:** The perception of when a shape seems to stand out from surrounding space or creates the illusion of being solid.
- **Divider:** An adjustable tool, similar to a compass, that has points at both ends and is used for measuring.
- **Drybrush:** A watercolor painting technique that uses a small amount of water to draw with the brush.
- **Fine-point markers:** These are drawing pens of varying size and color with free-flowing ink.
- **Fixative:** A liquid that's usually sprayed over a finished piece of artwork to preserve it and prevent smudging.
- **Floral painting:** Artwork focused primarily on presenting a pleasing rendering and less on scientific accuracy. A floral painting may include a background or have an impressionistic style. *See also* **Botanical art** and **Botanical illustration**.
- **Foreground:** This is the part of the artwork that appears to be closest to the viewer (the opposite of background).
- **Foreshortened:** The perspective of an object seen at a distorted angle, often coming towards the viewer.
- **Form:** An element that has length, width, and depth and appears three dimensional.
- **Gesso:** A water-based paint used to create a hard surface to draw or paint on.
- **Gestural:** An energetic, expressive sweep of the artist's hand deliberately emphasizing movement.
- **Gouache:** A water-based paint with an opaque quality that comes from white pigment or chalk in the paint.
- **Gradation:** A gradual change in value from dark to light, one color hue to another, or one texture to another. A gradation can occur over a short or large span but should be smooth.
- **Graphite:** A form of carbon found in the lead of a pencil compressed to varying degrees of hardness.
- **Hand-eye coordination:** The ability of your eye to coordinate the information received to control and direct your hands in the accomplishment of a given task, such as drawing or painting.
- **Helping hands tool:** A tool with adjustable movable clips used to keep your specimen in place.
- **Highlight:** An area or spot that's highly illuminated.
- **Hot-pressed paper:** This is paper manufactured with a smooth surface finish.
- **Illustration board:** Surface made by mounting sheets of drawing paper on both sides of a stiff backing, such as a heavyweight paperboard.
- **Kneaded eraser (putty rubber):** A soft eraser that can be shaped by hand and used to remove graphite.
- **Lifting:** The process of removing medium (paint or graphite) from the painting's surface.

- **Lightfastness:** The ability to resist UV rays and fading, core durability, and resistance to water.
- **Local color:** This is the color of the object itself. It's the color that isn't changed by light, shadow, or reflections.
- **Mapping:** The technique of defining areas of differing colors in your art.
- **Masking fluid:** A liquid product that's applied to the painting's surface where it dries and repels paint.
- **Mottling:** When a surface has irregular spots of varying values and sizes it's referred to as *mottled*.
- **Opaque:** When light does not easily pass through a surface or paint, it's called *opaque*.
- **Palette:** A surface on which to put and mix your paints.
- **Papillae:** Tiny outgrowths located on the surface of a petal or a leaf.
- **Perspective:** A system or process of representing the way elements appear to get smaller and closer together the farther away they are from the viewer.
- **Pigment:** The coloring ingredient of paint that's insoluble and when applied, impart their color by staying on the surface.
- **Plate finish:** This is a paper having an extremely smooth finish that's made using a metal plate.
- **Proportion and scale:** The size, location, or amount of one element in relation to another in the artwork. They help the viewer to make sense of the artwork.
- **Reducing glass:** A glass lens that allows you to see your artwork from a distance perspective of reduced size, like a magnifying glass in reverse.
- **Reference:** These are the supplies you can refer back to when drawing or painting. They can be your specimen, written color notes, and photos.
- **Reflected light:** Light that bounces from a source or surface other than the primary light source.
- **Scientific accuracy:** This is artwork that's scientifically and botanically correct. Parts of the specimen are portrayed in an accurate way so that the plant can be identified.
- **Sepal:** A leaf-shaped structure that's found in flowering plants.
- **Shadow:** A shadow is a dark area where light is blocked by an opaque object.
- **Silverpoint:** The technique of drawing with a silver wire on a prepared surface, which can be either a gessoed board or paper.
- **Specimen:** A sample of a flower or plant that you use as your subject. Botanical artists collect specimens so they can get a better look at something to study it.
- **Staining:** Refers to those colors of paint that can't easily be removed and leave a "stain."
- **Style:** When artwork is distinctive and recognizable to a particular artist, it's considered the artist's *style*.
- **Technique:** The method, procedure, or way something is done. For example, the "technique" of drybrush.
- **Tonal color:** The color that's lighter or darker than the local color—the colors that have changed as a result of light hitting the subject.
- **Tone:** Another word for *value*, the lightness or darkness of a color.
- **Tracing paper:** A thin, transparent paper used to sketch and make revisions before transferring to the drawing or painting surface.
- **Transfer paper:** A carbon paper used to apply a drawing to another surface.
- **Translucent:** When light can pass through a material, it's translucent.
- **Values:** The lightness or darkness of tones and colors.
- **Vellum:** A prepared animal skin used to paint on that's archival and gives the artwork translucence.
- **Wash:** A solution made by diluting paint with water.
- **Watercolor:** A fluid and transparent water painting medium that contains pigments in a water-based solution.

“Narcissus Bulb”
Narcissus papyraceus
silverpoint
4.5" (11.5 cm) high

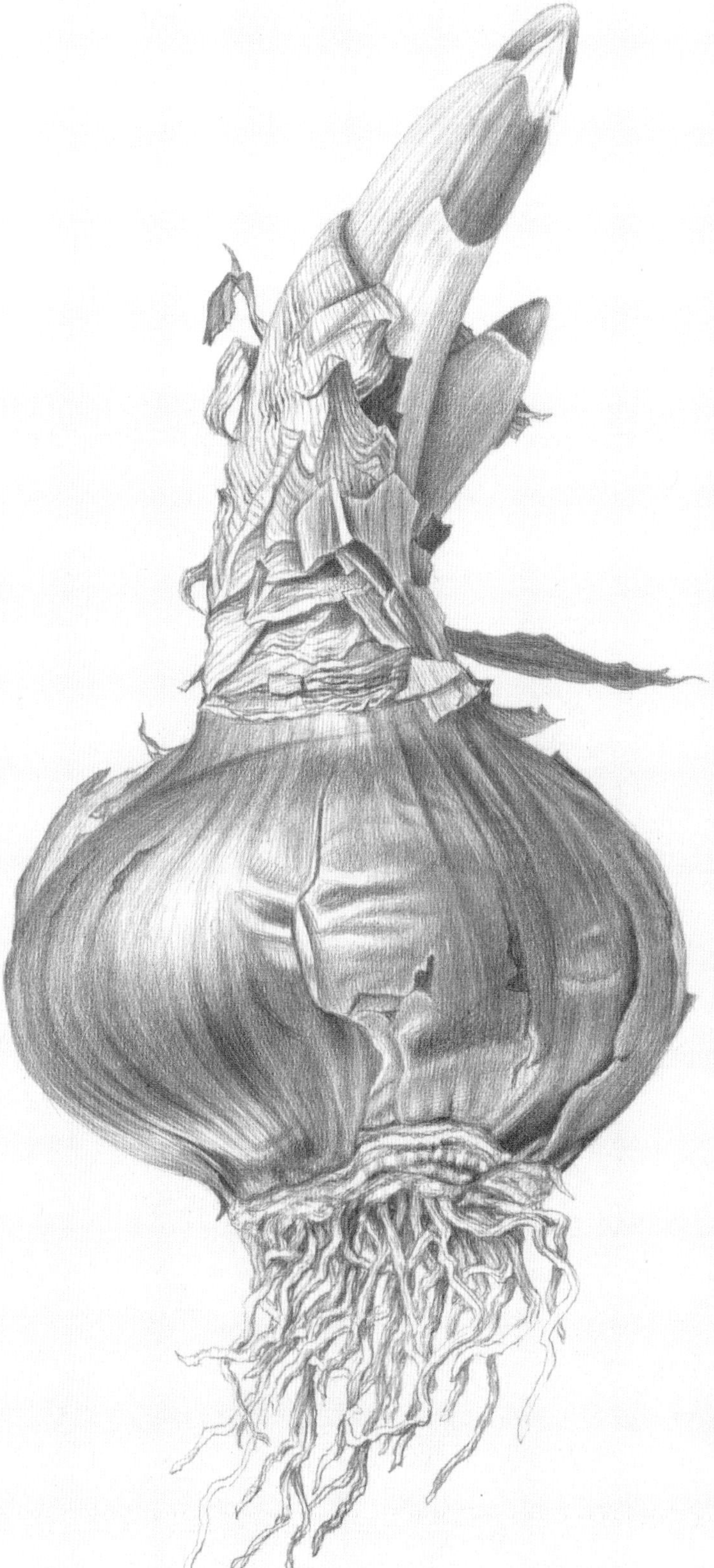

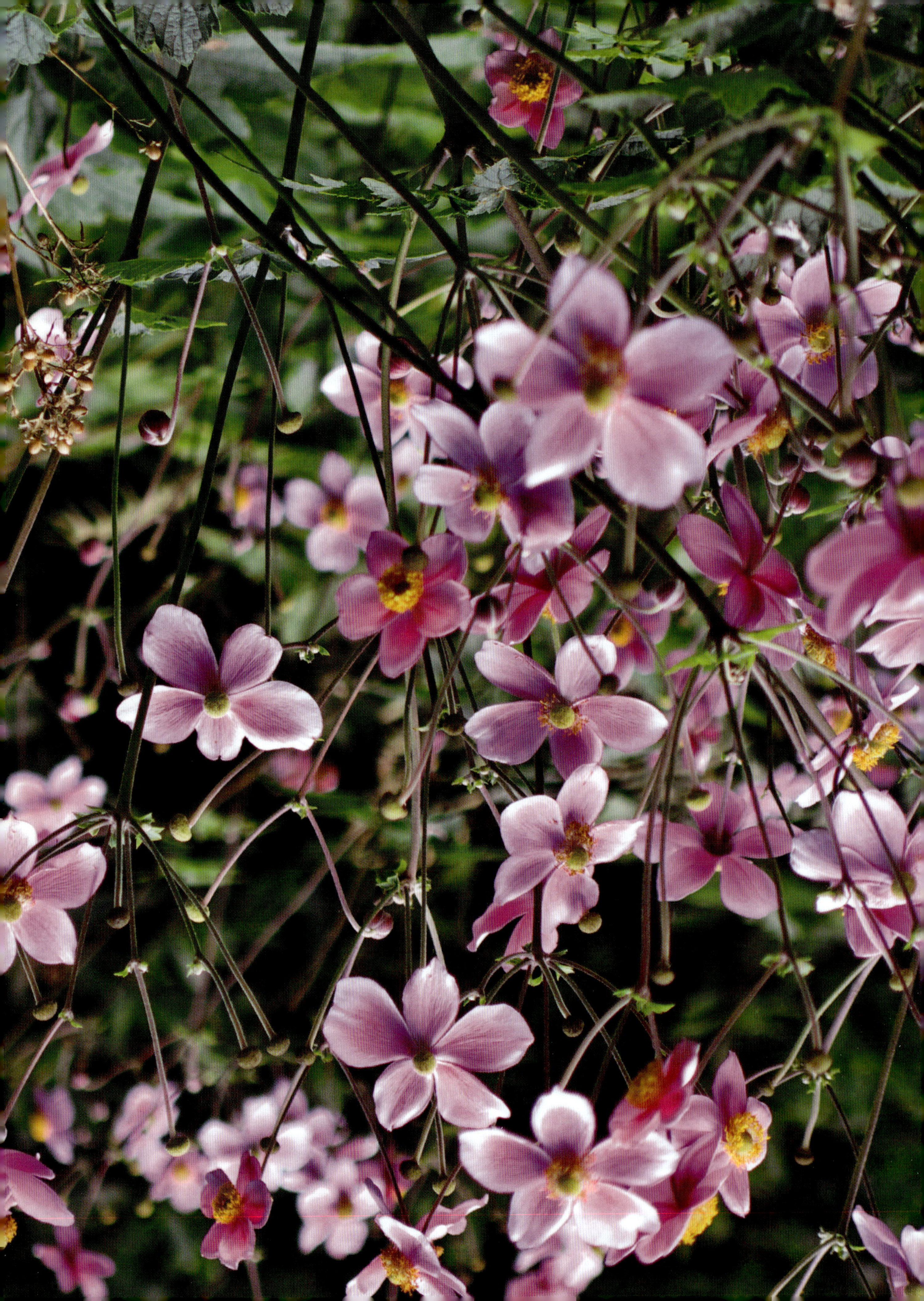

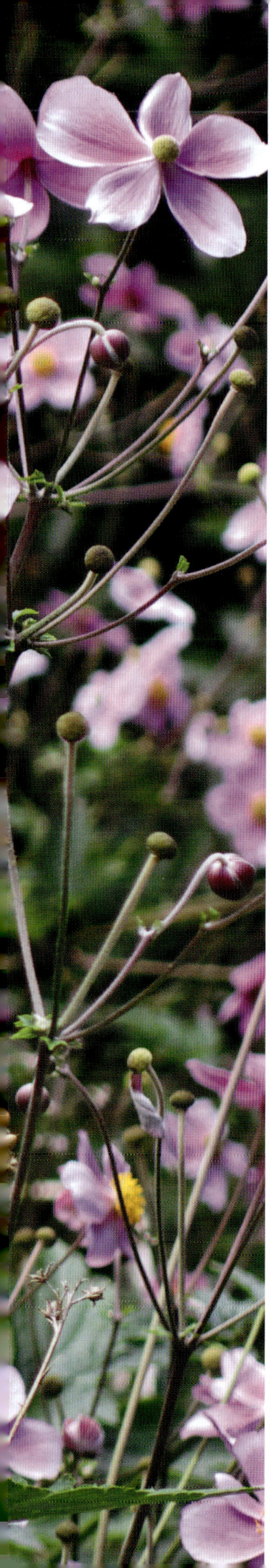

1

DRAWING *Botanicals*

Proficiency in drawing is by far the most important quality needed in creating traditional botanicals. Hours spent observing and *drawing what you see* will be of enormous benefit later when you work with the added complexities of applying paint.

With drawing, we can eliminate those questions and concerns and focus on what we see in the specimen before us. Choose a simply shaped flower or leaf that appeals to you. You're going to be looking at it for a long time. Look through your garden; have your eyes open during a walk in the woods or even in the produce aisle at the grocery store. You never know when you'll find that perfect peach to draw!

MEDIUMS AND SUPPLIES

What's nice about drawing is that the supplies are simple, inexpensive, and easy to transport.

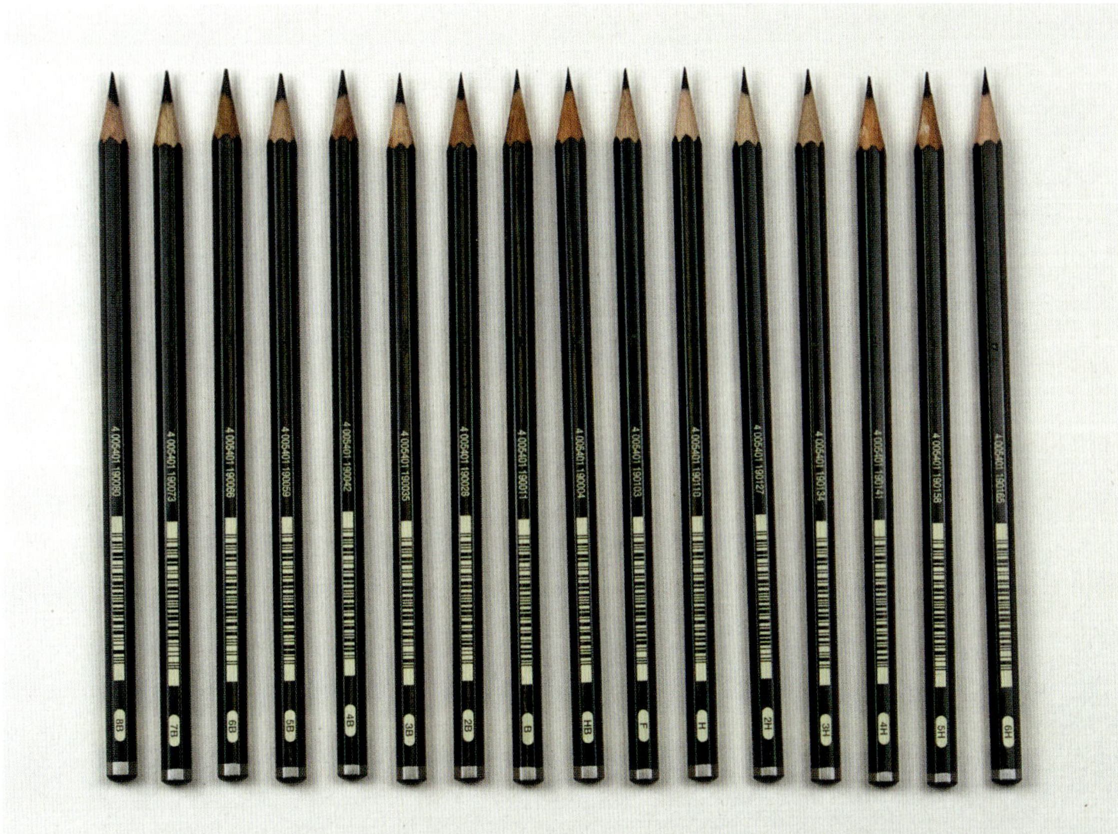

H pencils are hard, B pencils are soft, and an HB pencil is in the middle.

GRAPHITE PENCILS

Graphite pencils are graded numerically to identify their hardness or softness and how they will respond on your paper. Soft pencils have a lower clay content and appear darker, while hard pencils will leave a lighter mark. For this reason, soft pencils will need to be sharpened more often, whereas with a hard pencil, you can obtain a very sharp point that will last a long time. The letter *H* indicates a hard pencil, and the letter *B* designates the blackness of the pencil's mark and is a softer lead. The higher the number indicated on the pencil, the harder it is. For example, a 2H pencil will leave a light mark, whereas a 9H pencil will be significantly harder and lighter. A 2B pencil is soft and will leave a dark mark; an 8B pencil will be much softer and leave a significantly darker mark. An HB pencil is the same as a standard No. 2 pencil and is in the middle of the hard and soft pencils range on the scale.

For the purposes of botanical drawing, a softer pencil like an HB or B can be used for a more gestural loose sketch. When more precise lines are needed, a harder pencil such as a number 2H can be used. Generally, I only use a select few pencils: an HB, a 2H, a 6H, and an F. Each is used for a different purpose.

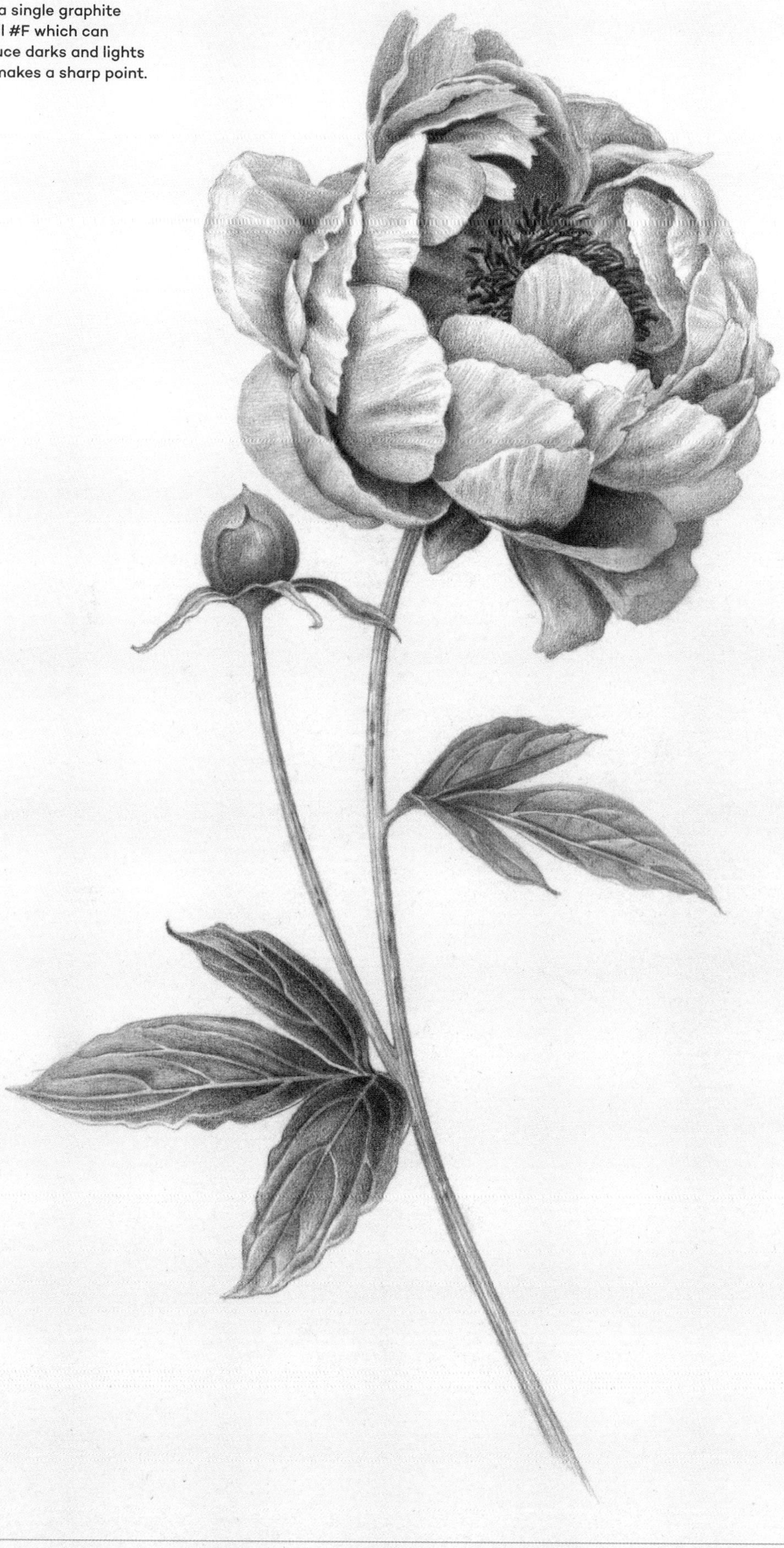

Peony (*Paeonia*) was drawn with a single graphite pencil #F which can produce darks and lights and makes a sharp point.

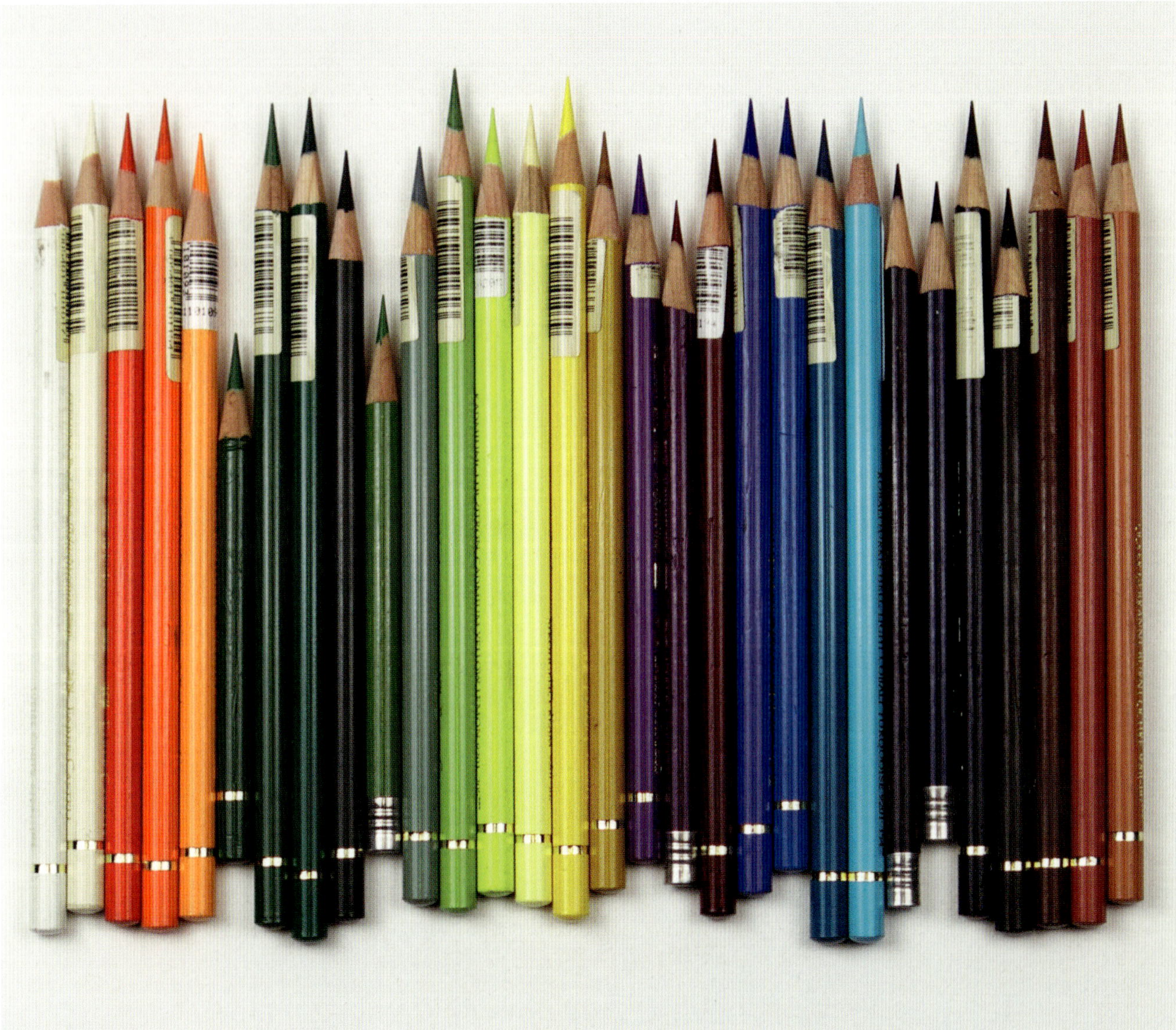

COLORED PENCILS

Colored pencils have a core of colored pigment and an outer wood casing. They may be made of wax, pigments, binding agents, and additives. They may be oil-based or water-soluble. Artist-grade pencils have a higher concentration of pigments than student-grade pencils. They are graded for *lightfastness,* which is the ability to resist UV rays and fading, core durability, and resistance to water.

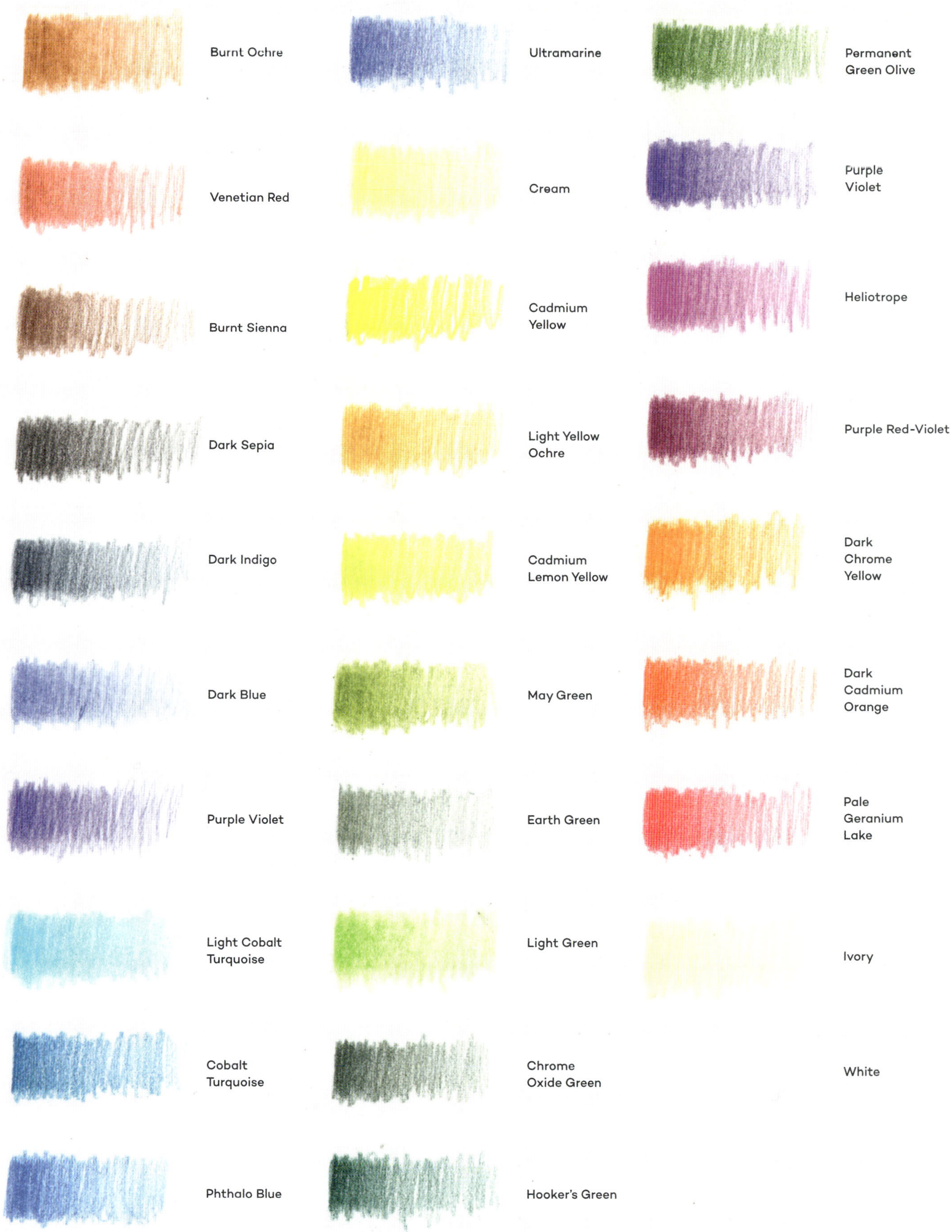

Faber-Castell colored pencils (opposite) and a color chart to use as reference when choosing colors.

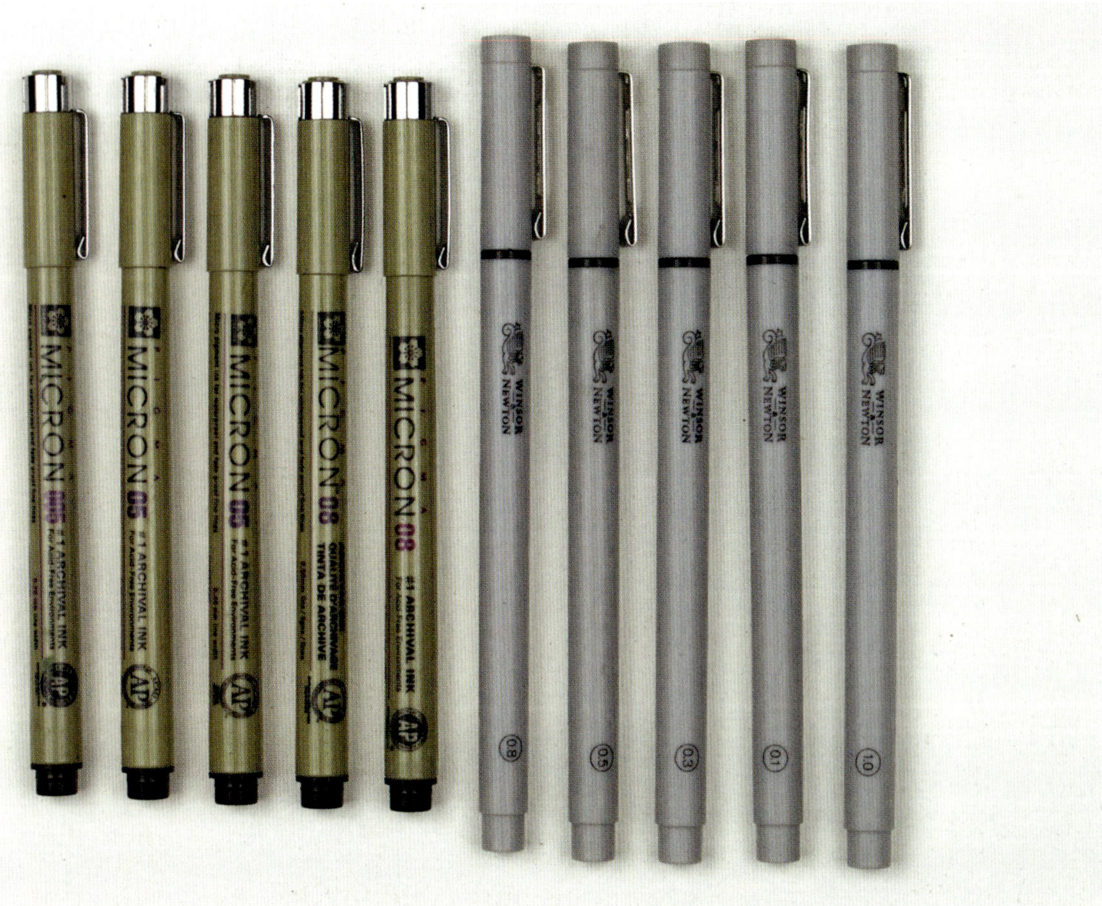

Fine tip markers are available in different colors and varying sizes.

FINE POINT MARKERS

Fine point markers are available in different thicknesses and colors and are a convenient replacement for the pen and ink used years ago. No longer are drips and spatters a concern. Good quality pens will be archival, fade-resistant, and smudge-, water-, and bleedproof, meaning that they won't bleed through the paper. Pens are available in different colors and come in a range of tip, or nib, sizes from 005, which is the smallest, to 08, which is the largest.

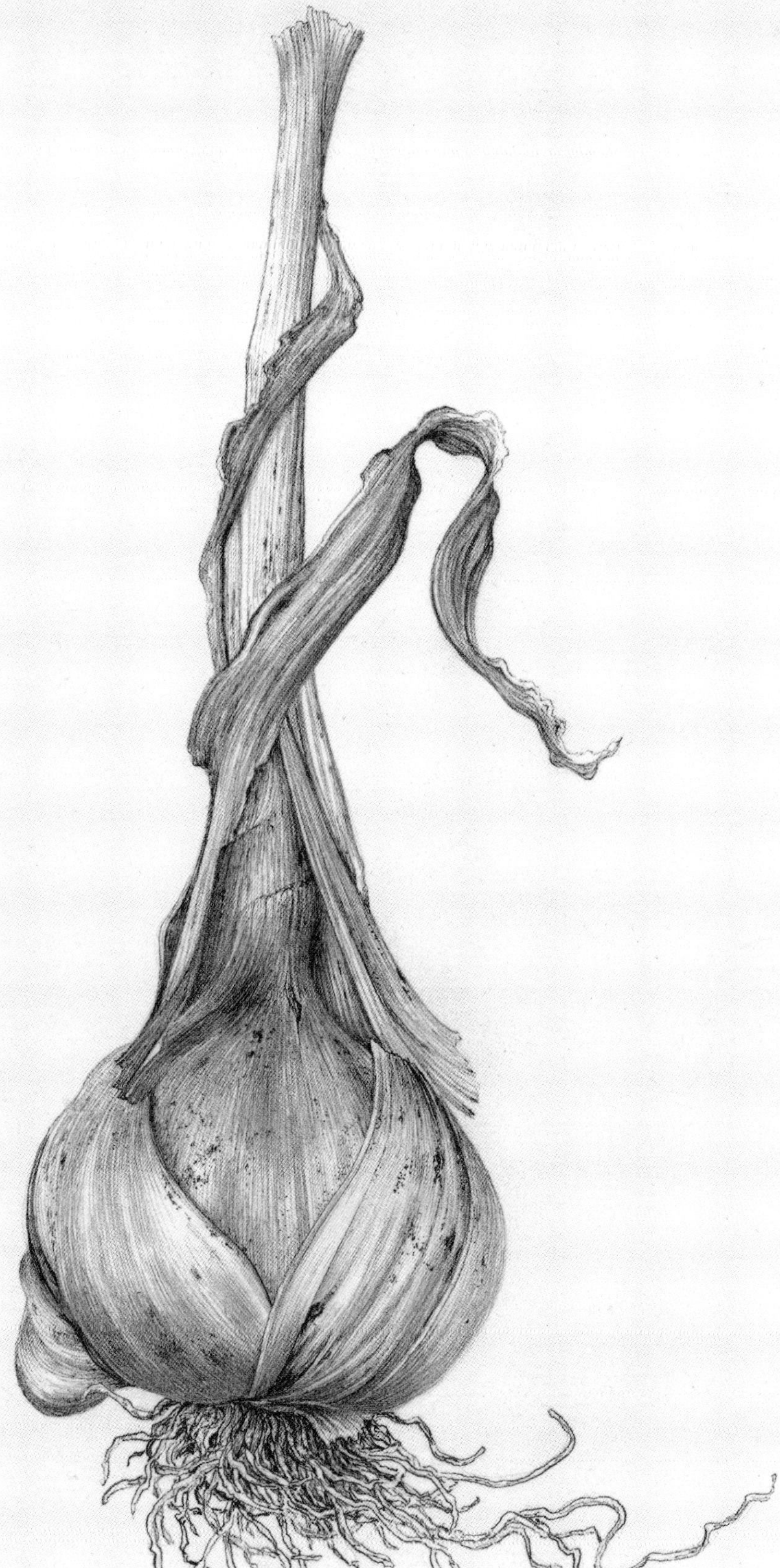

A garlic bulb drawn with fine point marker.

"Scottish Thistle"
Onopordum Acanthium
silverpoint on paper
9.5" x 12" (24.1 cm x 30.5 cm)

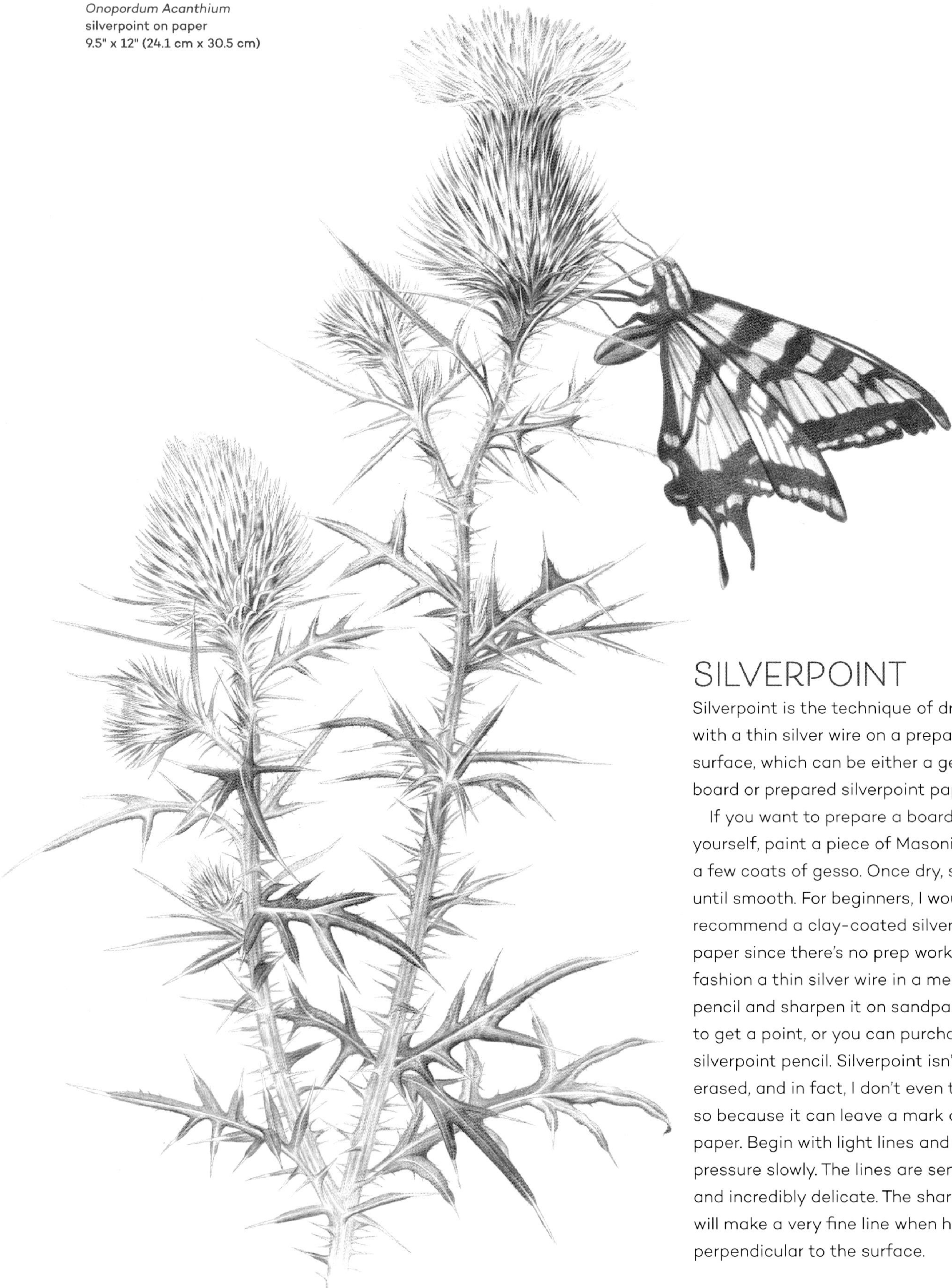

SILVERPOINT

Silverpoint is the technique of drawing with a thin silver wire on a prepared surface, which can be either a gessoed board or prepared silverpoint paper.

If you want to prepare a board yourself, paint a piece of Masonite with a few coats of gesso. Once dry, sand until smooth. For beginners, I would recommend a clay-coated silverpoint paper since there's no prep work. You can fashion a thin silver wire in a mechanical pencil and sharpen it on sandpaper to get a point, or you can purchase a silverpoint pencil. Silverpoint isn't easily erased, and in fact, I don't even try to do so because it can leave a mark on the paper. Begin with light lines and increase pressure slowly. The lines are sensitive and incredibly delicate. The sharp tip will make a very fine line when held perpendicular to the surface.

Drawing with the silver wire on its side will produce a wider line.
Using more pressure will make a darker line.

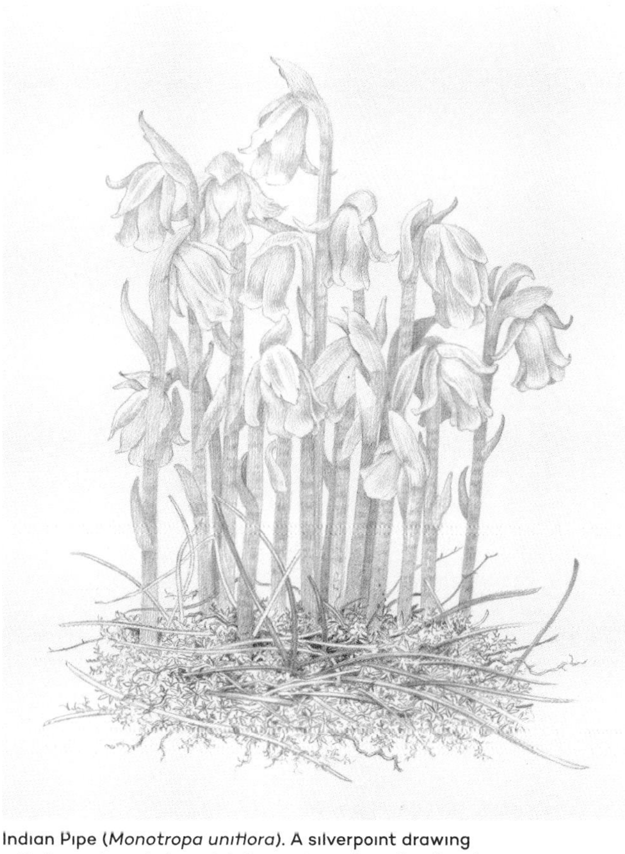

Indian Pipe (*Monotropa uniflora*). A silverpoint drawing will always be subtle and delicate. Over time, the silver/gray drawing will tarnish to a warm sepia.

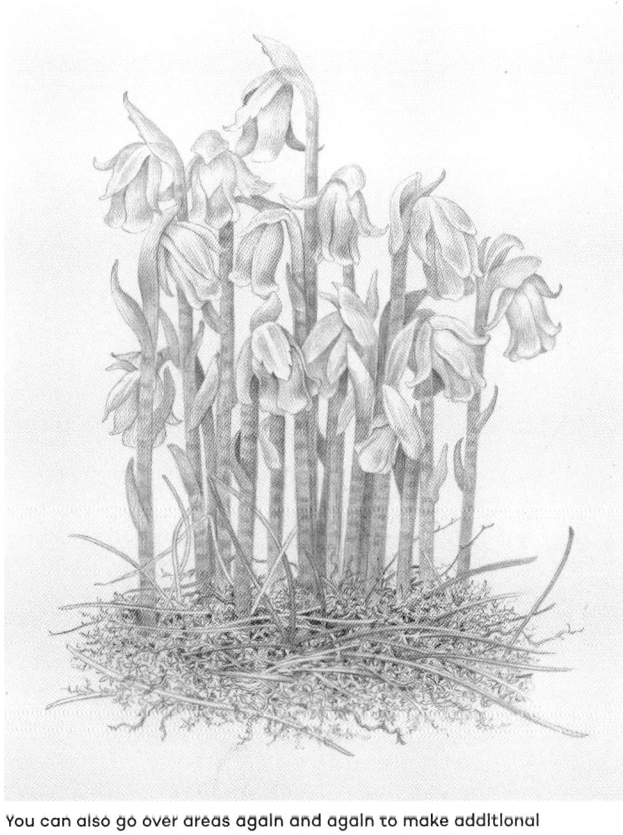

You can also go over areas again and again to make additional layers and darken values, though the final results will never be as dark as graphite.

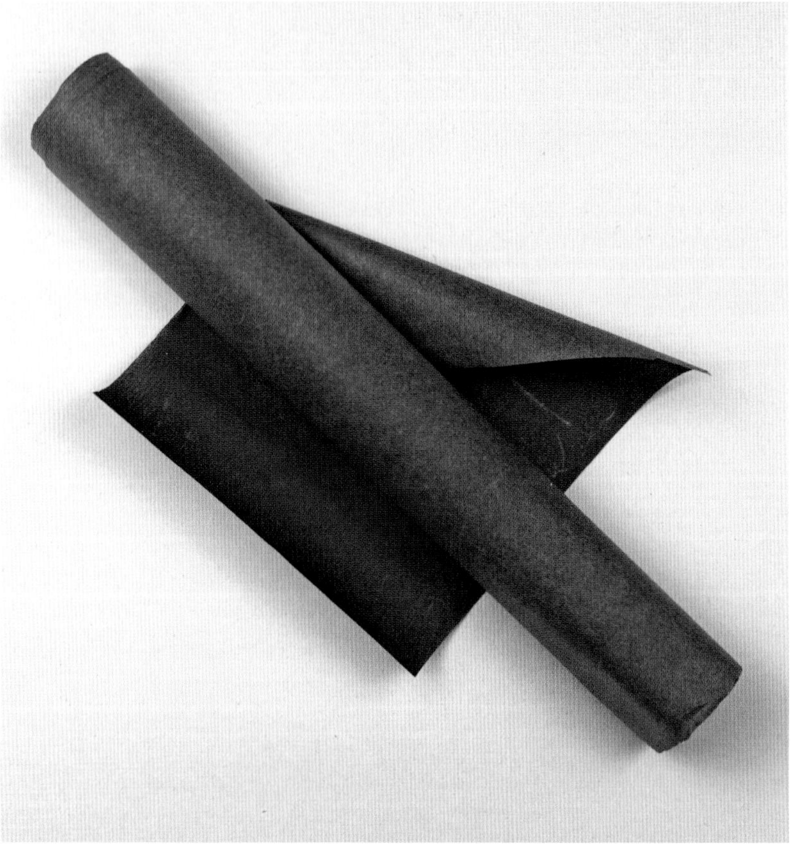

Saral paper is a brand of graphite paper that is used to transfer your sketch to your finished drawing or painting surface.

Above right: It can be difficult to get an even tone on rough-textured drawing paper. A paper with a smooth surface is more suitable for a realistic drawing.

PAPER

Drawing papers are distinguished by the tooth, or texture, they have and the weight, or thickness, they are.

While a hot-pressed paper is smooth, a cold-pressed paper has texture. Graphite will settle into the crevices of a cold-pressed paper, but it will glide on top of a hot-pressed paper. For detailed work, which is what botanical artists are looking to achieve, I would recommend a hot-pressed paper. A straight line looks more exact and straighter on the smooth paper as opposed to going into the hills and valleys of a cold-pressed paper. Using harder pencils results in more precise lines, whereas softer lead pencils tend to make less-defined lines and more dust!

Tracing paper can be used when you want to contemplate positioning of elements in your drawing. For example, a leaf can be drawn on the tracing paper and the angle of it repositioned until you're satisfied with how it looks before you add it to your drawing.

Transfer Paper Transfer paper, also known as graphite paper, is used to transfer your final sketch to the finished art surface. The paper is placed between the two surfaces with the transfer paper's graphite side down then the sketch is traced with a 6H pencil and transferred.

Silverpoint Silverpoint adheres to a smooth gessoed surface which can take some work to prepare. Alternatively, paper made specifically may be purchased. The paper's surface is very smooth. Note that silverpoint cannot easily be erased.

ERASERS

There are many different types of erasers available, but I really only use two or three. My two favorites are the standard gray kneaded eraser, sometimes called putty rubber, or a Sakura electric battery powered eraser, the SumoGrip® EE-3000 Electric Eraser. The kneaded eraser is versatile as it can be fashioned into a point to pick up lead in a small space or pressed down in a blotting fashion to carefully remove graphite from a wider surface. By *kneading* the eraser every once in a while, the eraser exposes another clean surface ready to pick up more lead. The Sakura electric eraser works like magic in picking up graphite in a tiny area. Because this eraser spins in one small space, you can pick up the area you want to remove without disturbing the rest of your drawing. The third eraser that can be helpful is the Tombow MONO zero precision eraser. It too has a tiny eraser, but it's a manual tool, as you yourself provide the motion to remove the graphite.

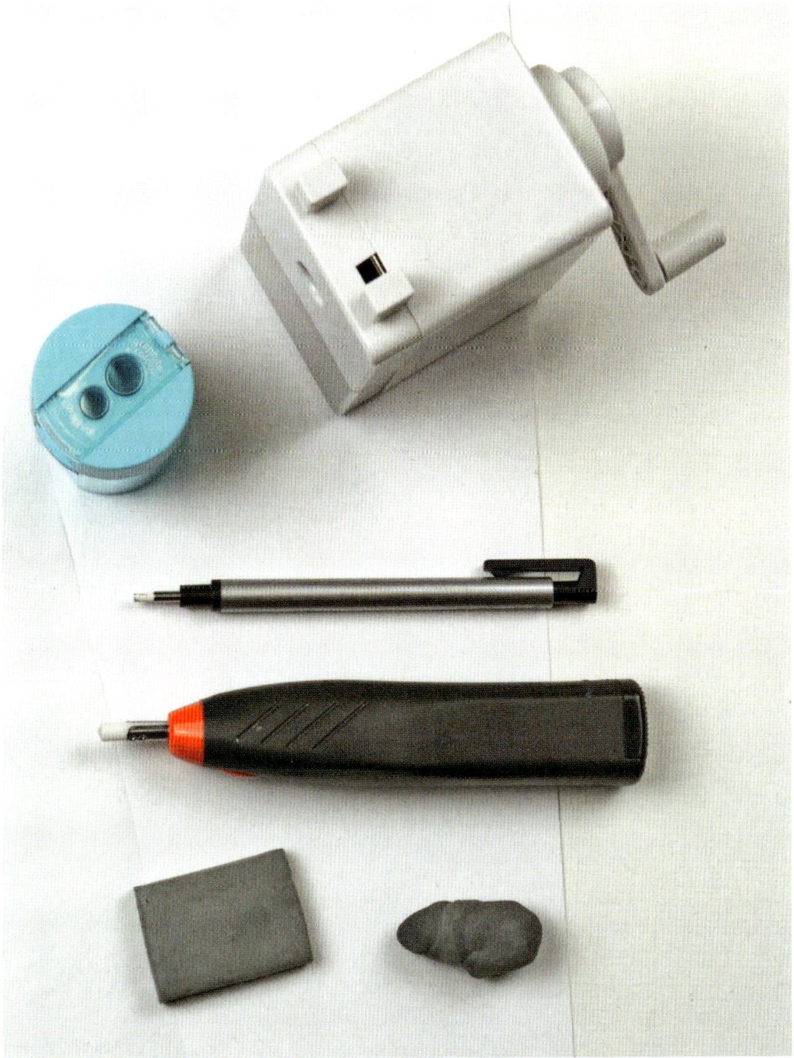

Sharpeners and erasers. Shown here are the Stadler, and Muji pencil sharpeners, and Sakura, Mono Tombo and kneaded erasers.

PENCIL SHARPENERS

There are numerous types of pencil sharpeners on the market for both graphite and colored pencils. Many sharpeners work well to achieve a decent point on a graphite pencil. To make the point even sharper, rub the side of the point on a fine-grade sandpaper. For colored pencils, the MUJI Manual Pencil Sharpener works well and will give you a sharp point.

ESSENTIAL DRAWING TECHNIQUES

Spending time drawing will be most beneficial to you but there are techniques and tools that can help your work to advance, be more precise, and make your practice more enjoyable. Your reference materials, drawing techniques, and the actual set-up of your workspace all affect the final result of your work.

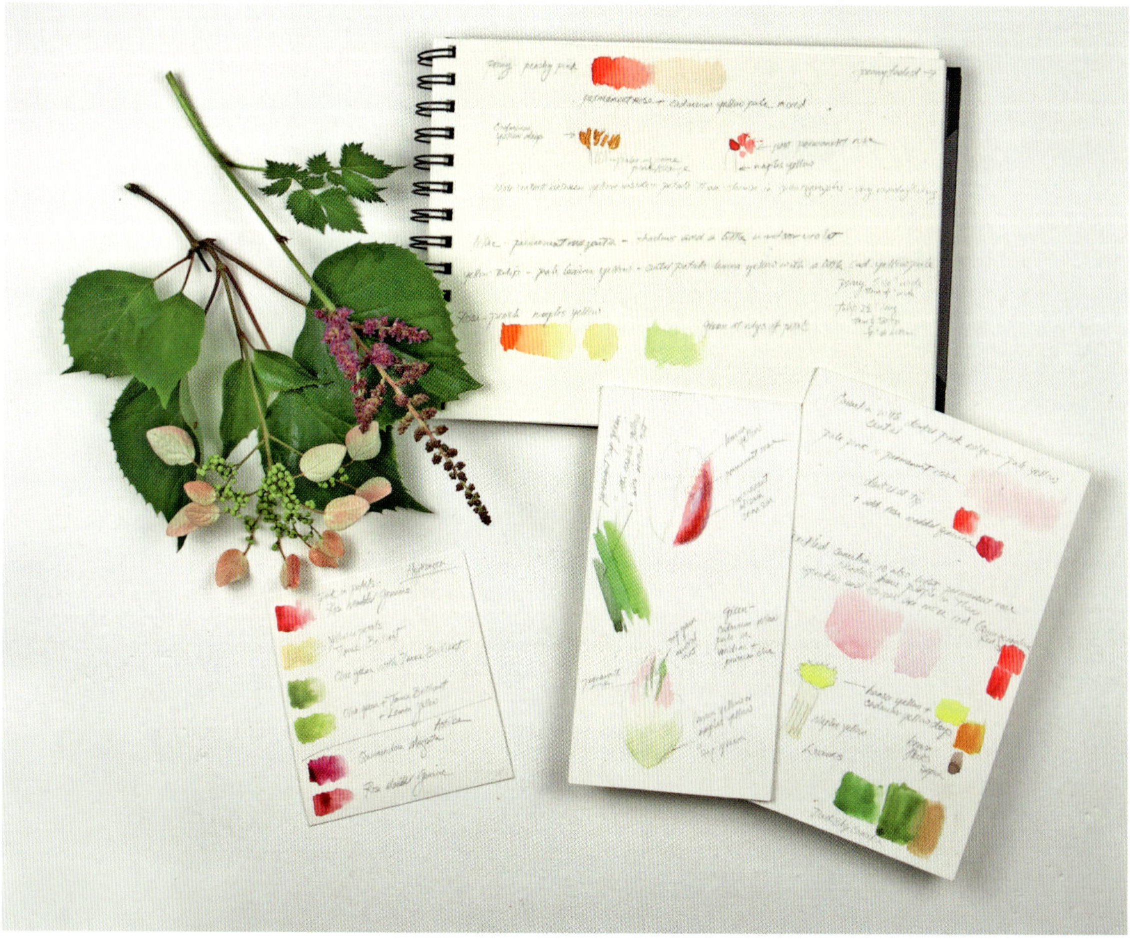

A photo may be helpful to see how light creates shadows and highlights on your subject. It may, however, fail to portray tiny hairs on a stem, and this is where your notes come into play. They can help you remember colors and textures that may not be seen in a photo.

LIVE SPECIMEN

The most important thing needed in creating botanicals is our live specimen. We want to keep our live subject alive for as long as possible! Put your flower in a refrigerator overnight to keep it fresh. Don't leave it in a warm room or in sunlight. You might even want to coax opened petals closed again with twine or tape. I've kept flowers, such as tulips, for many days with this method. After they were carefully held closed with Scotch tape (sticky side out) in the fridge overnight, they slowly opened once again the next day, enabling many more hours to paint!

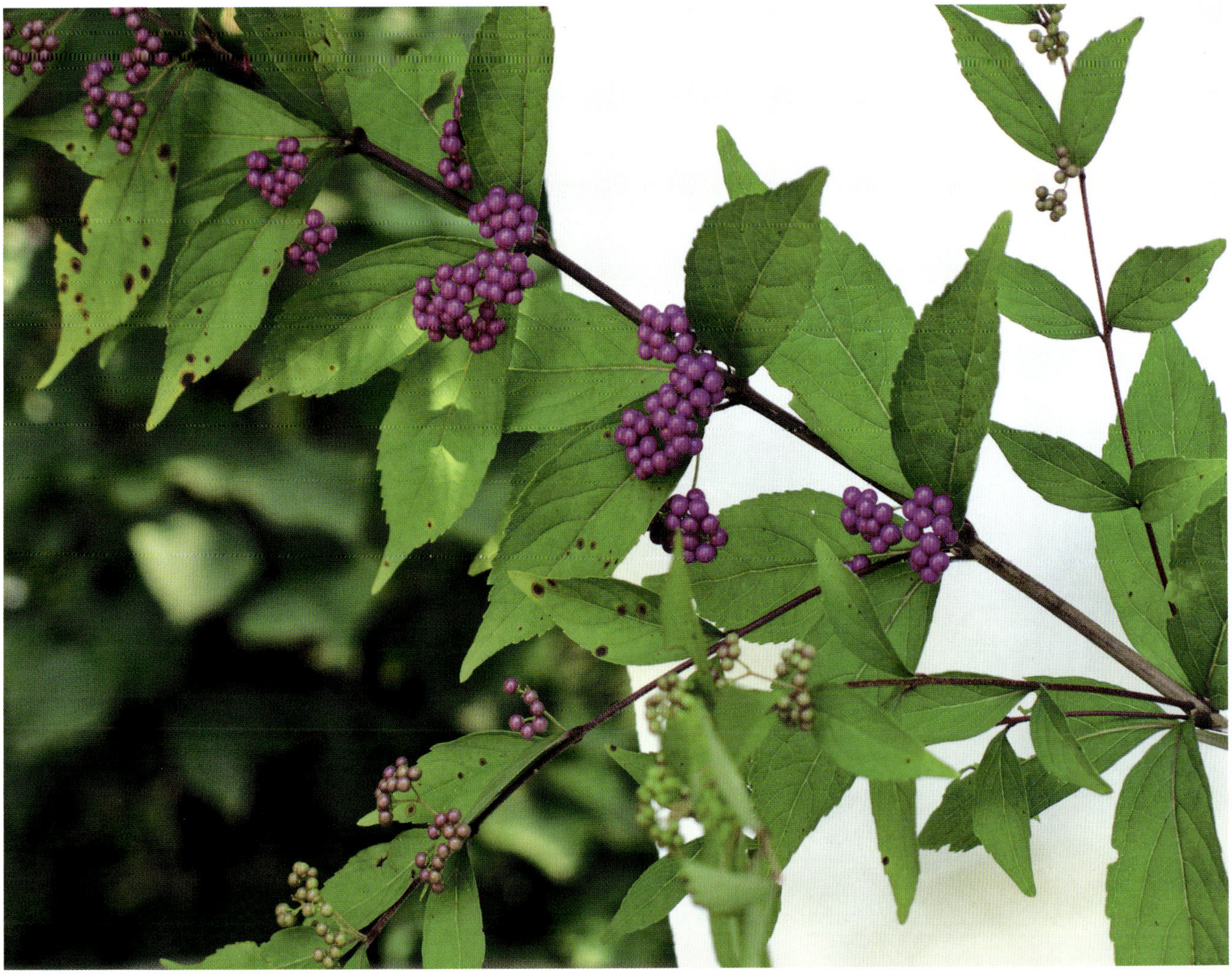

WORKING FROM PHOTOGRAPHS

Photos should be considered just another tool to help see your botanical subject accurately. They are never to be a substitute for seeing the real thing. Nuances of color and detail are often not accurate in a photo, but having a photo for reference can help to remember the highlights and shadows on your flower before it wilts! Do make sure you're taking the best photo possible. Choose your subject carefully, without broken or bent petals. Place a large white piece of cardboard behind the subject. This will help to show how the light hits the edges of your flower or leaves and which are dark and which are highlighted.

Most often, photographing in bright shade works best, but take many photos in different locations. Choose a sunny day, but in an evenly shaded location (not dappled light). You'll find that taking them in sunlight will give you shadows that are too harsh. Make sure the form of your subject is emphasized and does not look flat. Take many photos at various angles. Different elements of the plant can always be put together in the sketch stage (remember to be accurate to the plant). Always keep in mind that if something looks strange in the photo, it will undoubtedly look strange in your artwork!

In this photo, you can see how placing something white behind your subject makes it easier to isolate it from the background.

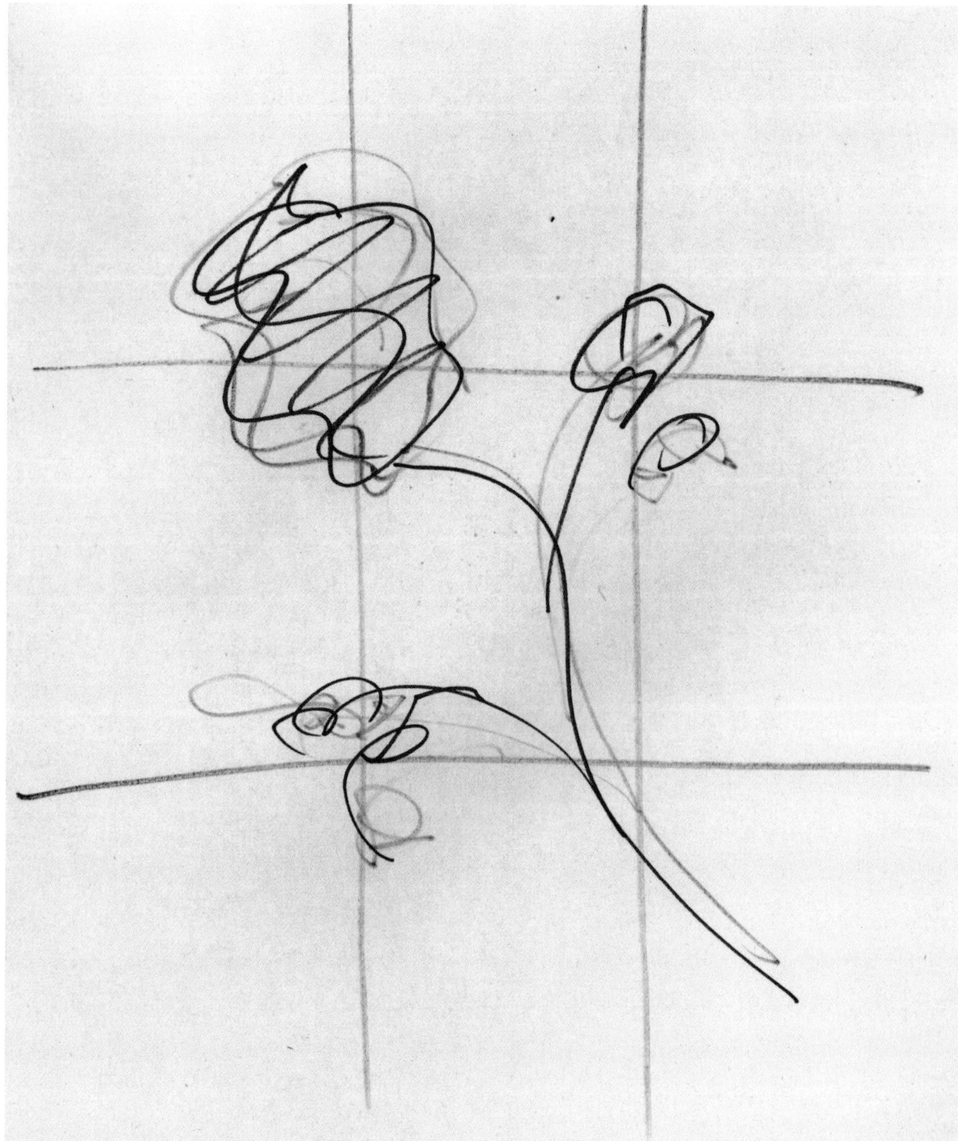

LOOSE GESTURAL DRAWING

A loose gestural sketch is a good way to plan the placement of elements in your design. I often make a sketch on tracing paper to visualize different compositions. One simple trick is the *rule of thirds*, where the paper is divided into three sections, both horizontally and vertically, and the primary element is placed where the lines intersect. Also consider how the viewer will look at your art, how their eye will travel through the image, and where the weightier elements will be placed. At this beginning stage, you can create movement and emphasize the most important elements you want to portray.

Once you're satisfied with your basic loose composition and your sketch becomes more detailed and complete, you can use tracing paper to transfer it to the surface you'll be painting on. The finished detailed outline sketch should indicate any shadows and the most predominant details, such as veining and bumps. This mapping of important areas will help guide you when you begin your final piece.

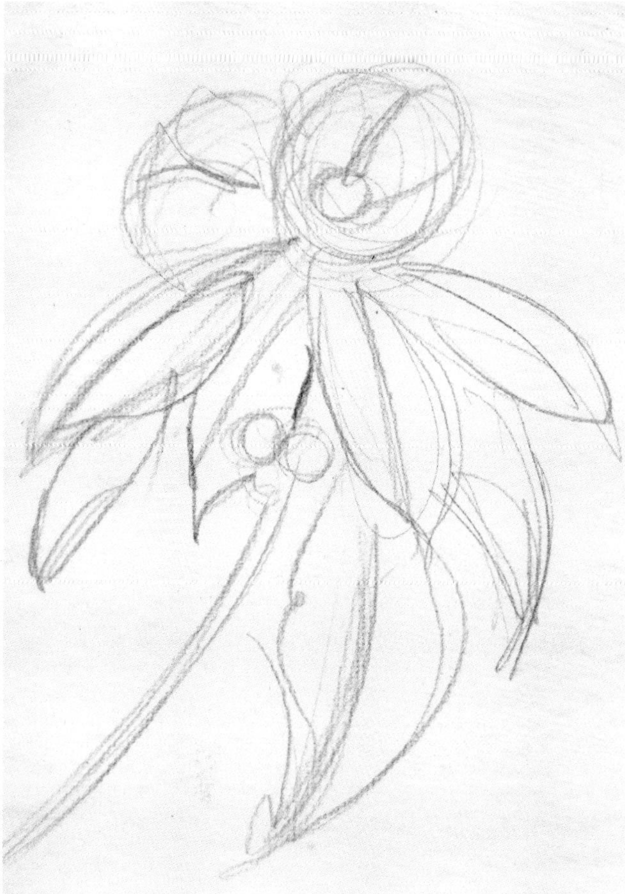

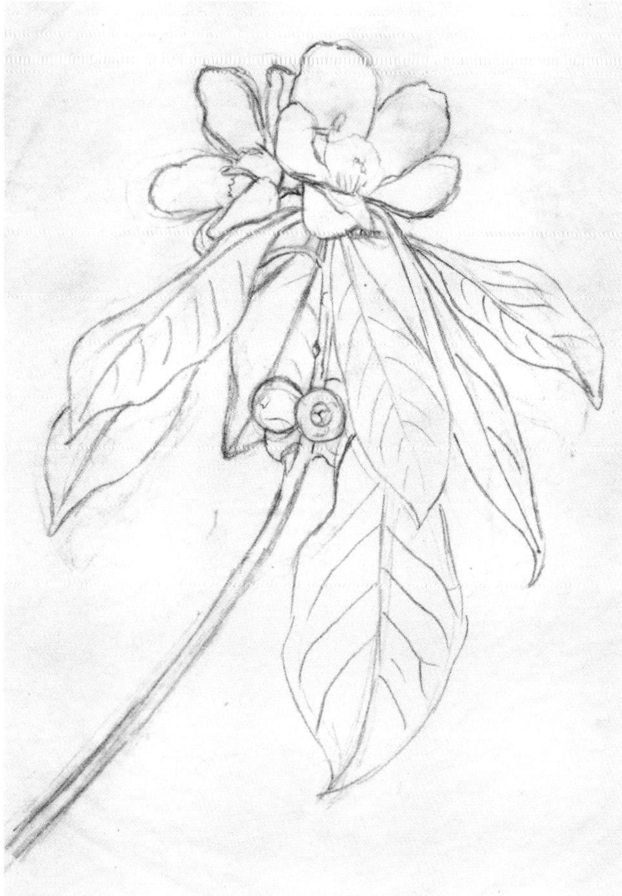

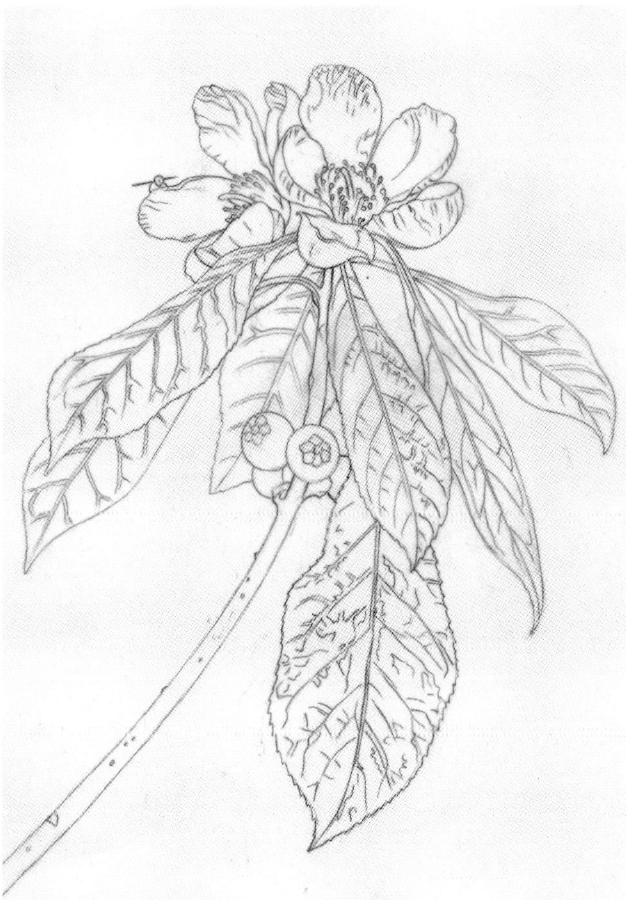

These sketches show the progression from loose gestural to a more refined image used to transfer to the painting surface.

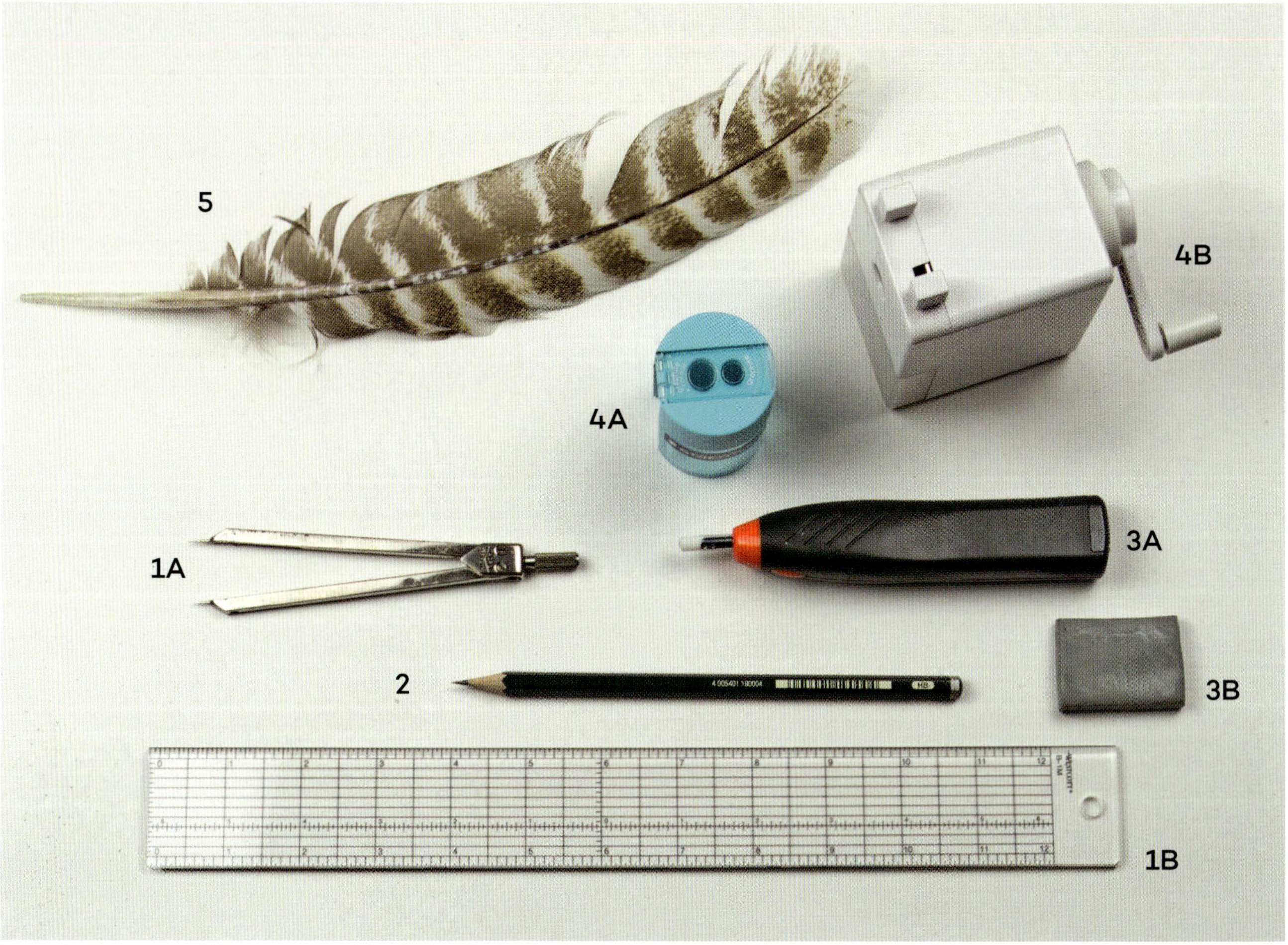

Supplies

1. Dividers **(A)** or a clear ruler **(B)**
2. HB pencil
3. Eraser, electric **(A)** or kneaded **(B)**
4. Pencil sharpener, manual **(A)** or hand crank **(B)**
5. Feather

PRECISE MEASURING

Drawing precisely from life entails lots of measuring to create a drawing similar in size to your actual subject. For a more contemporary feel, some botanical artists push the scale of their art to be larger, but for our purposes of explaining drawing from life, we will be drawing very close to the size of the subject in front of us. By measuring and lots of erasing and adjusting, an exact drawing of your subject can be achieved. This rewarding concept entails lots of practice. Once it *clicks*, you'll understand this concept of measuring and drawing from life, and at some point, you should even be able to make informed decisions as to correct proportions!

There's no steadfast rule as to where to start measuring, but I can tell you what works best for me.

The drawing supplies you'll need are dividers or a clear ruler, an HB pencil, a kneaded eraser, pencil sharpener, and a smooth hot-pressed drawing paper.

Setting Up

When drawing from a live specimen, it's important to set up your workspace so that you're comfortable, have good lighting, and have a white background behind your subject. Doing everything you can to simplify the image you're looking at will be beneficial.

If you want cast shadows, place the object on a flat white surface. If not, raise your subject up and position a flat white background behind it. A piece of foam core on a picture easel can be helpful. Use your imagination as to how to hold your subject in place. A vase, a flower frog, or a *helping hands* tool—adjustable devices with clips for holding objects while your own hands

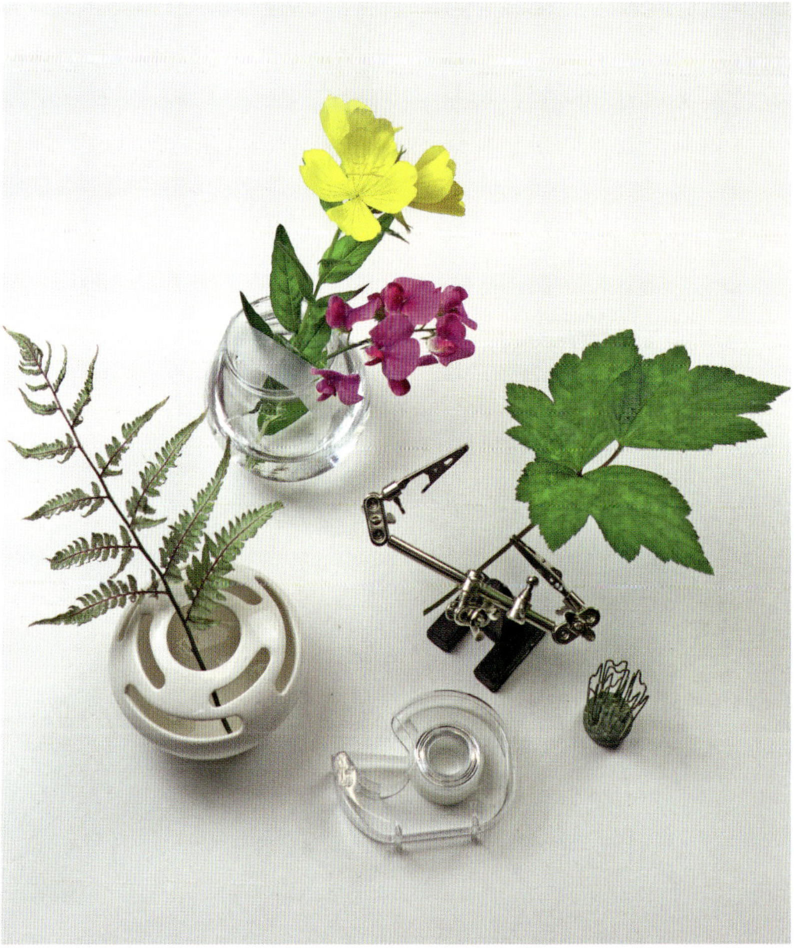

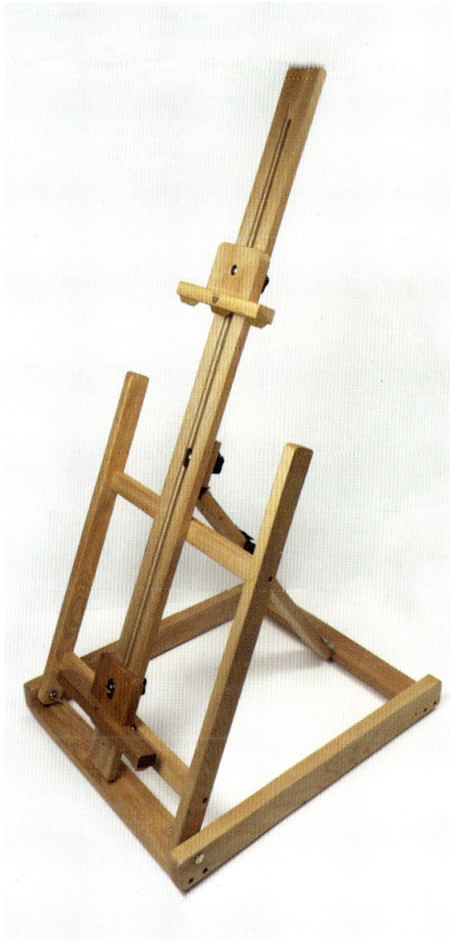

are occupied—all work well. Place tape across the top of your vase to secure delicate stems.

Use an adjustable lamp with a daylight bulb. Positioning it from the upper-front left often looks the most natural.

Before you begin, decide where you would like to position your subject on your paper, as it can be frustrating to find out later that you can't fit everything on your page. First consider the size of the entire specimen, then determine its placement on the page.

- Arrange your subject just as you want it to appear on the page. Be aware of any elements, such as leaves, that may look too foreshortened or odd. If you can position your subject in a pleasing way, this is the time to do it because from this point on, we don't want to move anything! For this reason, it's helpful to secure everything in place with tape.

- Don't forget to take a photo of your subject. Put a piece of white paper behind it so there are no background distractions and the darks and lights of the edges will be clear. A piece of foam core on a picture stand works well for this. Make sure your camera is angled exactly the same way that you're going to be looking at your subject while drawing. This photo will be invaluable because your flower or plant will inevitably shift with time!

Options for setting up and arranging your drawing subjects—flower frog, vase, and helping hands—plus transparent tape for keeping them in place.

Above right: I prefer to work vertically rather than flat on a table, so I can see what I'm drawing most similarly to how I see the subject in front of me. A tabletop easel at an 80- to 85-degree angle works well for this.

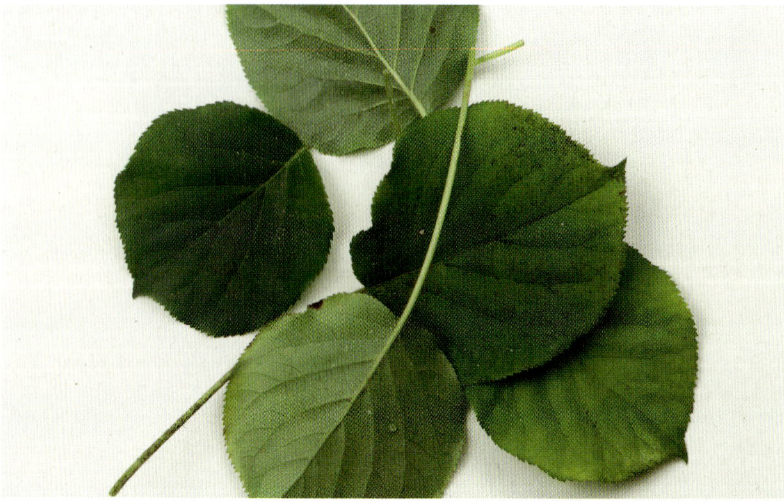

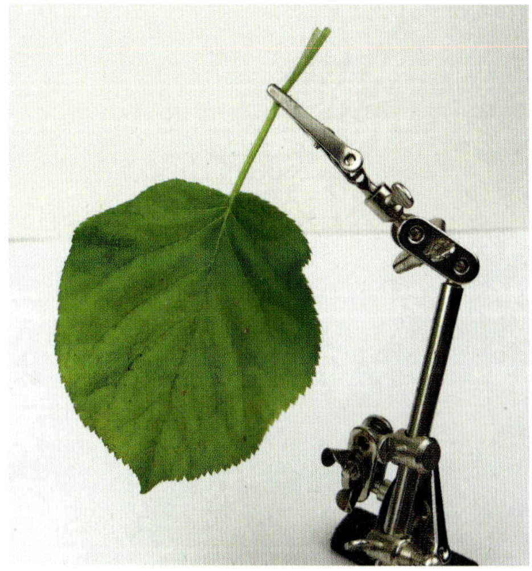

The climbing hydrangea leaf has distinct veining, irregular contours, and serrated edges. The contours and veining become most apparent when the leaf is lit from the side.

The Measuring Process

1. Sit a comfortable distance from your subject so that when you extend your slightly bent arm towards it, you're about 3 inches (7.6 cm) from the subject. If you're right-handed, use your left hand to measure.

2. Imagine a flat vertical plane in front of the subject at this 3-inch (7.6 cm) distance—as if there were a vertical piece of glass 3 inches (7.6 cm) in front of the subject. Each time you measure, you'll be bringing your slightly bent arm up to this flat vertical plane. (If this all seems confusing to you, practice measuring a simple small box instead of a flower until you understand the concept.)

3. Make sure to use a sharp HB pencil. Raise your dividers or clear ruler up to the longest span in your subject (for example, across the diameter of a flower from tip to tip of the longest petals). Remember to keep your dividers or ruler on the same plane as the imaginary glass. This is the single most difficult concept for students to grasp when drawing and measuring from life. The more natural inclination is to angle the dividers when measuring and to actually touch the flower you're assessing, but that isn't the correct technique.

4. Picture the numbers on a clock and superimpose those numbers onto the glass in front of your specimen. Let's say the angle of that line you've measured goes from the 11:00 position to the 4:00 position. You would then take your dividers or ruler to your drawing paper at that same 11:00 to 4:00 angle and put a dot with an HB pencil on your paper at those two positions. Be sure to double-check this measurement. Then, go to the next largest span in your subject and repeat the process. Go up to your imaginary glass, measure two points, and then figure out what angle on the clock it is. Mimic that angle on your paper. Then, compare and check the first two points you put down on the paper to the second two. Repeat until you've documented your subject's critical drawing points. See figs. A–F for examples of essential measuring spans on a leaf:

- the entire width **(A)**
- each half from the midrib to the edge **(B and C)**
- from the center to the tip of the stem **(D)**
- from the center to the base where the stem emerges **(E)**
- from the center to the tip of the leaf **(F)**

A

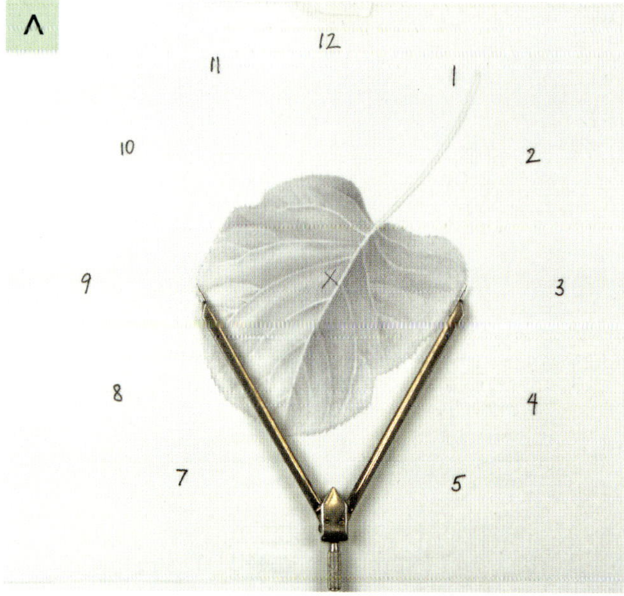

B

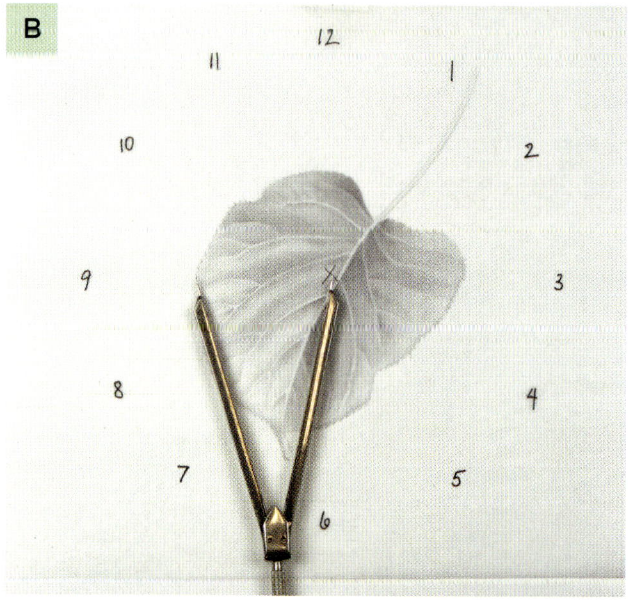

C

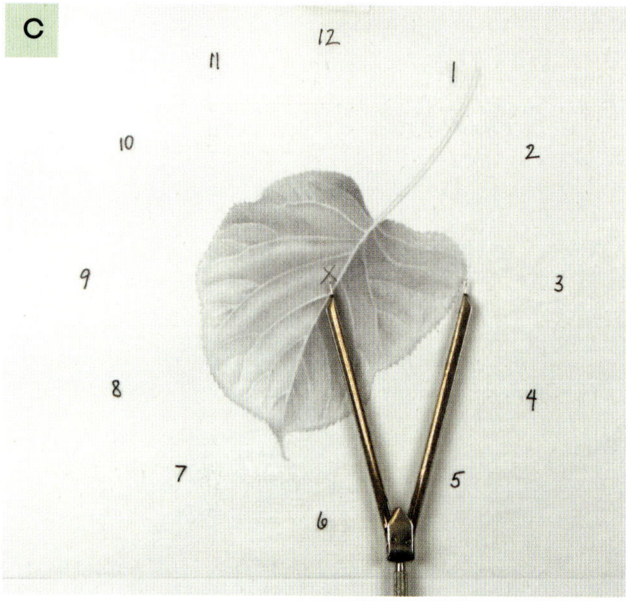

D

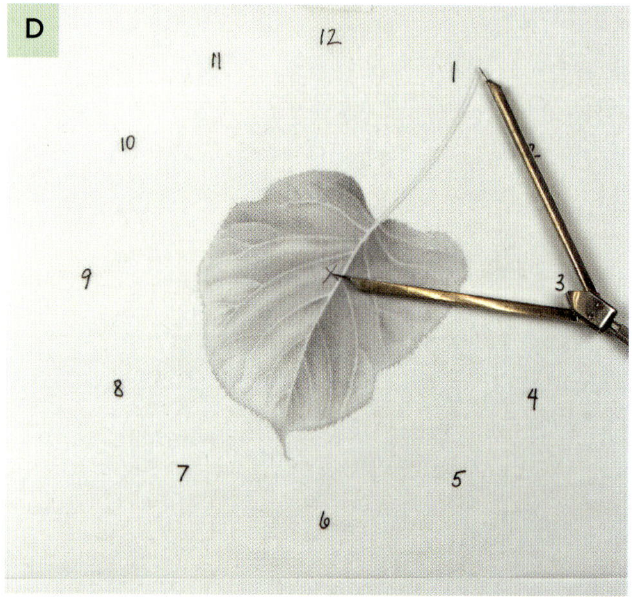

E

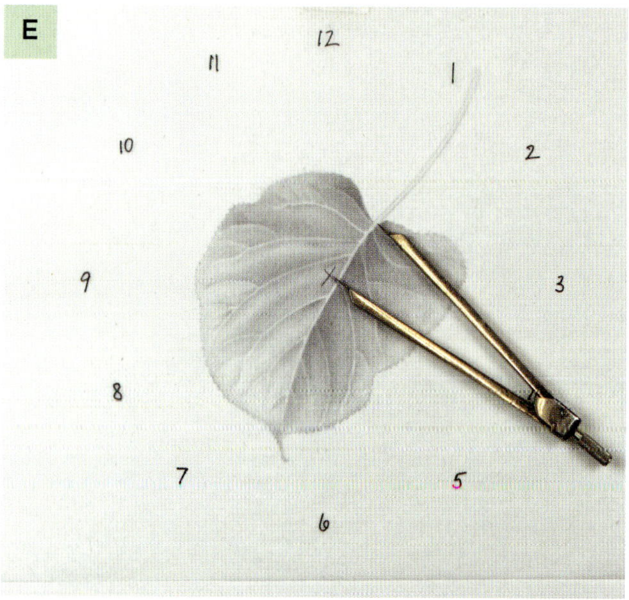

F

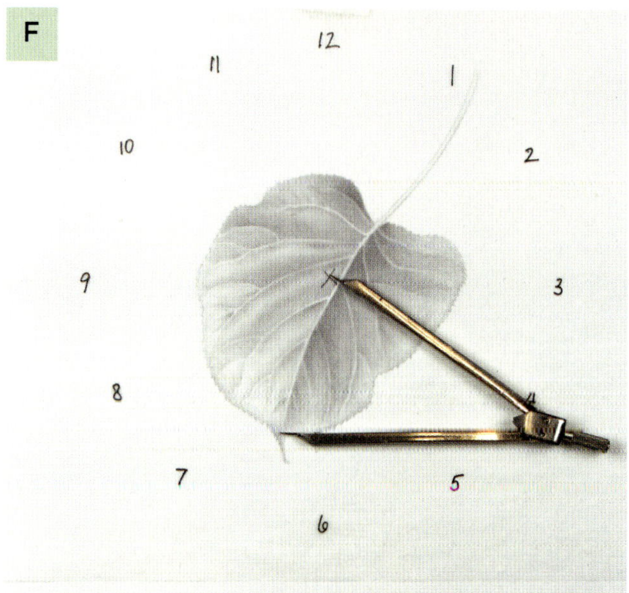

Many variables can prevent things from measuring up correctly, so a lot of erasing and double-checking can go on. A feather or makeup brush can whisk the frazzles away. Keep in mind that this is a slow, deliberate process that can't be rushed.

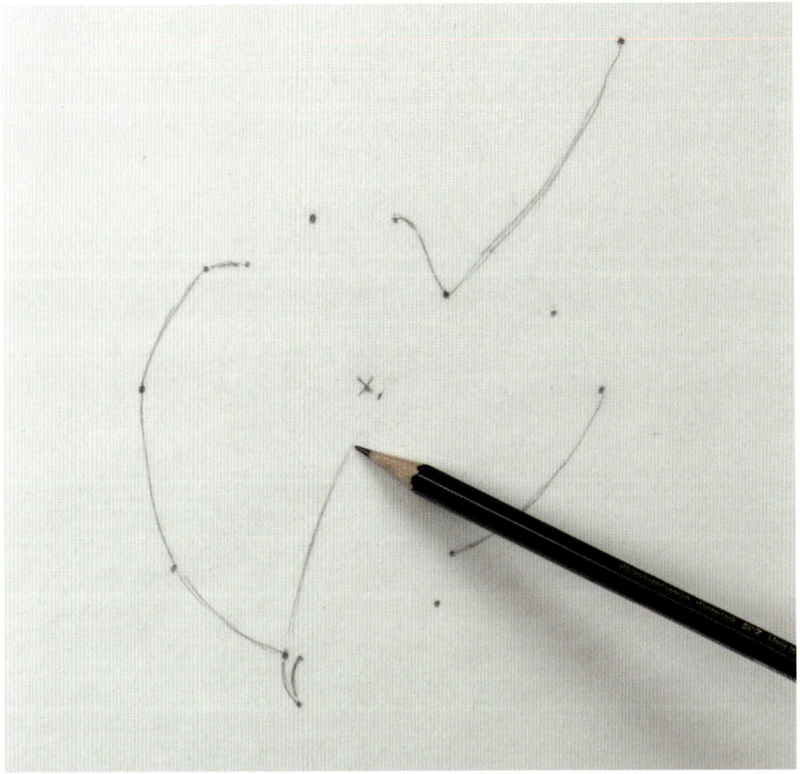

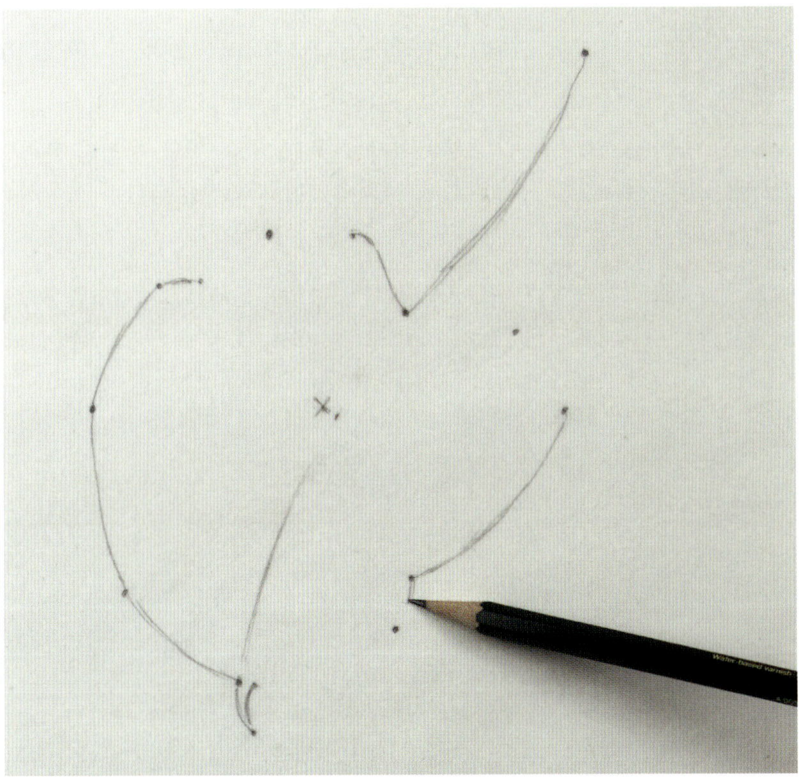

Mimic the curves you see between the dots.

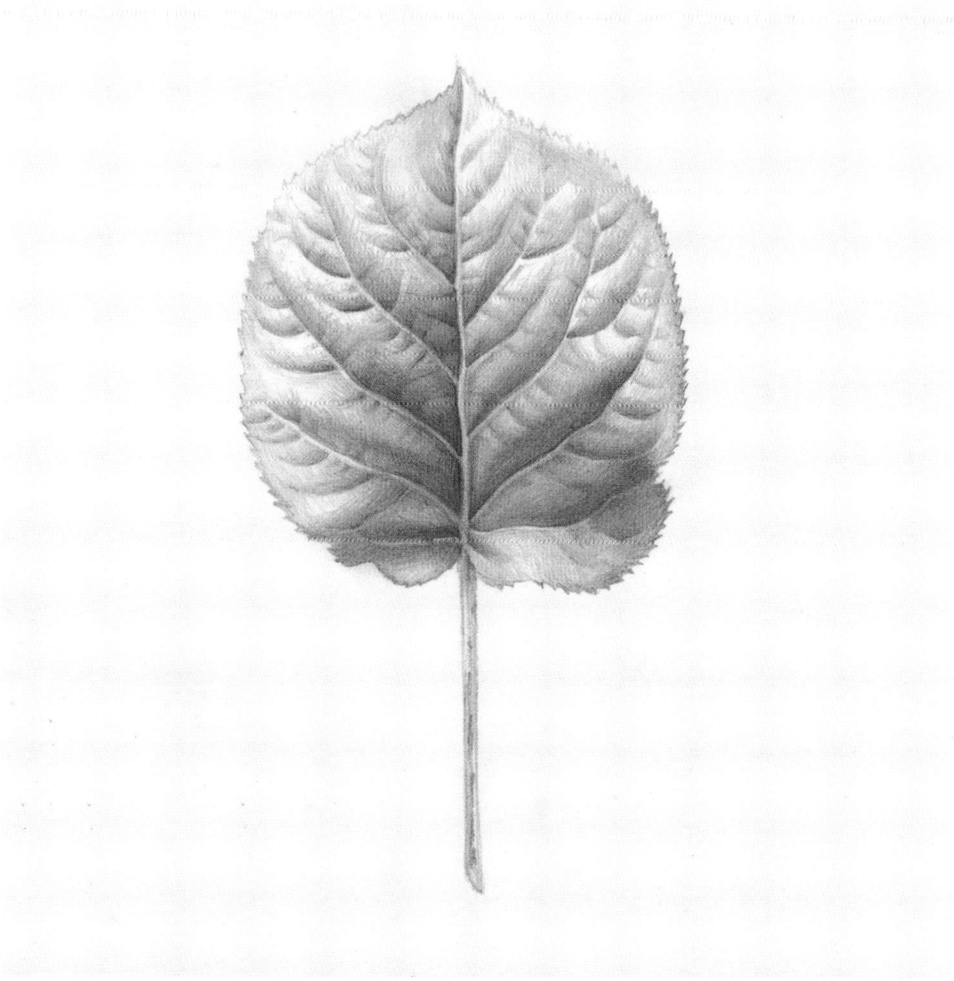

Notice where light hits the surface of this leaf, creating highlights, shadows, and dimension.

VALUES, SHADOWS, AND HIGHLIGHTS

Value is the lightness or darkness of tones and colors. In something that's black and white, the highlight is white, the shadow is black, and the mid tone is a middle gray. This middle gray or *local value* is the essential value of the subject without the addition of shadows or highlights. When looking at something in color, it's easiest to visualize its value in black and white without the distraction of color.

The goal in a successful drawing or painting is to have a full range of values. Dark values should be in harmony with light values and have a full range in between. Dark values add depth to your subject, and without contrast, your work will appear flat and lack realism. The full range of tonal values will make your work sing.

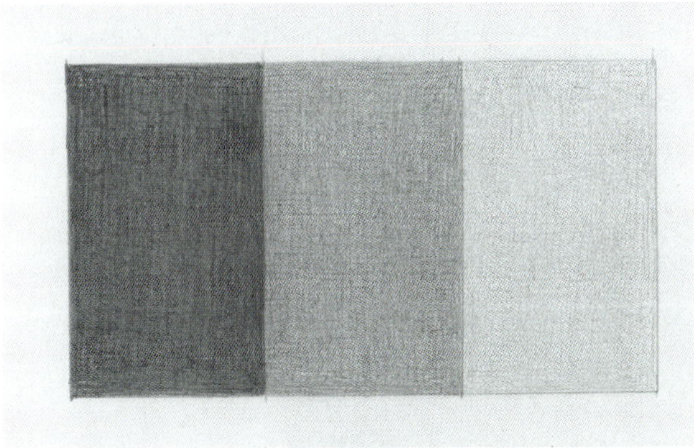

Dark, medium, and light tones with an HB pencil.

In graphite, highlights may have a light tone or maybe even no graphite at all. The darkest shadows can be achieved with a softer pencil or by layering or applying more pressure. You can practice values in graphite by using a single HB pencil and varying the pressure applied.

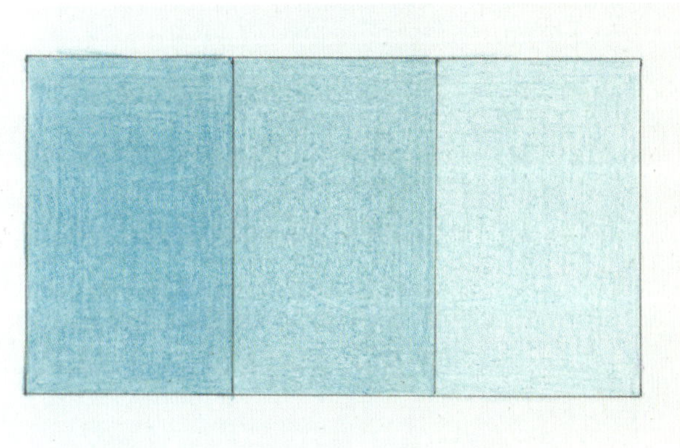

Dark, medium, and light tones with colored pencil.

Values and Overlapping

As shown in this graphite drawing, an overlapping leaf may be darker or lighter than the leaf below, depending on contours and lighting.

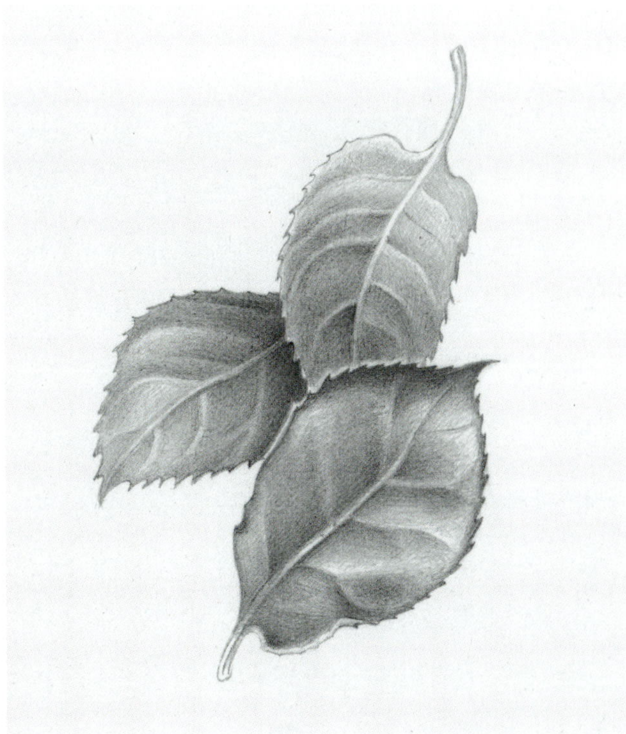

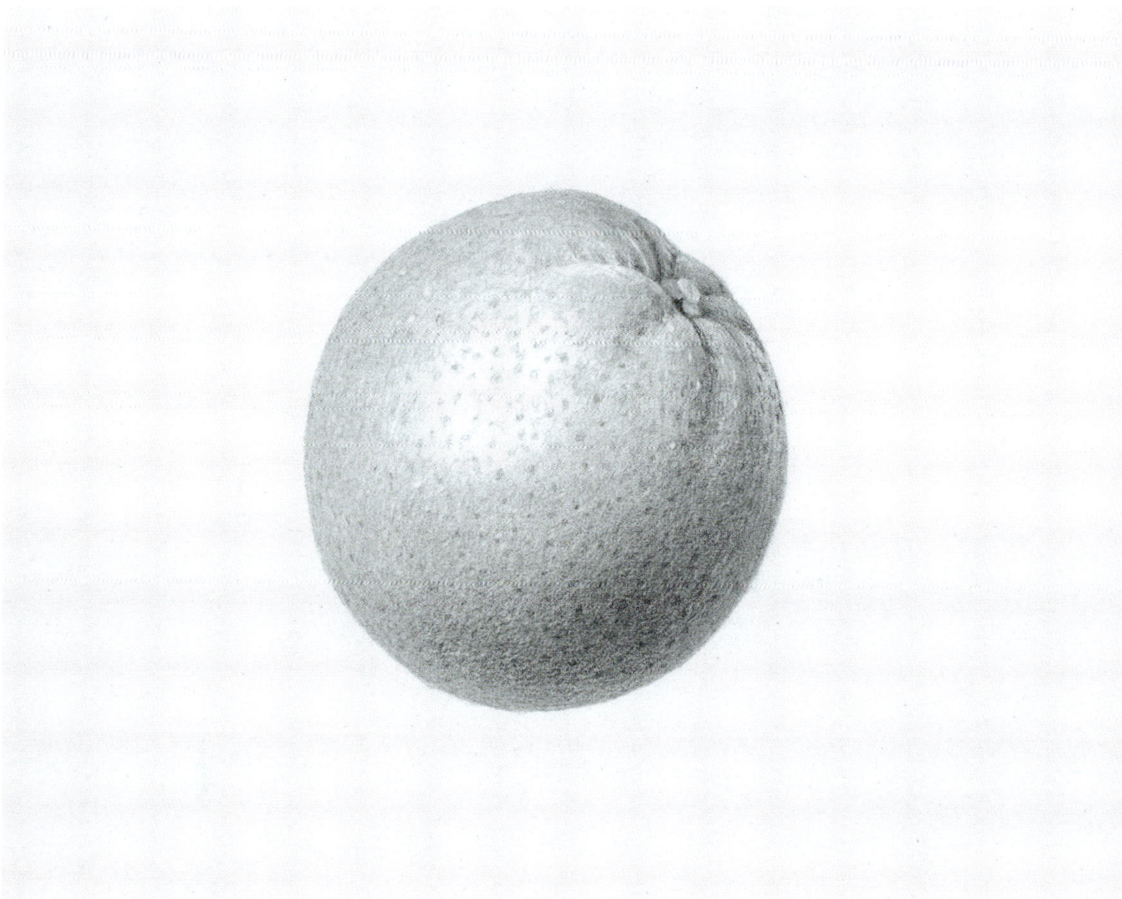

Graphite drawing of an orange showing shadow, mid tones, and highlight.

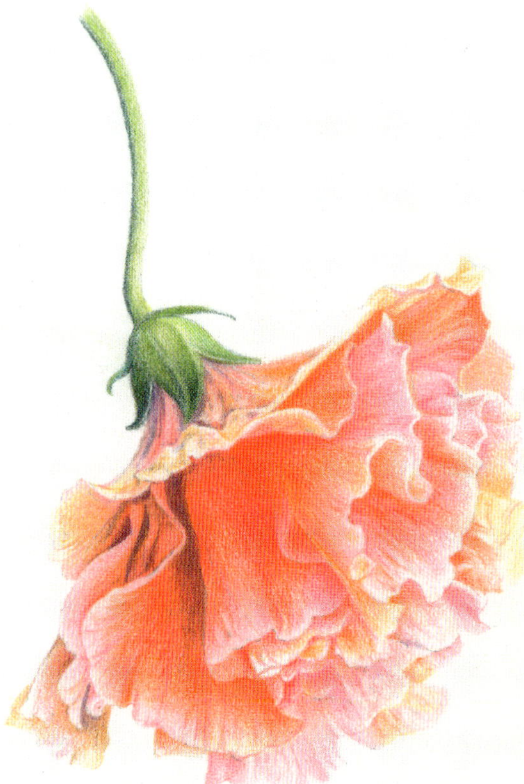

Drawing of hibiscus flower with colored pencil showing shadow, mid tones, and highlight.

GRADATIONS

Gradations are a gradual change in value from dark to light, one color hue to another, or one texture to another. Volume and curved or rounded forms, space, distance, and atmosphere can all be created with gradations. For the purposes of botanical art, we most often want to recreate the smooth gradations in a petal or leaf.

To make a smooth gradation with a graphite pencil, make horizontal overlapping lines all going in the same direction. Gradually move your hand down the page, applying less pressure and spacing the horizontal lines further apart as you go. The goal is to have the darkest value at the top and gradually fade out at the bottom. When making these lines, hold the pencil at an angle so that a wider and softer line is made. By going over this area repeatedly and filling in the white areas, a smooth gradation is created.

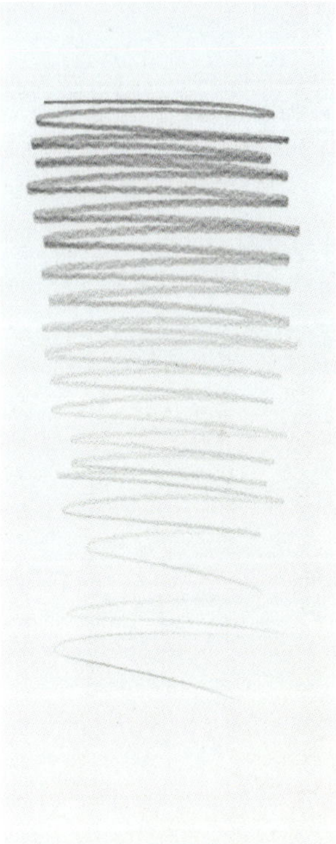

An exaggerated gradation shows more pressure and lines closer together where it's darkest.

The gradation becomes even and smooth by filling in the lighter areas.

The same building up of color and smoothing done with colored pencil.

After crosshatching to build up the colored pencil, use a wax-based colorless blender pencil to smooth and fill in the white spaces in the paper.

LIFTING GRAPHITE

When you've decided a value is too dark or you want to create a small highlight or adjust a color, lifting may be the way to go. Lifting graphite is easier than lifting with paint, but the same principle applies. Removing from a large area is more difficult than a small one. You have a choice of erasers to use when lifting graphite. If you wish to create a white dot in a dark area, the electric eraser will quickly pick up all graphite wherever it touches. If you want a light area that isn't as pronounced, a point can be fashioned from a kneaded eraser and carefully be worked into the area. The small Tombow MONO precision eraser can do this as well.

When lifting graphite from a larger area, I find flattening the kneaded eraser and pressing it onto the area you want to lift works well. You'll probably need to go back in to even the tone when doing this.

An electric eraser can also remove graphite lines from a transferred sketch on the surface of the paper you're going to paint on. The electric eraser is a great choice because it only disturbs a tiny area and removes the graphite efficiently.

These same lifitng techniques may also be used with colored pencil but will not work with fine-tip markers or silverpoint.

Supplies

- HB pencil
- Eraser: kneaded, Tombow MONO precision, or electric

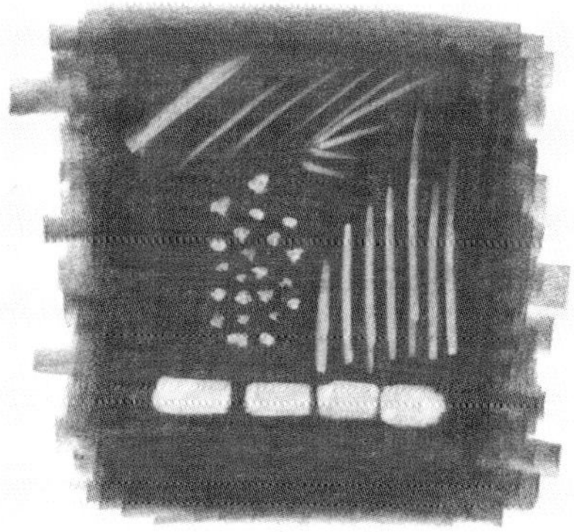

Graphite lifted with the electric eraser can make distinct small white spots and lines.

Effects made with the kneaded eraser on the left and Tombow MONO zero precision eraser on the right are more subtle.

A larger area can be lifted by flattening and pressing the kneaded eraser into the graphite.

DRAWING SUBJECTS AND MEDIUMS

Various drawing mediums can be used with botanicals. Whether the subject is delicate or roughly textured, you'll want to choose a medium that will give you the desired effect. Most important is to be able to get the detail needed with the medium you choose.

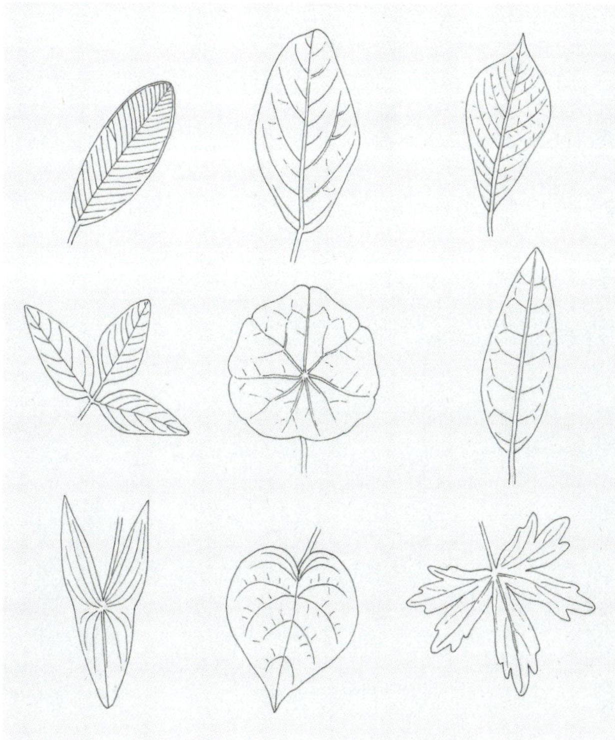

Before choosing a leaf to draw, be aware of the different variables that distinguish them from each other. Leaf shape and arrangement, edges or margins, and veins or venation patterns are all things to consider.

DRAWING LEAVES

Because in botanical art we're aiming for scientific accuracy, your drawing shouldn't stray from the leaf structure we're seeing. This is yet another reason why it's important to have the actual subject in front of you as reference and not just a photo, which may not clearly show all the details you need to see.

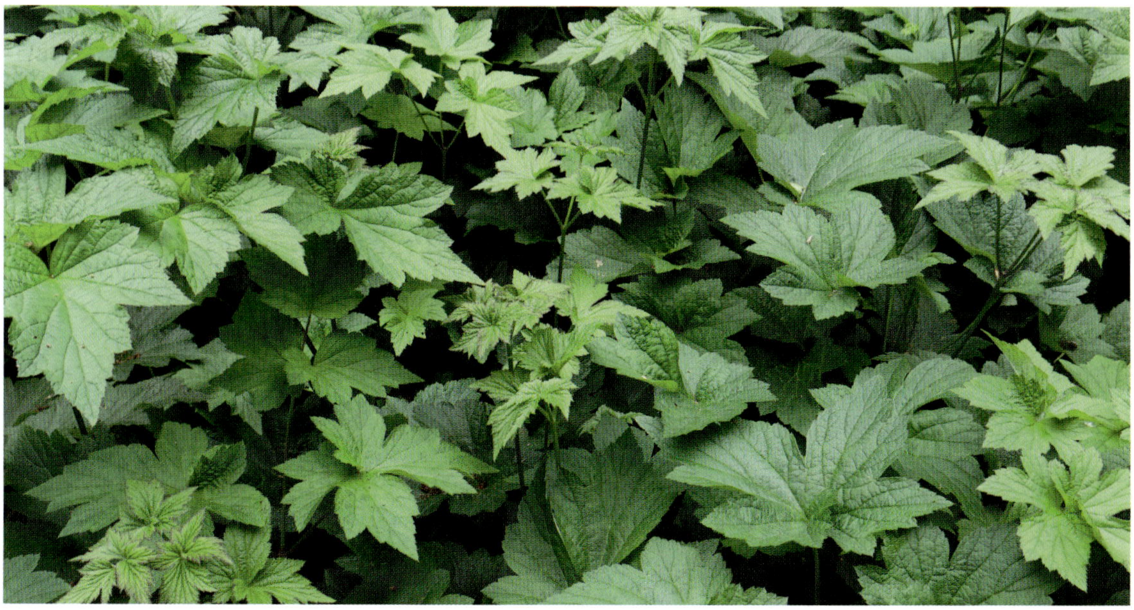

Leaves from one plant may look the same, but in fact, each is unique, so look carefully and choose the one with the most pleasing shape for your art.

Working in Colored Pencil

In the drawing demonstration for the leaf on pages 42–43, I use Faber-Castell colored pencils on Strathmore 500 Series Bristol Plate Finish (hot-pressed) paper, which is designed to capture lots of detail.

The same erasers used for graphite will also work for colored pencil (kneaded, Tombow MONO zero precision eraser, or electric). A burnishing pencil may be used towards the completion of your drawing to blend color together. These are wax pencils without color, sometimes called colorless blenders. A spray fixative for colored pencil can stop smearing.

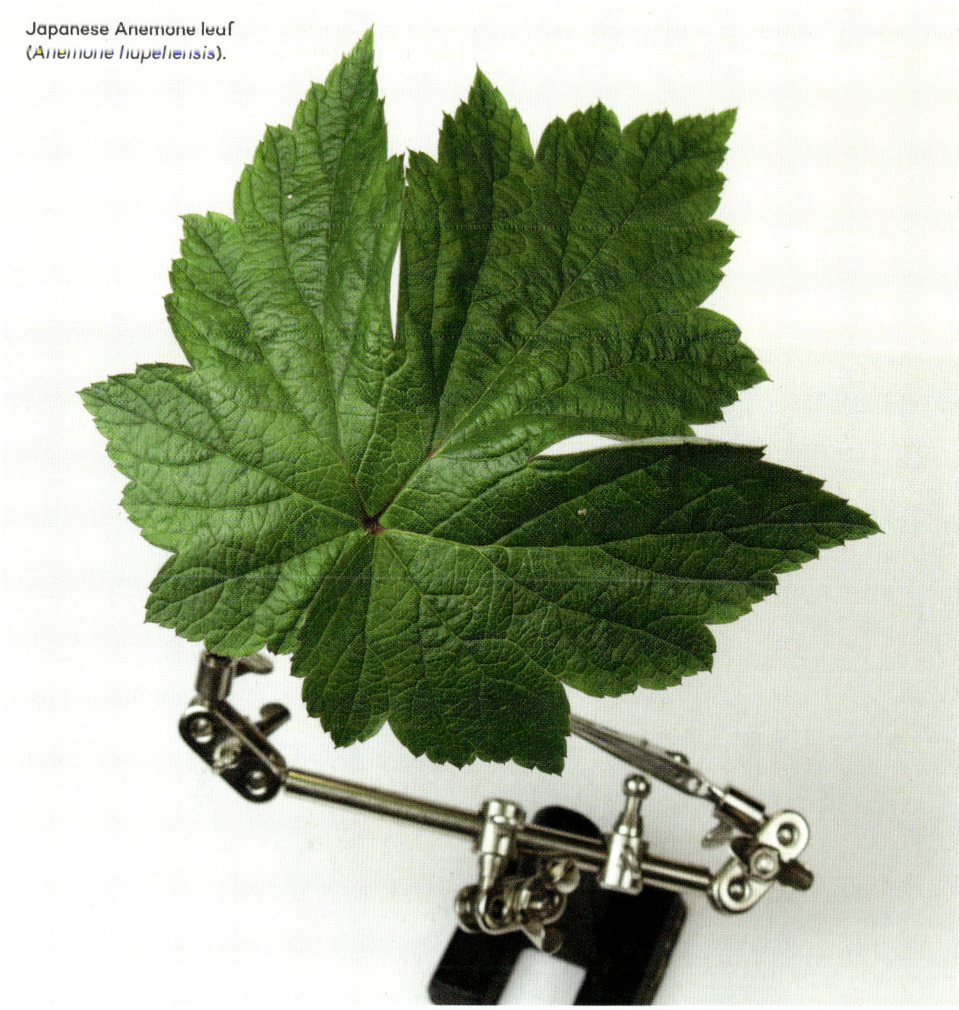

Japanese Anemone leaf (*Anemone hupehensis*).

Japanese Anemone Leaf in Colored Pencil

If you choose a leaf that has varying texture or color you will have lots of information to work with and your art will be more interesting. That was the reasoning for choosing this anemone leaf. The way your leaf is lit will help you to see the contours of the surface so adjust its placement carefully.

Supplies

- Tracing paper
- 6H pencil
- Hot-pressed Strathmore Bristol Plate paper
- Kneaded eraser
- Tombow MONO zero precision eraser or electric eraser
- MUJI Manual Pencil Sharpener
- Faber-Castell colored pencils in the following colors: Light Cobalt Turquoise, Green Olive, Chrome Oxide Green, May Green, Purple Violet, and Heliotrope
- Burnishing colorless pencil

1

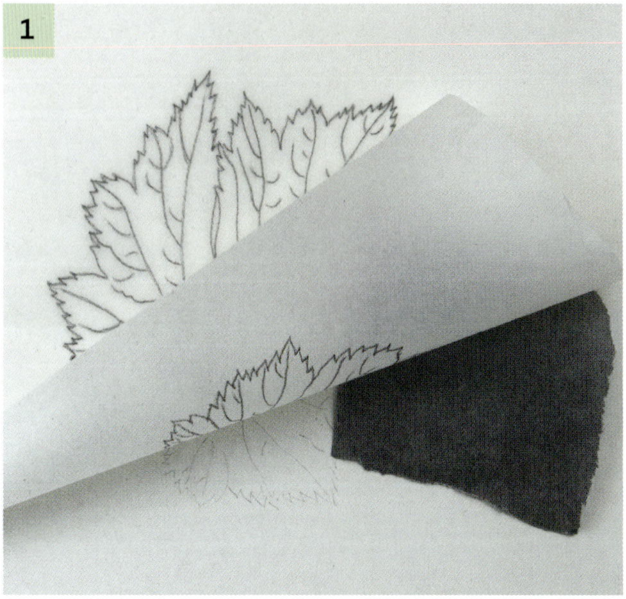

2

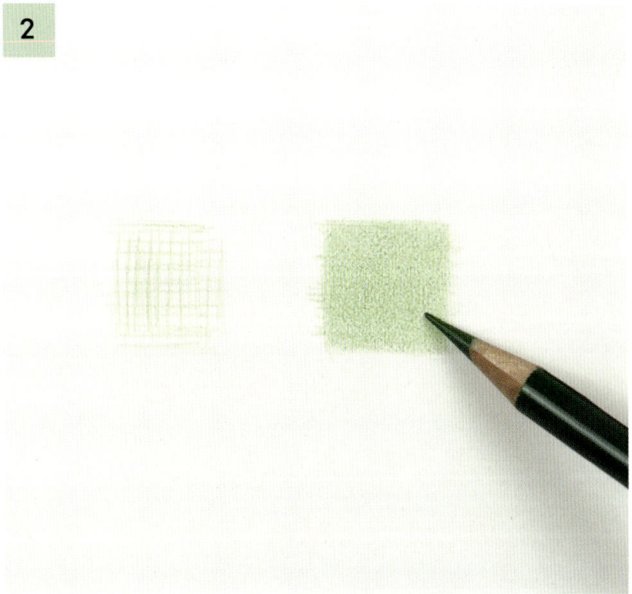

Edges

Make sure your drawing's edges accurately reflect your leaf's shape. If you use a solid line to outline a leaf, it will look "cut out" and not very realistic. Fading the edges in and out by making them darker and lighter, and perhaps not so perfect, will heighten a drawing's realism.

1. Draw the outline of your leaf, including veining, shadows, and any other significant markings. Then, transfer it to your paper in one of two ways: (1) outline the back side of the drawing with a soft graphite pencil, then turn it over, place it on your paper, and trace over the front; or (2) place a sheet of transfer paper (Saral) on your surface graphite-side down, place the drawing on top of it, and then trace it.

2. Using a very sharp pencil, apply a very light layer of color, moving the pencil in just one direction. Build up the layer slowly, putting hardly any pressure on the pencil.

3. For the second layer, apply lines in the opposite direction.

4. Use this technique to apply colors in various areas as you see them in your subject. This *mapping* approach defines the contours, shadows, and highlights in the leaf. Here, I used a pale aqua in the highlight areas, gradually layering darker greens in the shadows.

5. Build up color slowly until the values are where you want them. Defining the veining early on will help you stay on track. Experiment with gently blending with a paper towel or brush. As you work, be aware of your light source, which should remain consistent over the hills and valleys of the leaf's surface. In this way, you'll get an even tone.

6. Smaller details like red in the veining and ochre at the tips of the leaf are added later.

7. As you add more layers, you can add more pressure. Build up different colors in different areas. You may want to try the small Tombow MONO zero precision eraser to pick up highlights in small areas. Don't burnish or apply lots of pressure until you're happy with the colors you have. Once the surface has been burnished, it's difficult to add more color because there's too little *tooth*, or paper texture, left. When all the elements—values, colors, and details—seem right, your drawing is complete!

3

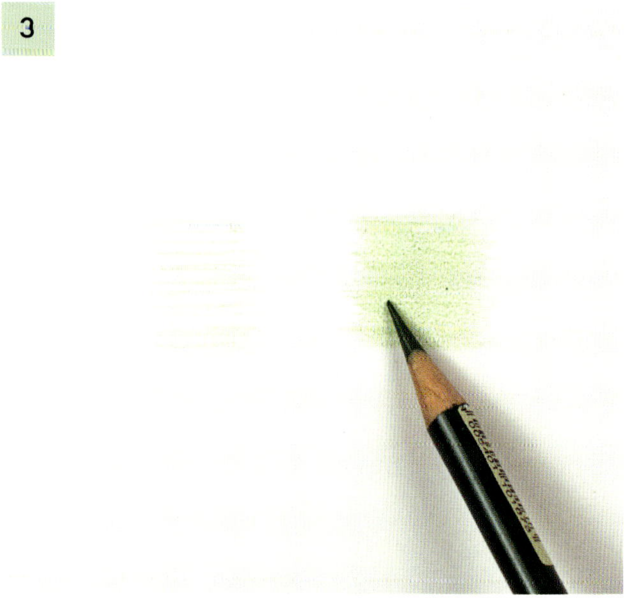

4

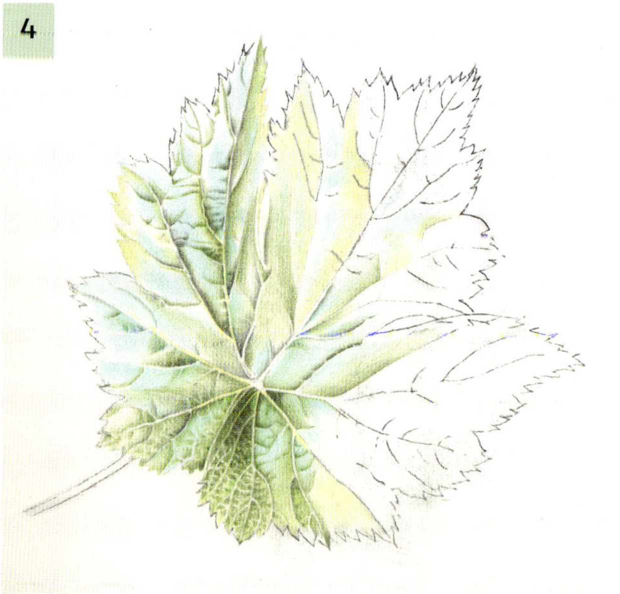

5

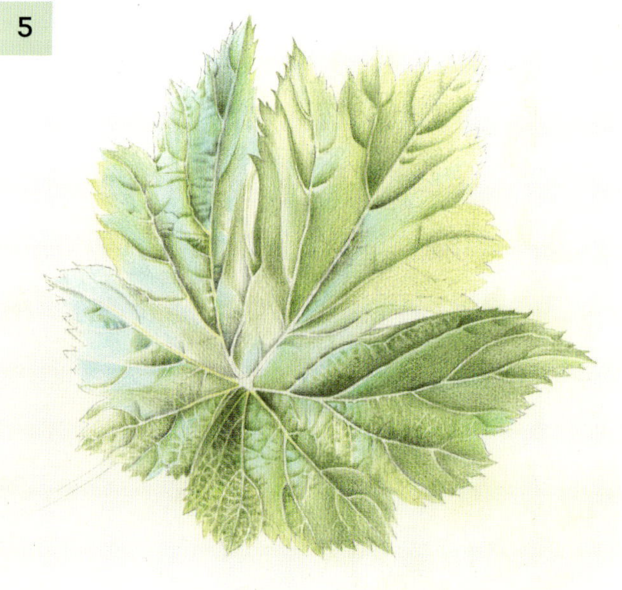

6

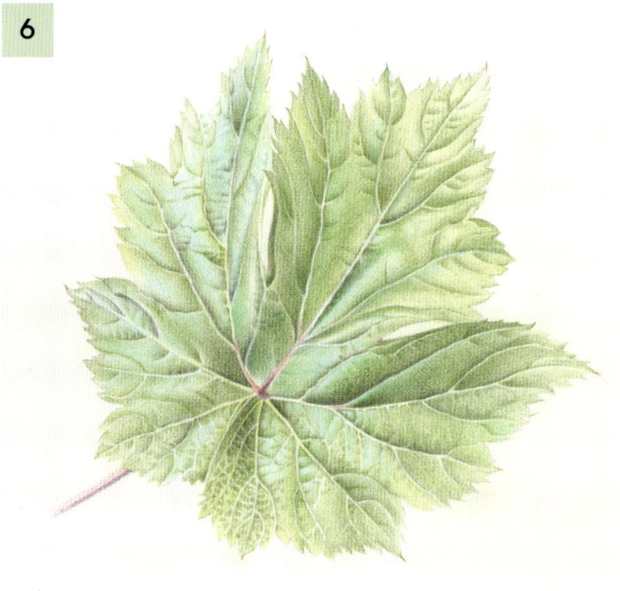

7

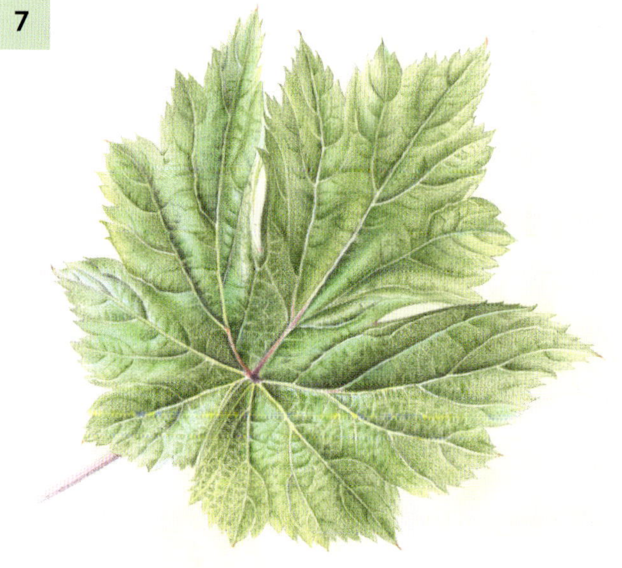

Japanese Anemone
(Anemone hupehensis)
drawn with colored pencil.

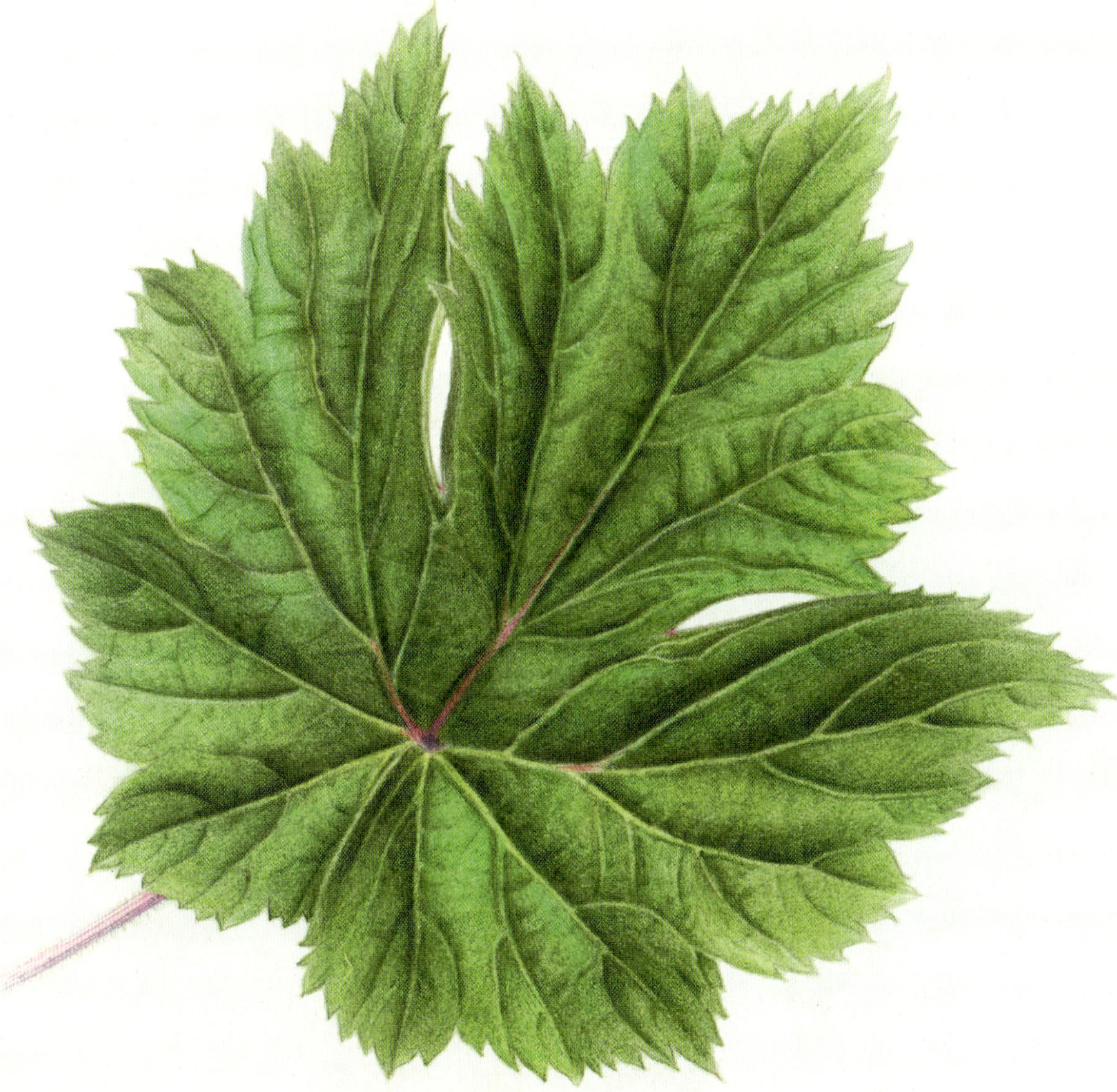

DRAWING FLOWERS AND PETALS

Flowers and petals often have a delicate surface texture with gradations that indicate their curving shapes. When they are light in value a delicate touch should be used. They may have ruffled edges or have deep veining. Be observant and mimic what you see.

Anemone coronaria **drawn with graphite.**

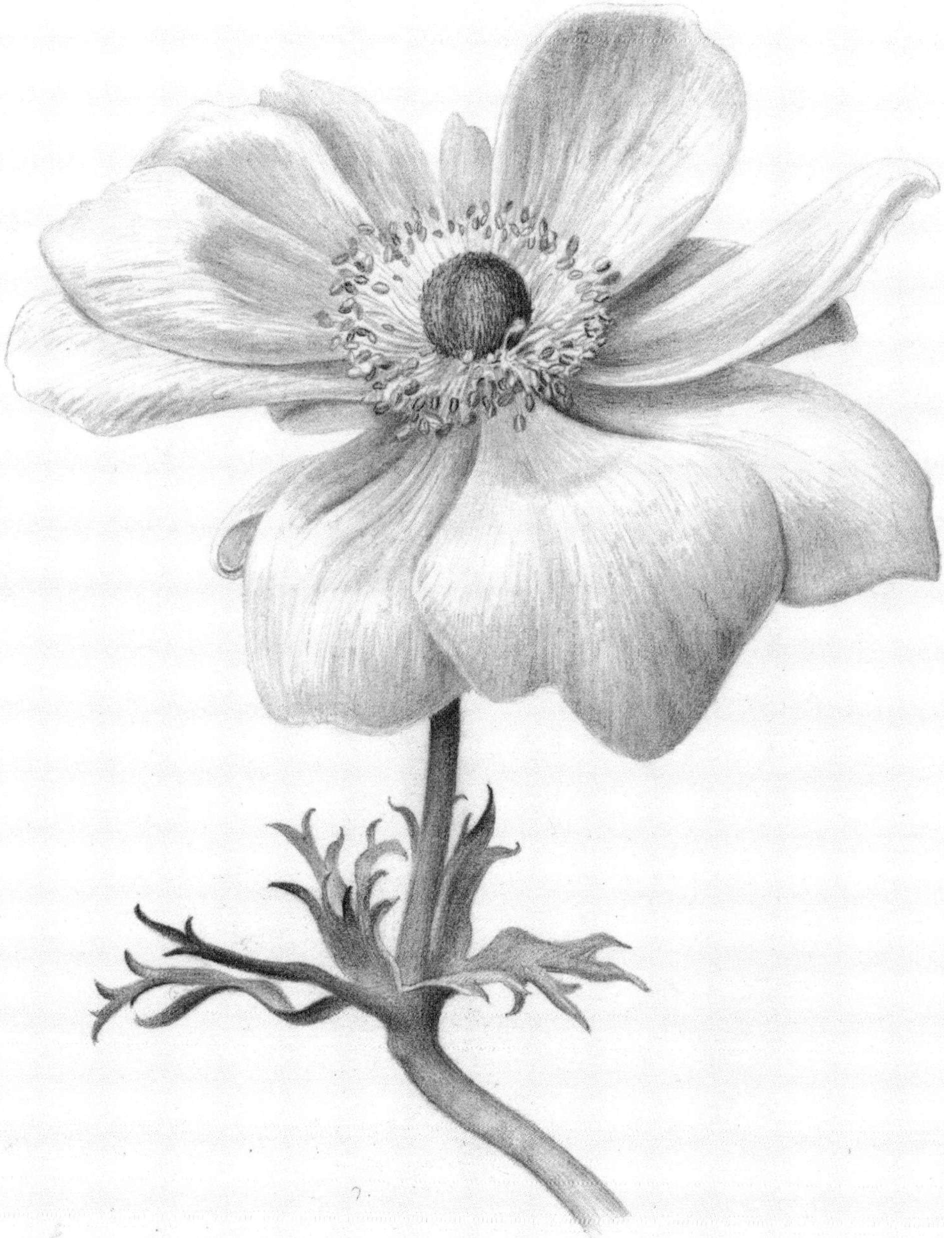

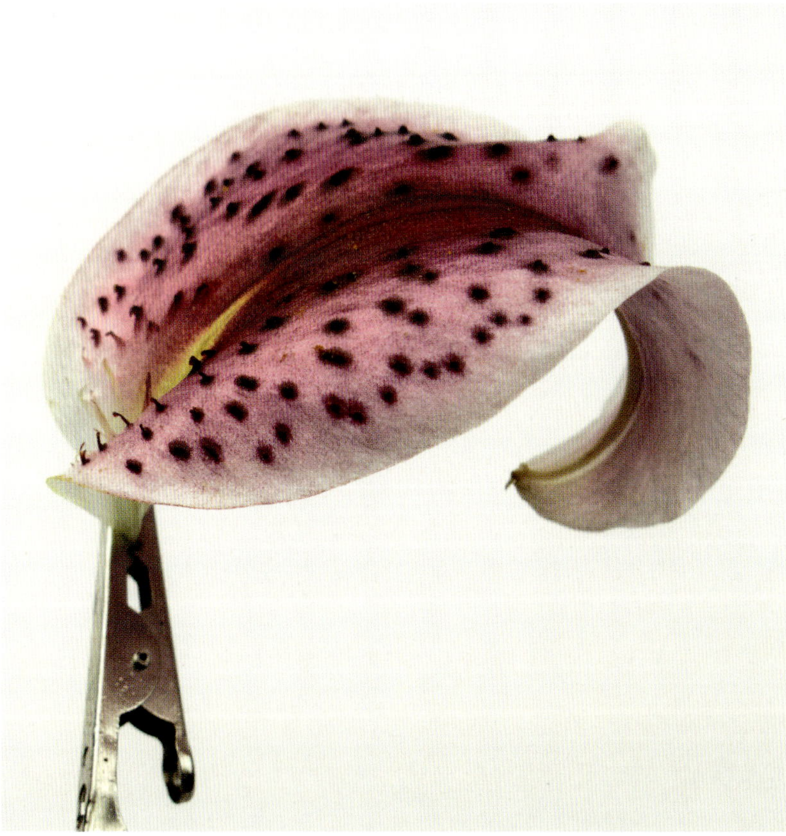

Lily Petal in Graphite

Choose an interesting petal with both dark and light colors and distinguishing details, like the lily (genus *Lilium*) flower petal above.

Supplies

- Tracing paper
- HB, 3B, No. F, 2H, and 6H pencils
- Hot-pressed drawing paper (Arches Illustration Board used here)
- Kneaded eraser

1. Draw the outline of your petal on tracing paper, highlighting the most predominant details, such as veining and spots, and any shadowed areas. Next, transfer your outline to a piece of hot-pressed paper. To transfer, use a soft 3B graphite pencil and trace over the lines on the back of your tracing paper, turn the paper over, place on your final drawing paper, and trace over the tracing paper once again with a very sharp 6H pencil. Your drawing will now be transferred with light lines to your final drawing paper. By using this method, there are no excess pencil lines, erasure marks, or damage to the paper.

2. Using a No. F pencil, fill in the bumps, or *papillae*, and any predominant veining. Begin shading in the darkest creases of the petal, moving the pencil in the direction of the creases. Hold the pencil point at a little bit of an angle to the surface of the paper, to make a softer line that will easily blend. Continue following the natural direction of the petal. To make the darkest spots, hold the pencil point at a more perpendicular angle to the paper and apply more pressure.

3. Once the dark areas are in, use a 2H pencil for the lighter shadow areas. Fill in and smooth the shadows already drawn with the No. F pencil. Then, continue to add darks to the veining, spots, and papillae. Pay particular attention to the light edges of the petal and where they fade in and out of space. In the lightest areas, there may be barely any graphite.

4. Continue to add layers of graphite to build up values and bring out the shape of the petal. The petal becomes more realistic as we darken and create contrast. The fine lines going in the direction of the petal's growth creates a delicate texture, while darker and more defined lines create the small protrusions on the petal's surface.

1

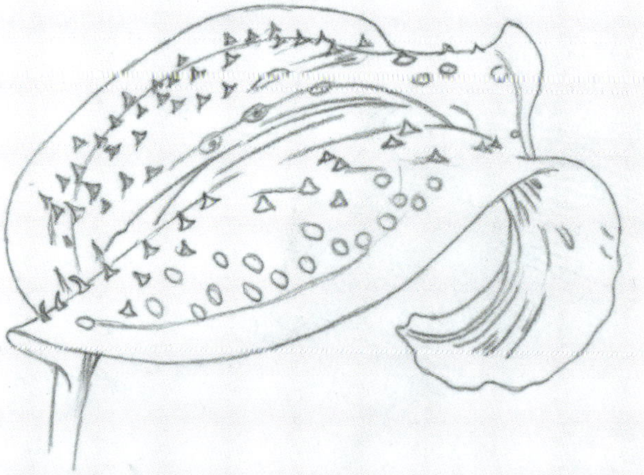

2

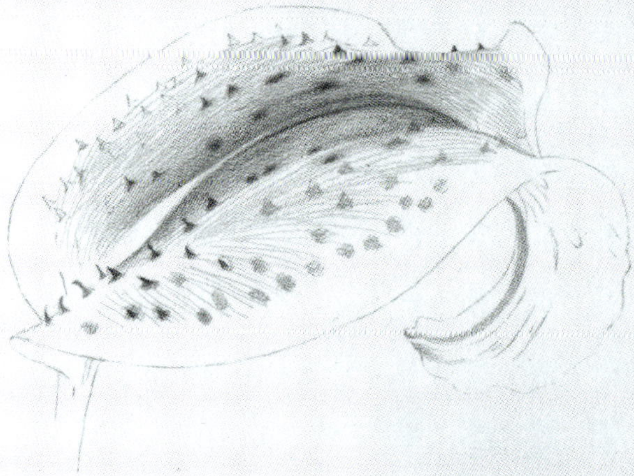

3

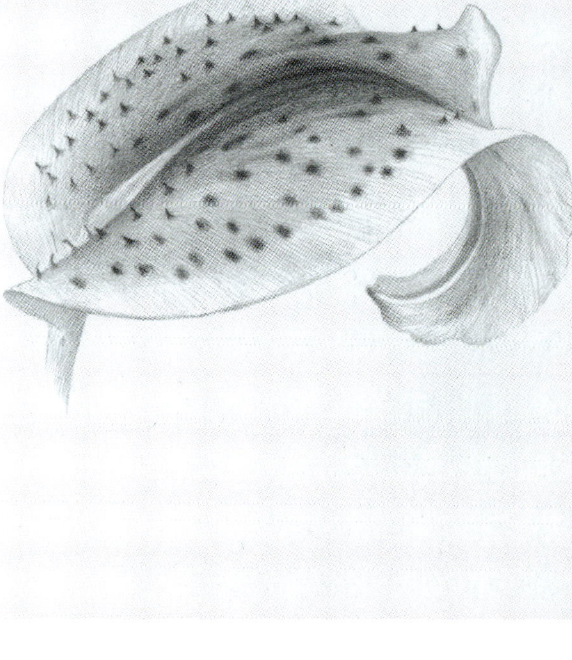

4

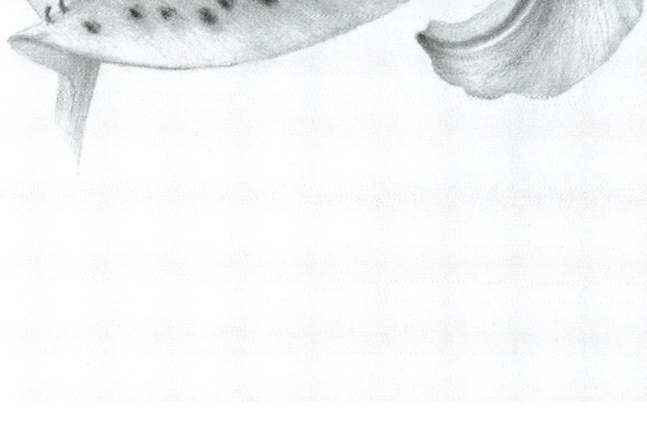

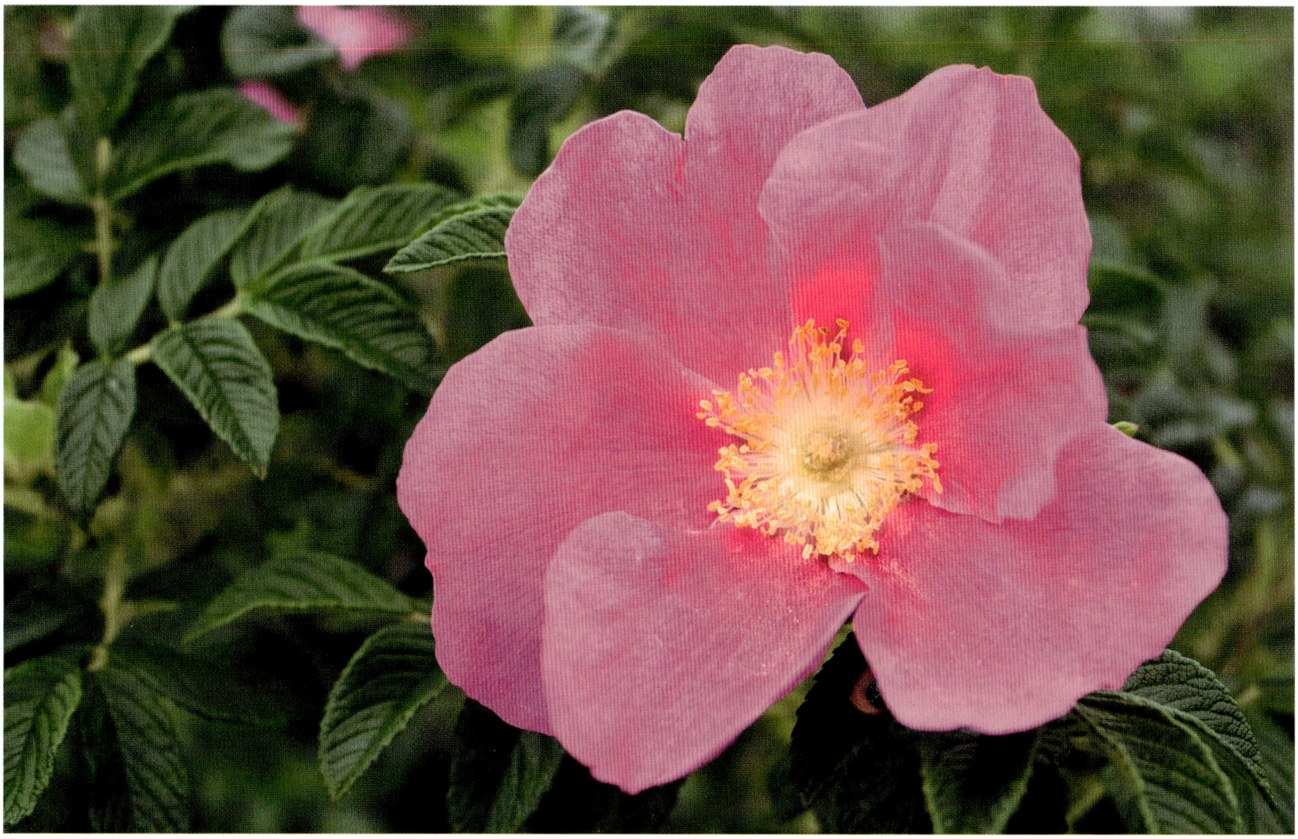

Beach Rose in Fine Point Marker

I created this beach rose (*Rosa rugosa*) sketch using both a photo and small cutting from the plant for reference. I chose this subject because the amount of detail involved made it an excellent choice for an ink drawing. For paper, I used a clay coated, *sealed*, pen and ink paper. I did not use a graphite sketch first, but instead drew directly on the paper. If you prefer, you can always make a light sketch on your paper and then erase the pencil lines after your ink drawing is complete.

Supplies

- Clay coated pen and ink paper
- Micron fine point markers, Nos. 08, 05, and 005

1. Draw the leaves and petals one at a time, comparing the proportions as the drawing progresses. To make the thicker lines, hold the marker at an angle or apply more pressure. To make the thinner lines, hold the marker at a perpendicular angle to the paper and apply light pressure.

2. Once the main outlines are drawn, add the finer details, showing veining and contours. Indicate shadows using fine lines and dots. Make the darker shadows with dots (stippling) applied close together. These shadows bring out the rounded shape and volume of the beach plums and contours of the leaves. Because the petals have less detail, apply the ink with a lighter touch so that they don't appear too heavy.

1

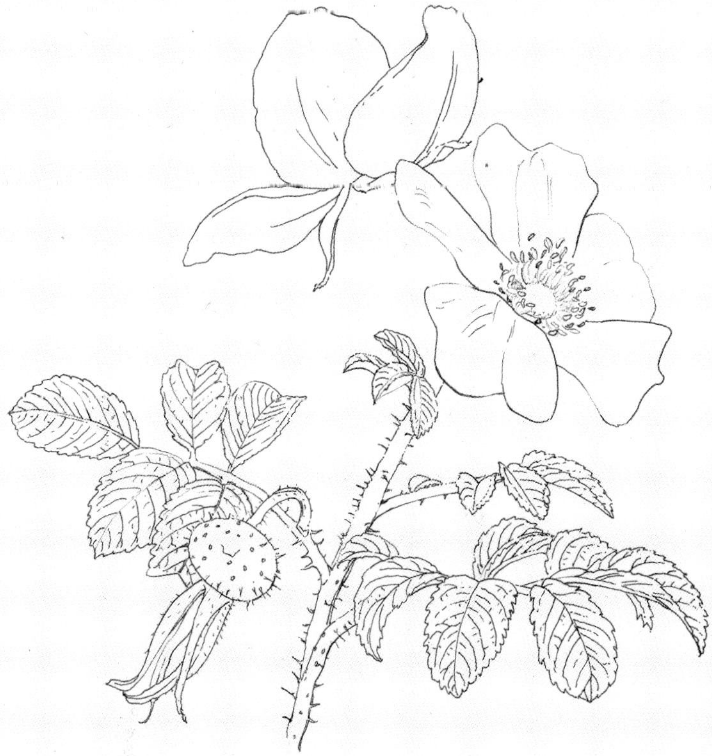

2

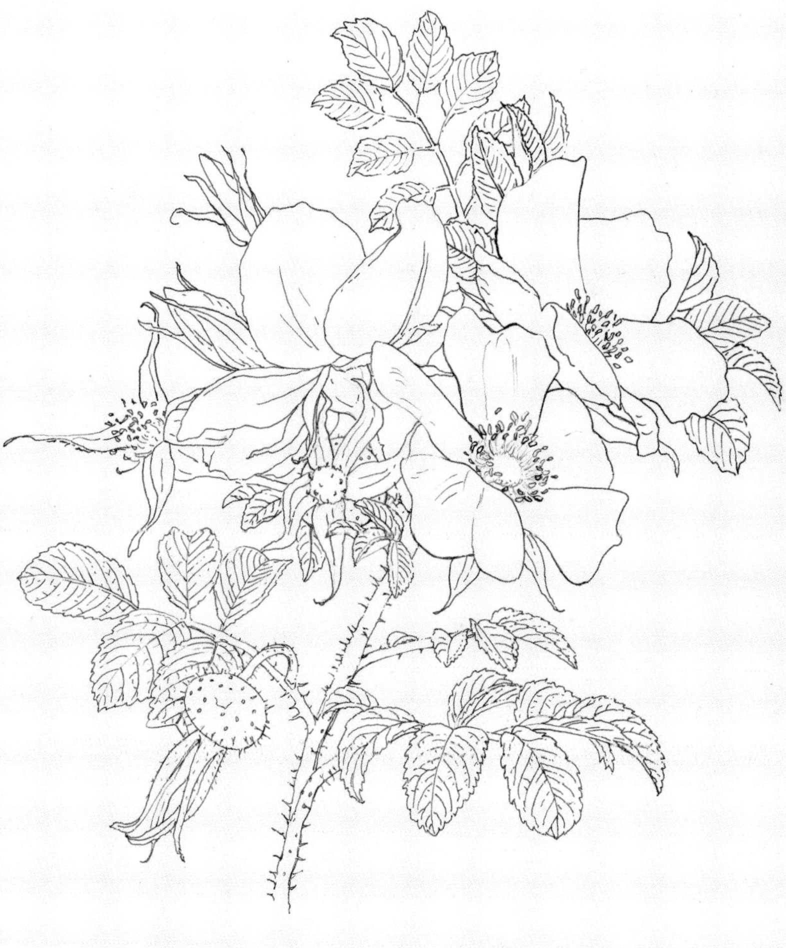

The completed marker drawing shows contours, lots of texture in the leaves, and stippled shading.

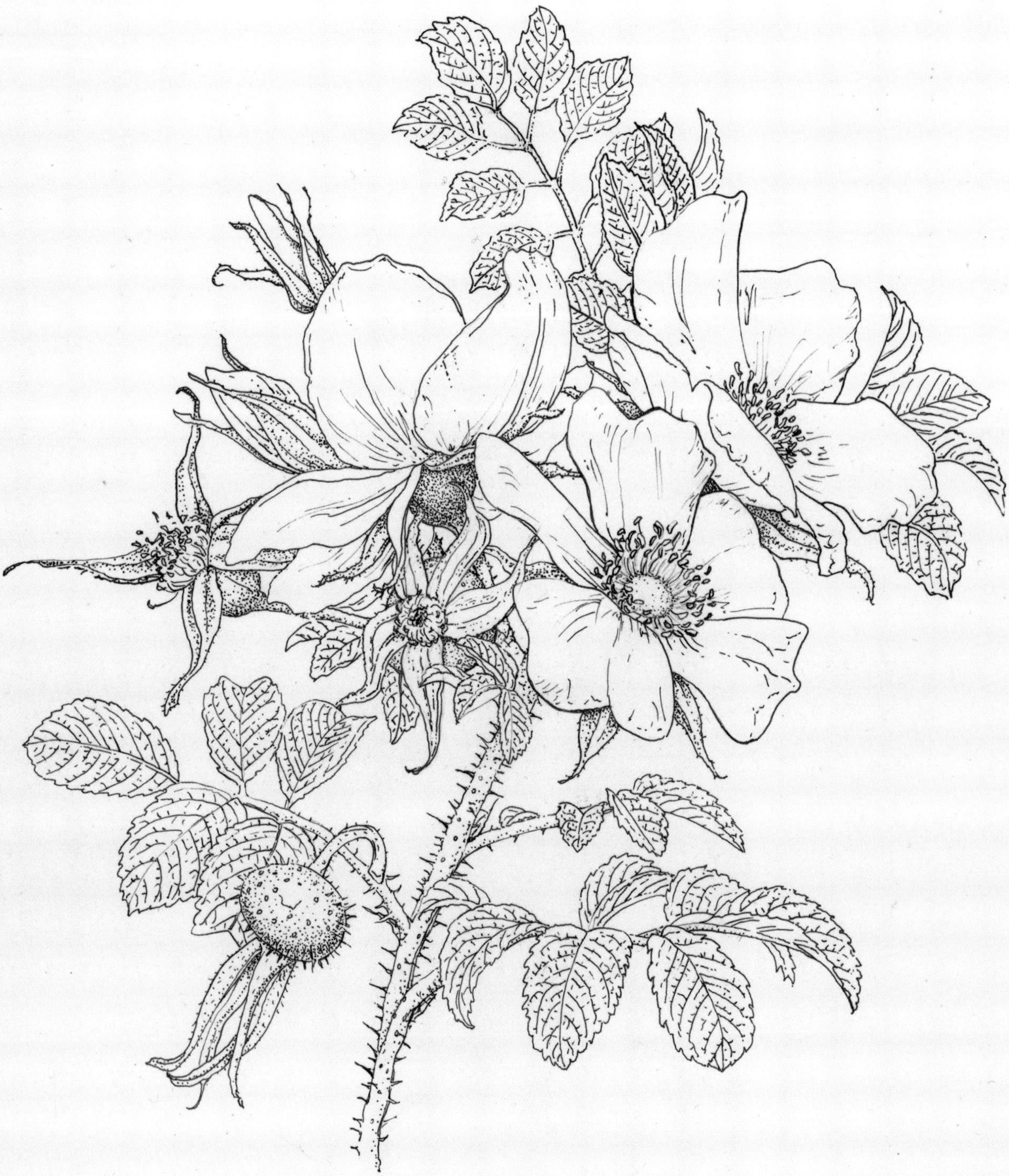

DRAWING FRUITS AND BERRIES

When portraying fruits or berries it is all about the many distinct textures they have. A banana has a matte surface so will not have the well-defined shiny highlight you would find on a strawberry. A fruit may have tiny hairs or seeds, be shiny or have bloom. For me this is what makes fruits interesting to draw.

Strawberry (*Fragaria ananassa*) drawn with colored pencils.

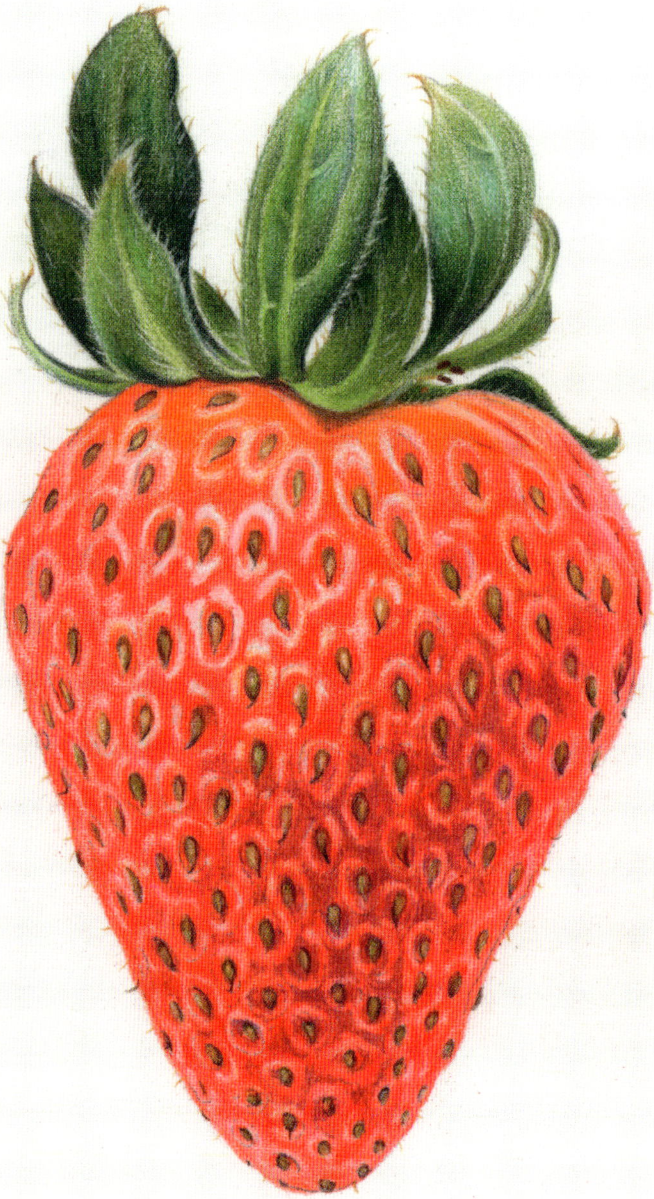

Blackberry in Colored Pencil

The blackberry was chosen to show how to create volume in each little segment with highlights, shadows, and reflected light. We can control the shiny surface by adjusting the value of the highlights and the sharpness of the highlights' edges. By doing this, each little segment looks round, has volume and texture.

Supplies

- Tracing paper
- 6H pencil
- Hot-pressed Strathmore Bristol Plate paper
- Kneaded eraser
- Tombow MONO zero precision eraser or electric eraser
- MUJI Manual Pencil Sharpener
- Faber-Castell colored pencils in the following colors: Dark Sepia, Dark Indigo, Pale Geranium Lake, Light Yellow Ochre, and Pink Carmine
- Burnishing colorless pencil

1. The highlights on the blackberry (genus *Rubus*) subject will change with each slight movement, so be sure to take a photo to record the original composition.

2. Once you finish the outline of each segment, draw in the highlights and shadows using Dark Indigo in the darkest shadows. This blackberry has intense deep blue-black color throughout most of the berry, so the color mapping process for this subject is simple.

3. Add Dark Sepia over the Dark Indigo to deepen shadows.

4. Use Dark Indigo to draw in gradations, one section at a time, comparing and mirroring the values you see in your subject. Since the value of the blackberry is so dark, use Dark Indigo over the entire surface of the berry, except for the whitest highlights. Define the edges using the sharpest point, and once the

1

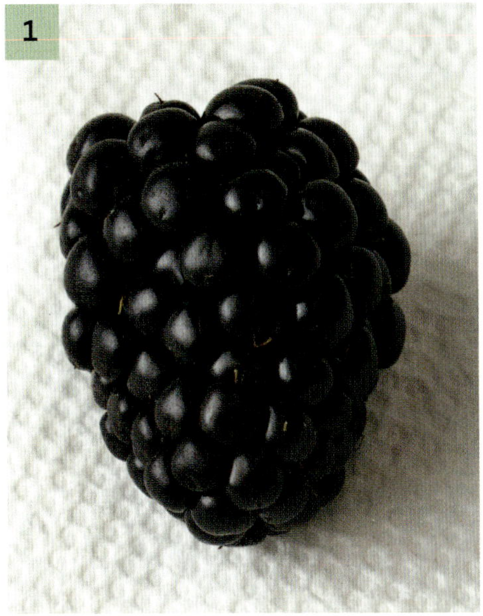

point begins to dull, use the wider line to cover larger areas. Make lines going in different directions (crosshatching), so the lead adheres to the paper, being careful not to press too hard. Continually turning the pencil will eventually create another sharp edge without needing to use a pencil sharpener.

5. Use Pale Geranium Lake and Light Yellow Ochre in the hairs. Layer Dark Sepia into the deepest shadows.

6. Lightly add Pink Carmine to the hairs and just a few segments to create pink undertones.

7. Burnishing helps to fill in the tiny spaces of white paper and deepen the values. When your drawing is complete, you may want to spray it with a fixative for colored pencil to prevent smearing. A workable fixative spray can also be used while you draw. You can draw on top of a workable fixative, but you won't be able to remove any pencil lines once it's been sprayed.

2

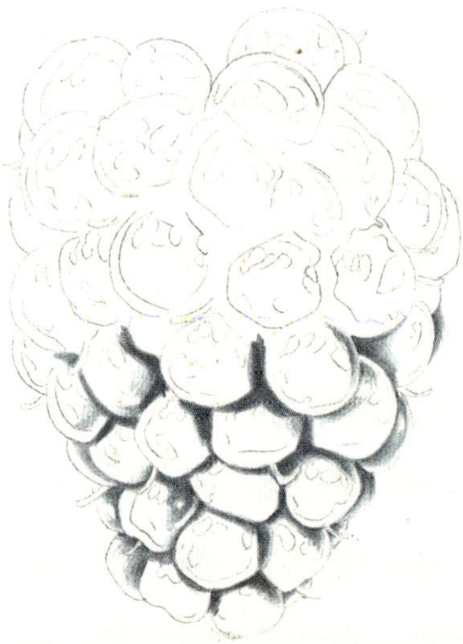

3

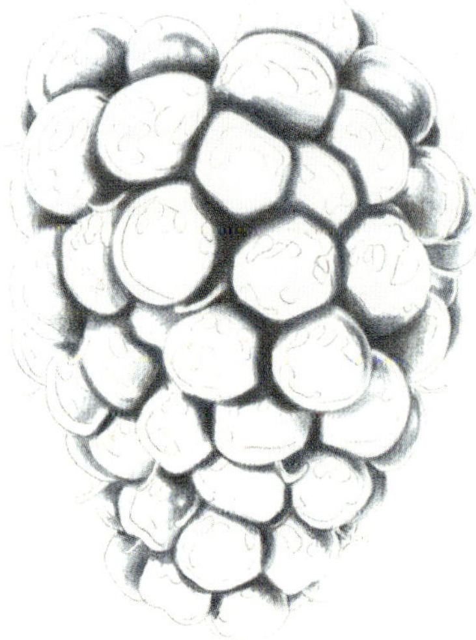

4

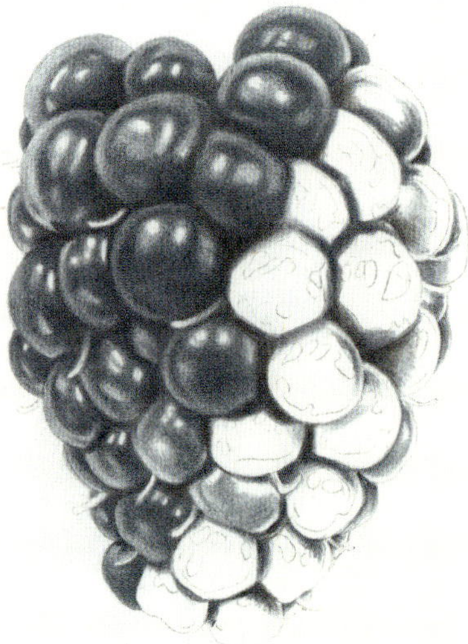

5

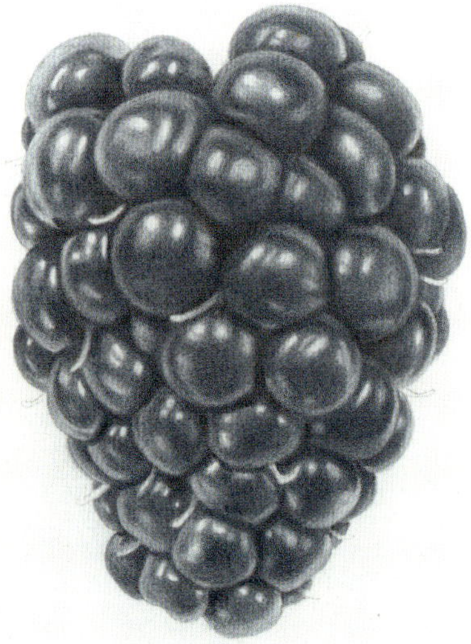

6

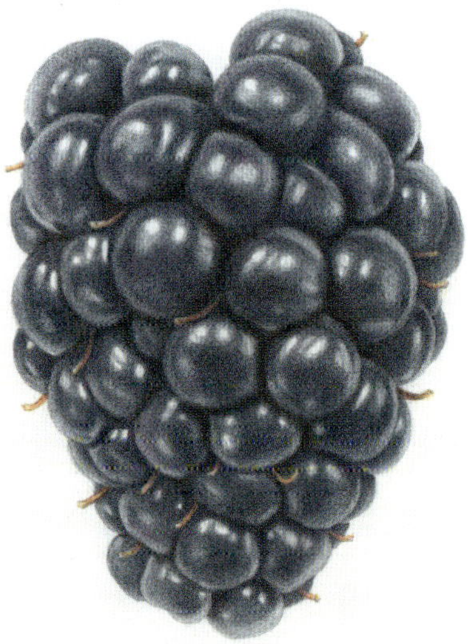

7

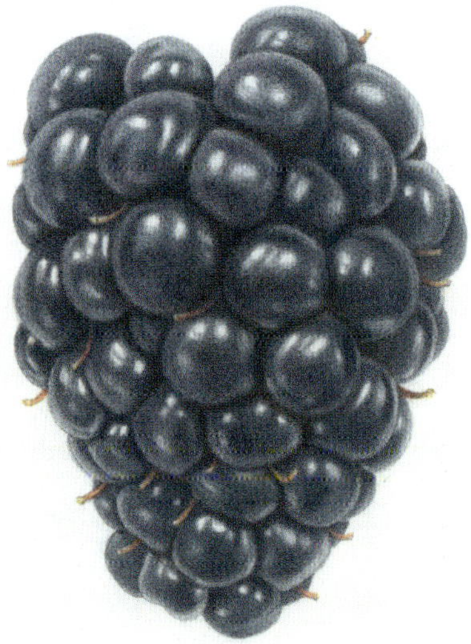

DRAWING STEMS AND BRANCHES

To be honest, stems and branches are my least favorite, although necessary, part of a plant to draw or paint. I would much prefer to portray a showy colorful flower. Once again, careful observation of your subject is important as the details are often not easily distinguished in a photograph. Because stems and branches don't wilt quickly, you'll find these easier to maintain and display than a flower.

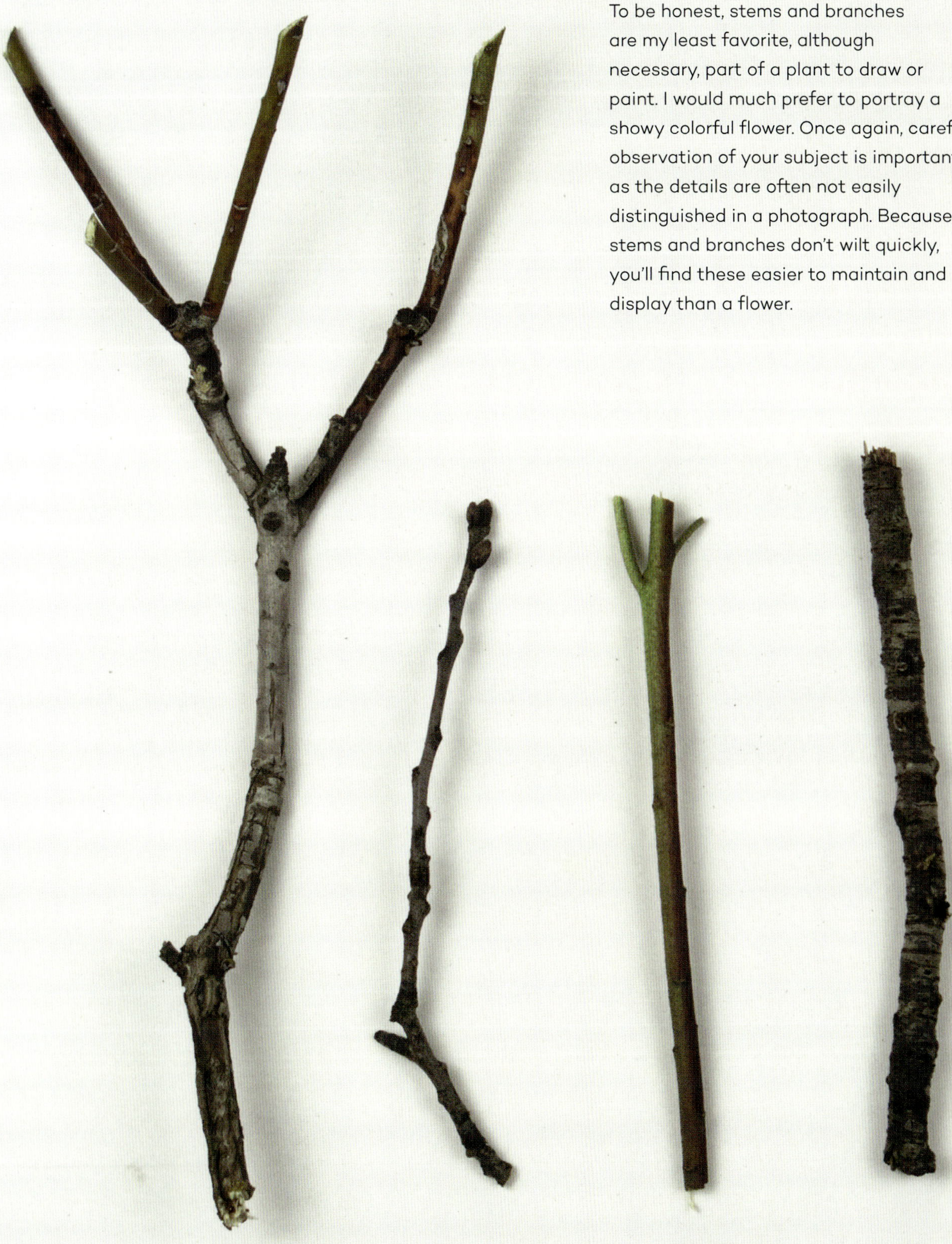

Each stem or branch is unique in both color and texture.

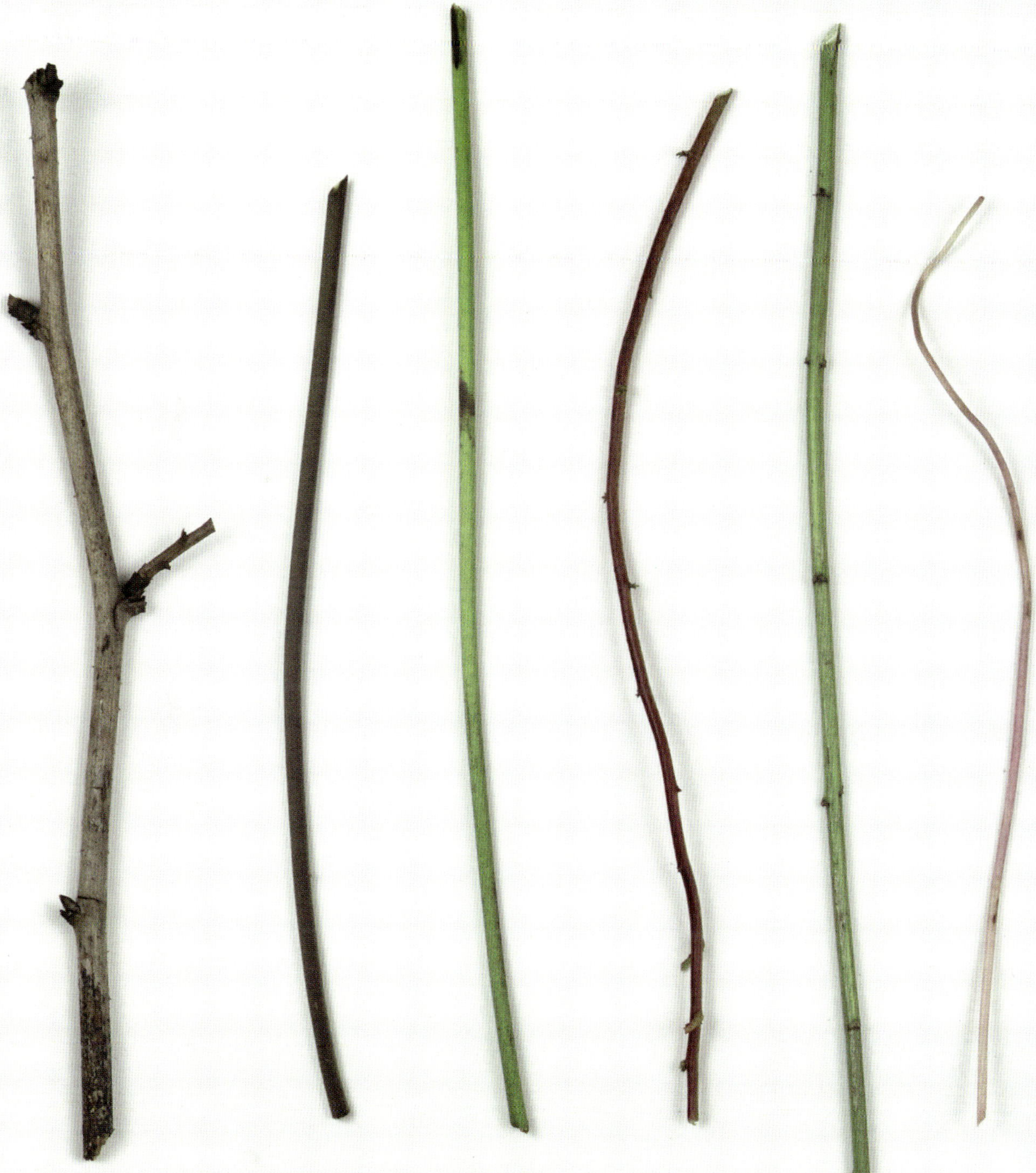

Stems often gradually change in appearance as they get closer to the flower. Make detailed written notations of your observations of these textures and colors. Notice where leaves come off the stems, how they are configured, and their distance apart.

Observe the texture so you can accurately convey the way the subject feels. Is the stem shiny, hairy, ribbed, or undulating? Whatever texture you observe, you'll try to portray by replicating what you see. A shiny stem will have a light highlight; a ribbed stem will have one or more indents running the length of the stem; a smooth stem will have even gradations; and a rough branch will be filled with a lot of contrasting textures.

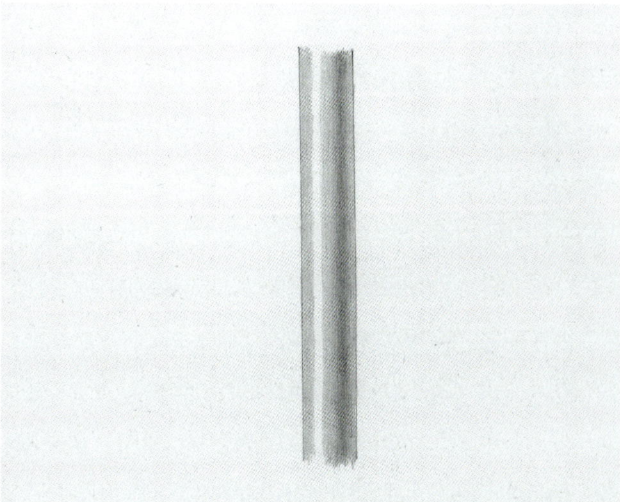

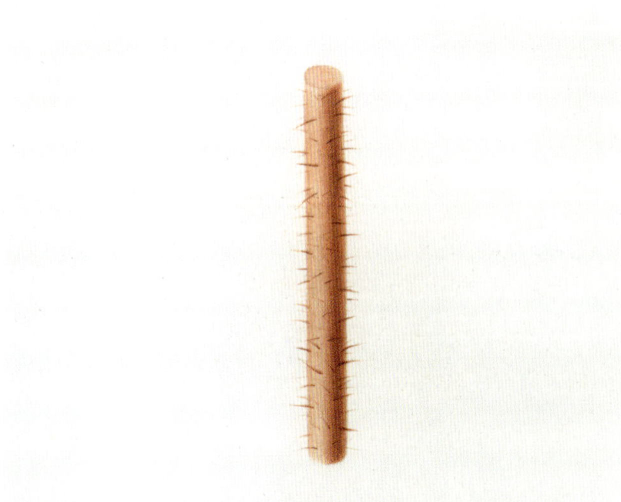

To simplify, think of a stem like a long cylindrical shape.
One side will have a shadow, and there will be a lighter highlight running along the length.

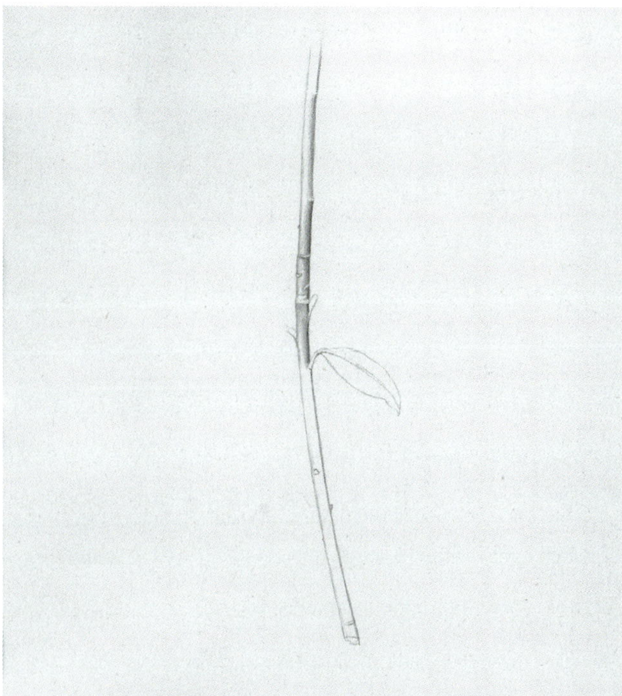

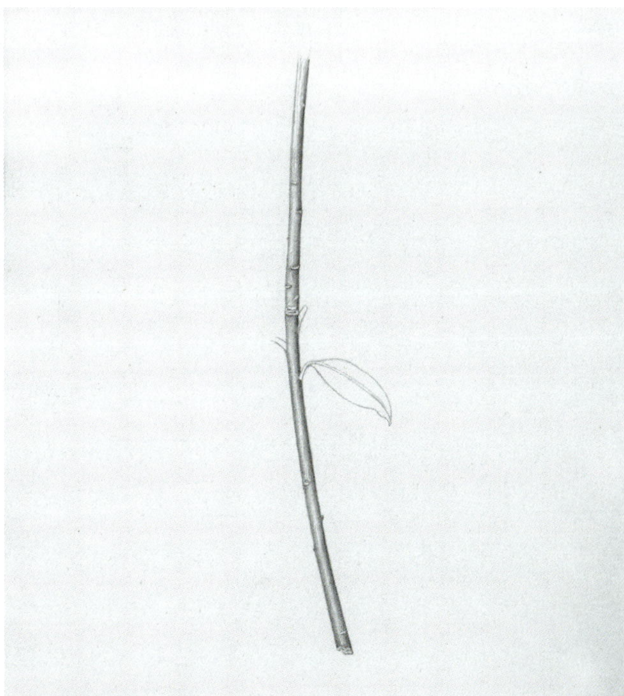

The rhododendron (genus *Rhododendron*) stem has small segments that can be drawn section by section, detailing the texture you see.

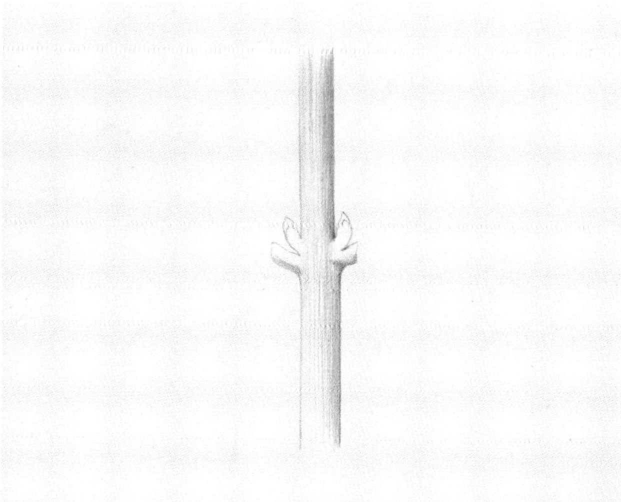

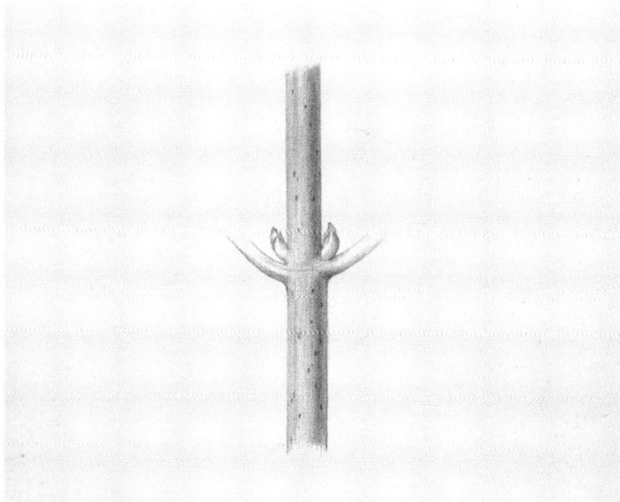

Long lines going in the direction of growth create shadow in this thick hydrangea (genus *Hydrangea*) stem.

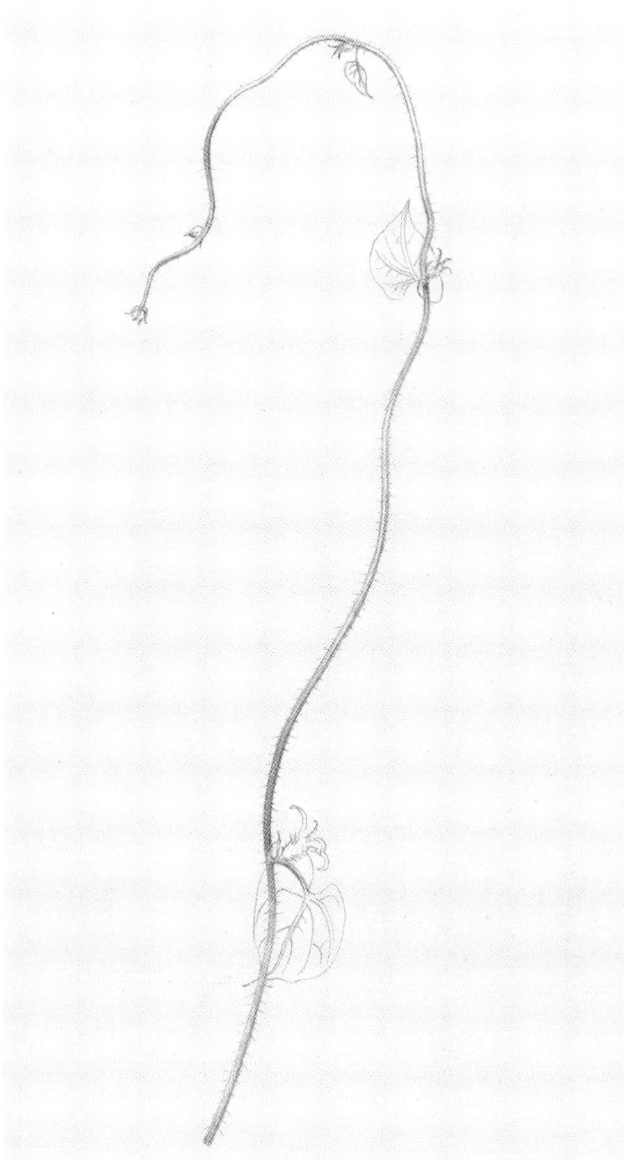

Light and shadow give this curving morning glory (*Convolvulaceae* family) stem movement. The fuzz on this hairy stem can be made using a sharp pencil point.

All three stems
shown together.

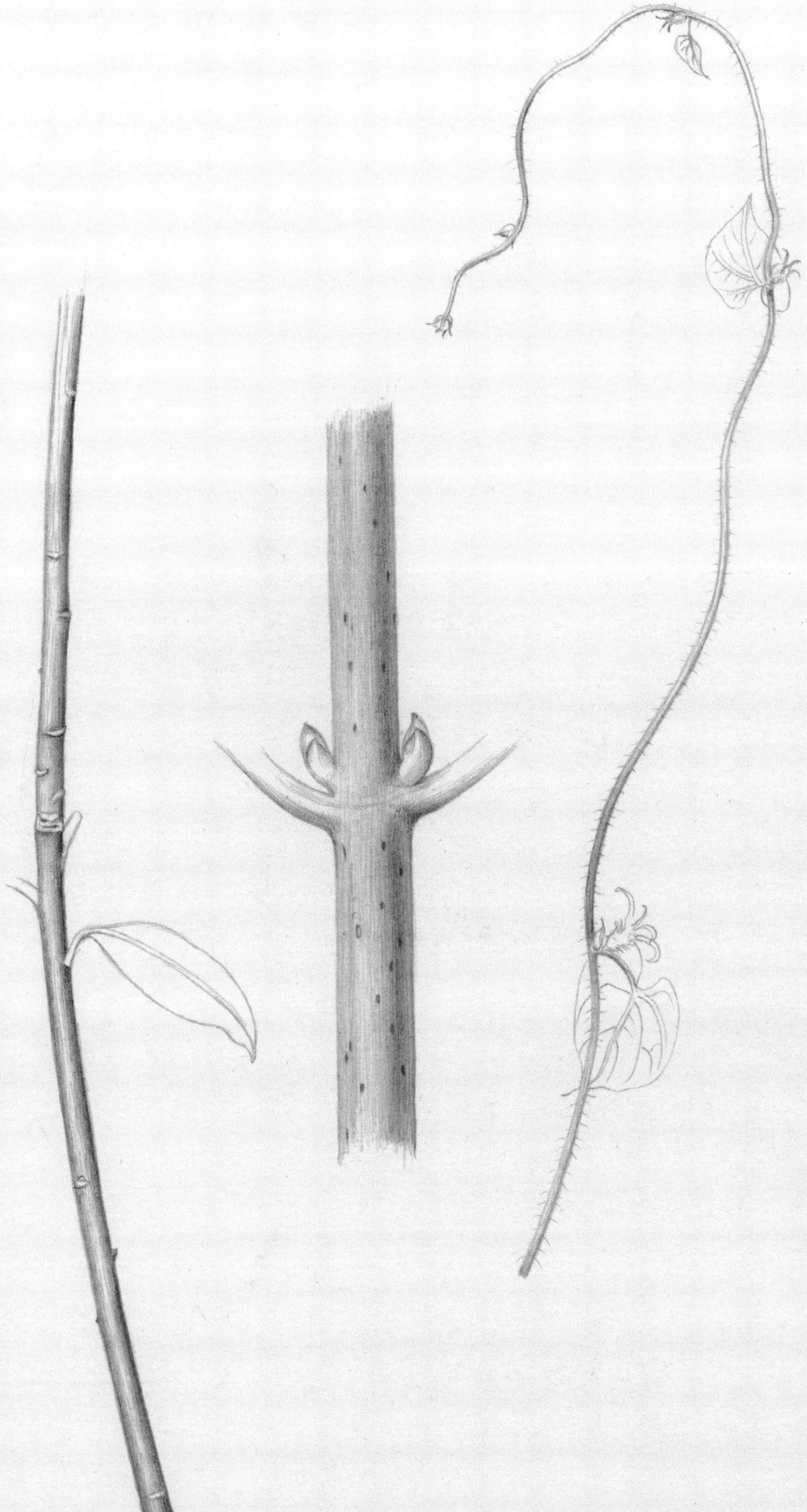

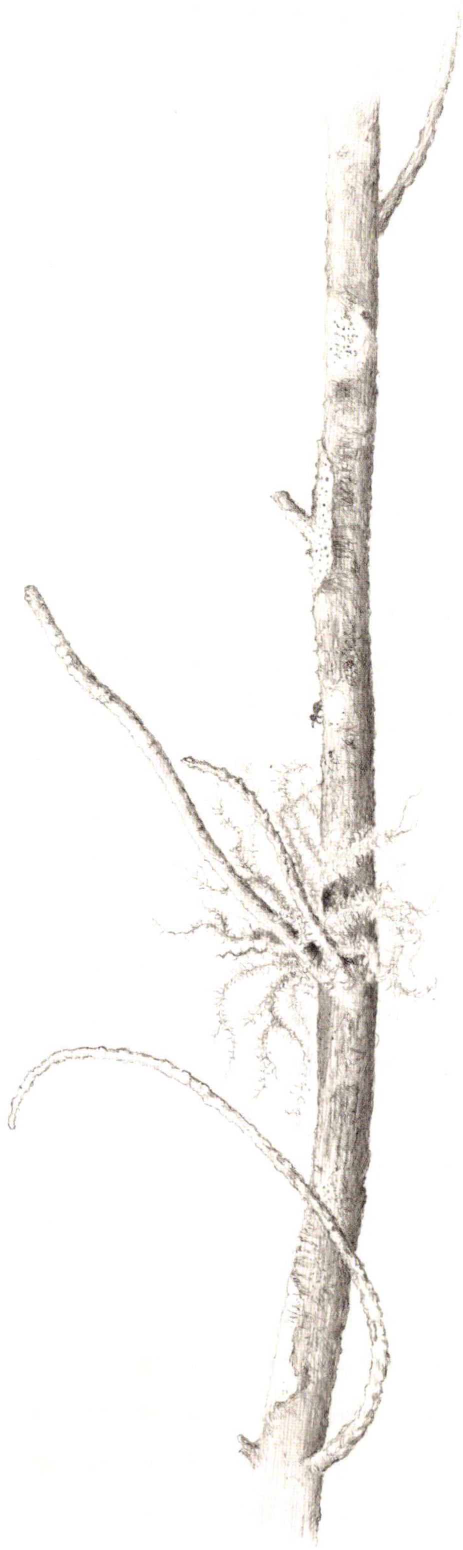

Lichen growing on a branch has lots of irregular and delicate texture to work with.

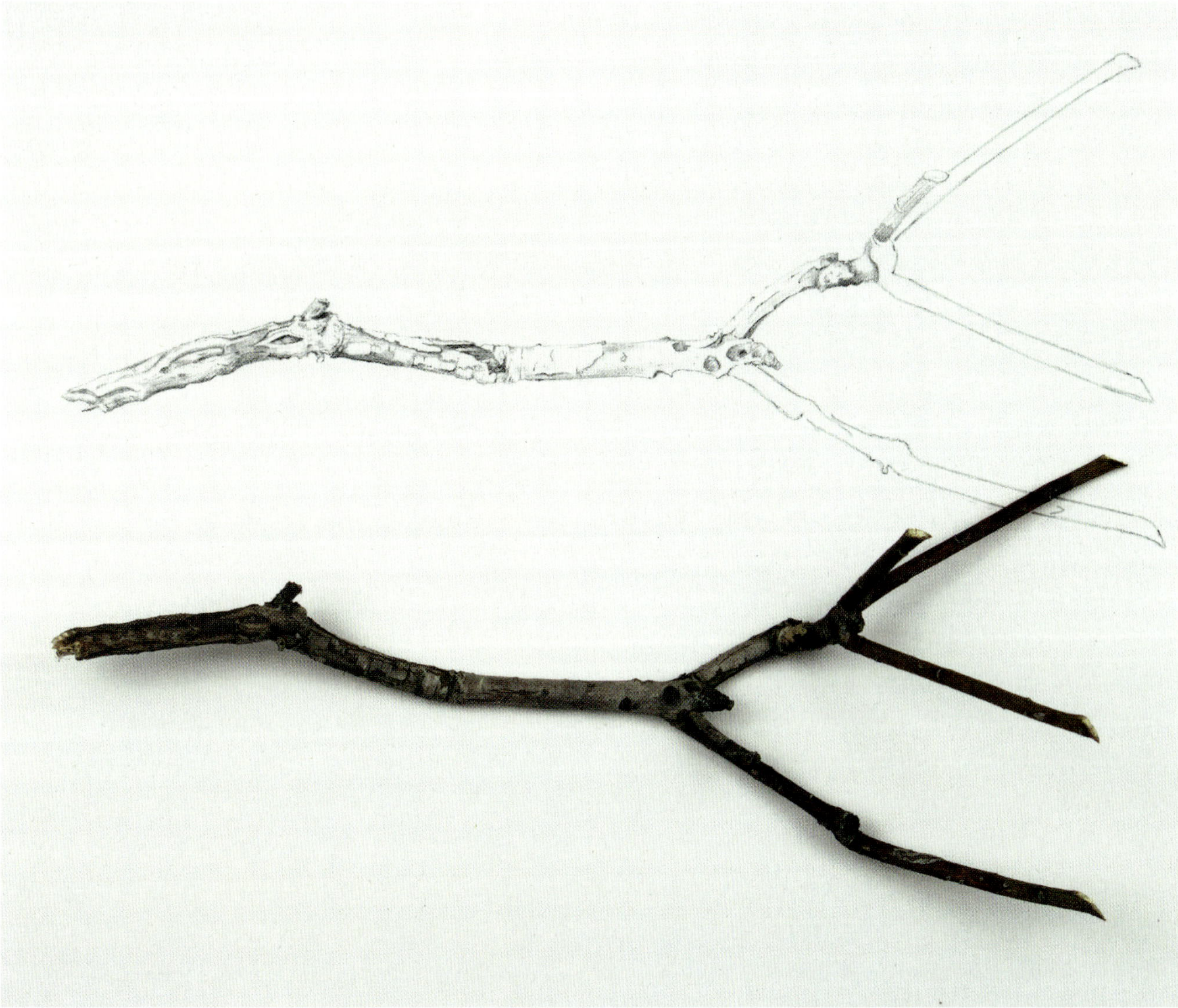

Because the details are so irregular and nondescript, this drawing is kind of like scribbling.

Branch in Graphite

This drawing of a small branch is a quick exercise easily done from life without using dividers to measure. Because the branch is stiff and holds its shape, you can hold it carefully with one hand and make a general outline of its proportions with the other hand. Then, you can more accurately draw in the branch's width just by eyeing it.

Here, I'm working from left to right, adding predominant markings, flaking bark, indents, and protrusions. Use a light touch where the values are lighter. Press down harder with a sharp point where you see the darkest shadows. A highlight and shadow will run along the length of the branch, so make sure a gradated shadow is drawn on one side to bring out the cylindrical shape.

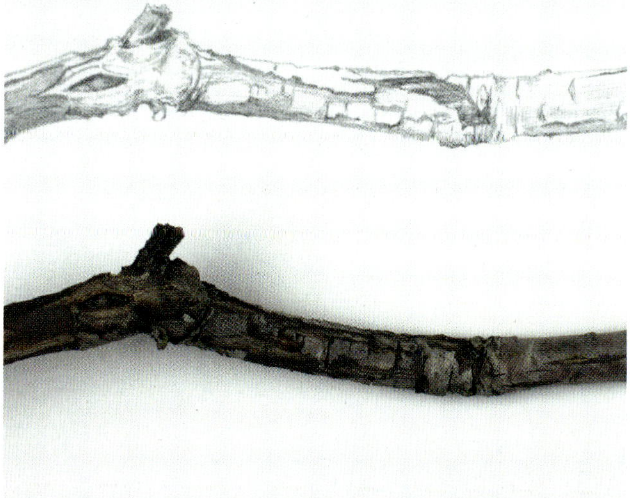
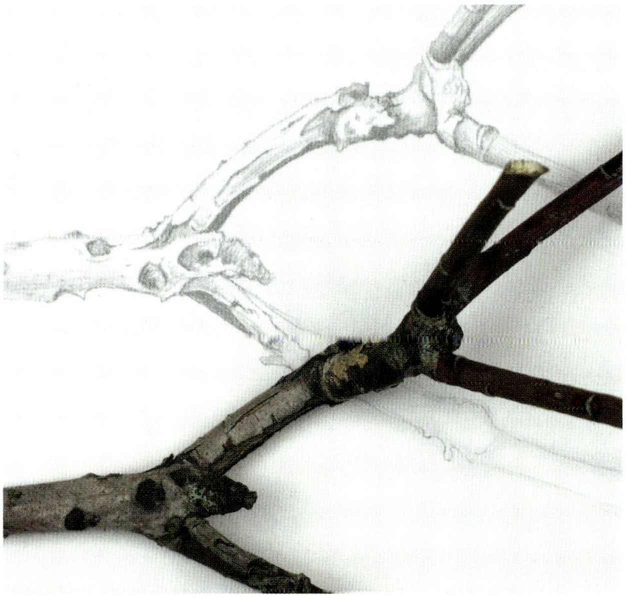

These photos show sections with more detail.

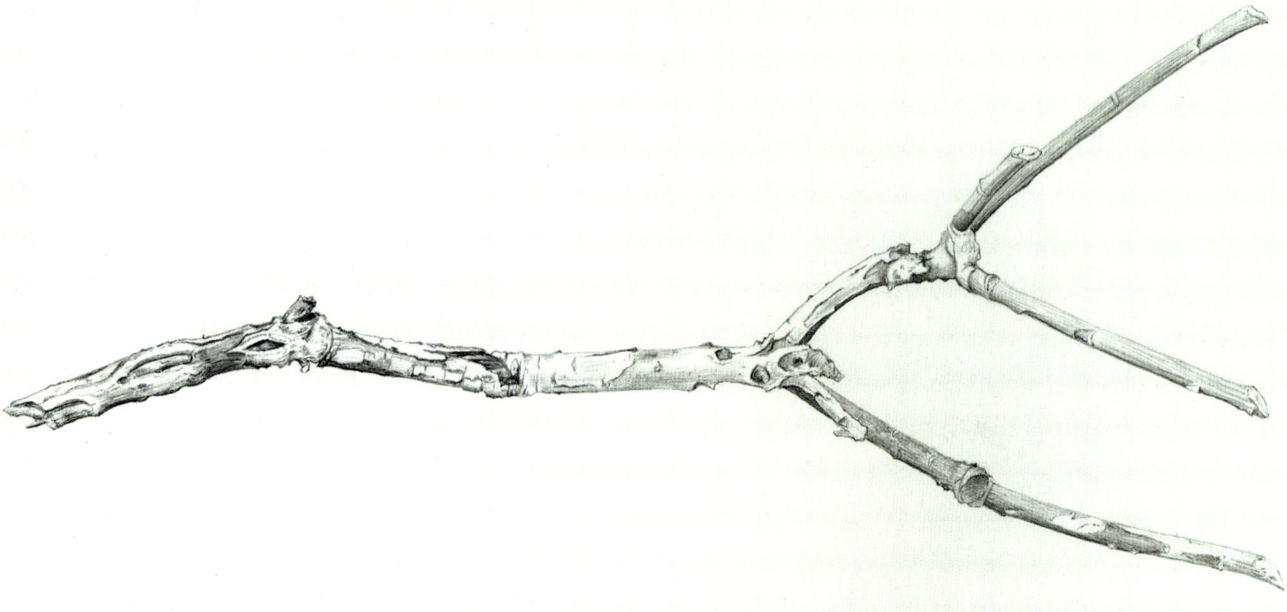

The completed drawing.

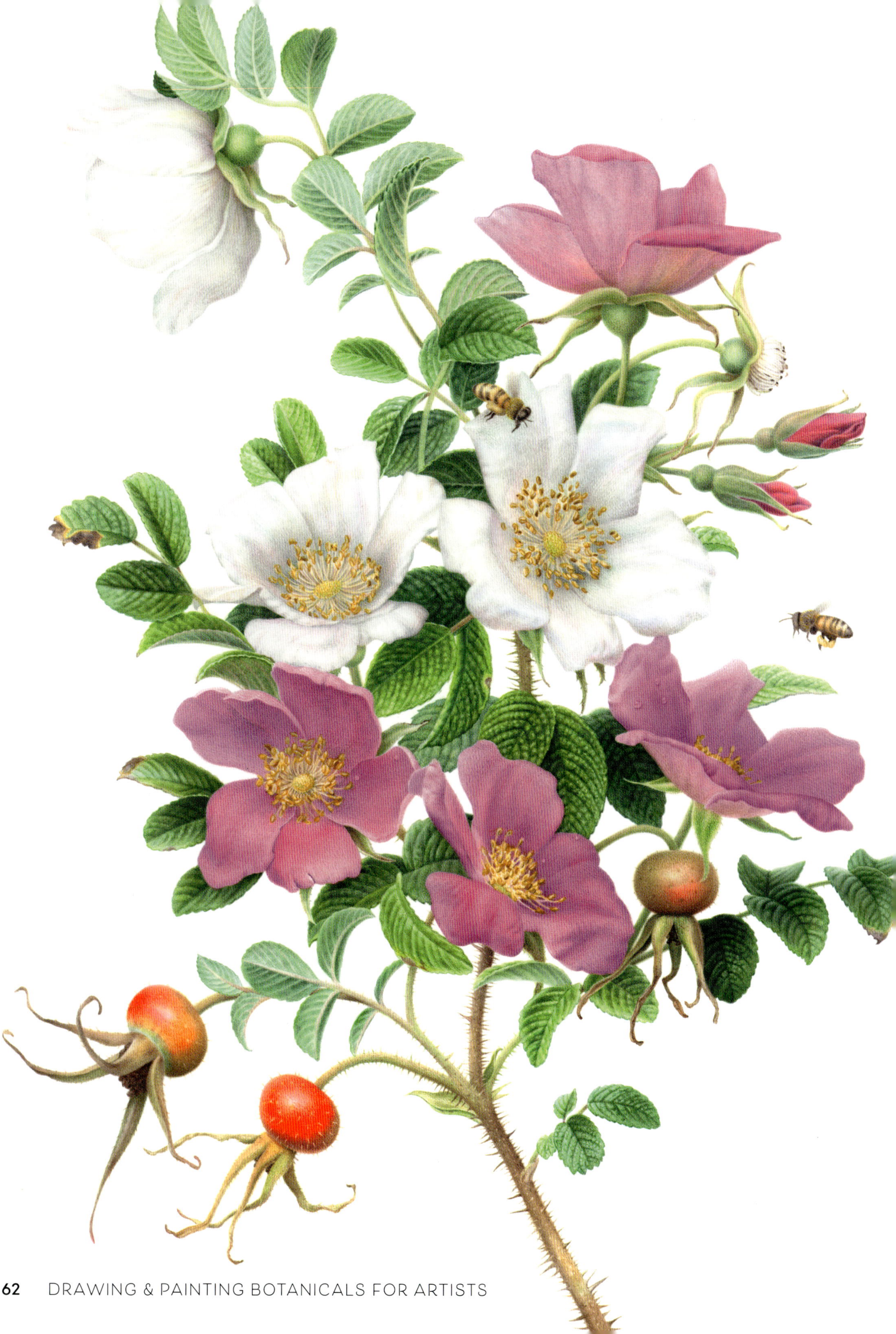

2

PAINTING *Botanicals*

In botanical painting, we use knowledge gained from drawing and add in the complexities of working with fluid color.

Prior to photography, botanical painting was the only way to document the world's varied plant life. Specimens were depicted accurately for identification purposes, and the colors used were an important part of that identification.

Most botanical paintings are created in watercolor—the medium that was used most often long ago and is still most popular today. Delicate washes accurately mimic the transparency of petals, tiny brushes can create the minute detail in a flower, and colors are matched to the specimen for accuracy.

MEDIUMS AND SUPPLIES

Botanical artists, focused on portraying detail, usually choose to work with a water-based medium because of the minute detail that can be achieved. Regardless of the medium, the supplies needed are the same. Paint, brushes, your painting surface, a palette, paper towels, and a cup for water are the basics.

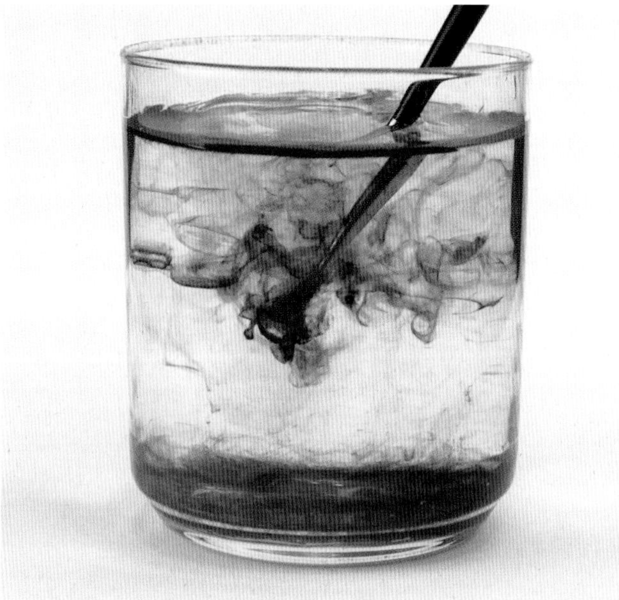

WATERCOLORS

Watercolor is made of pigments suspended in a water-based solution. The characteristics of watercolor have made it a traditional medium of choice for the botanical artist. The translucence of a delicate petal or leaf can be portrayed with washes of varying density of pigment applied to the paper. The paint has minute particles of pigment that are applied with sable brushes of varying sizes. Larger brushes are used at the beginning of a painting, and then the smallest of brushes are used for the details.

The botanical artist can achieve detail with watercolor unlike that achieved in any other medium. Both acrylics and oil have a denser quality and lack the translucence found in watercolor. As much as previous botanical artists have created amazing and detailed work, I believe that today's contemporary botanical artists surpass them in terms of detail and precision. Perhaps this can be attributed to better tools and products available to them, but they have taken the art of botanical painting to a whole new level.

Some watercolorists like to limit their palette to just a few colors and then mix everything they need from those few. Not me. I love color! And, I don't want to limit my palette. Even though it's true that most colors can be mixed from just a few, it can be easier to go directly to a clean, clear pigment that's already formulated. That isn't to say that I don't sometimes add a bit of another color to enhance it, because I usually do! I prefer professional watercolors in tubes rather than pans, but both work equally well. I fill an empty metal tin and plastic wells with my various paints. As they dry out, an eyedropper with water can be used to place a few drops in each section to moisten the paints. Even completely dried-out watercolor can be rewetted and used. A little watercolor goes a long way.

The easiest tool to help you with color mixing is something you can make yourself—a color chart of the paints you already have.

A small color chart that coincides with paints in your palette is convenient when choosing colors to mix.

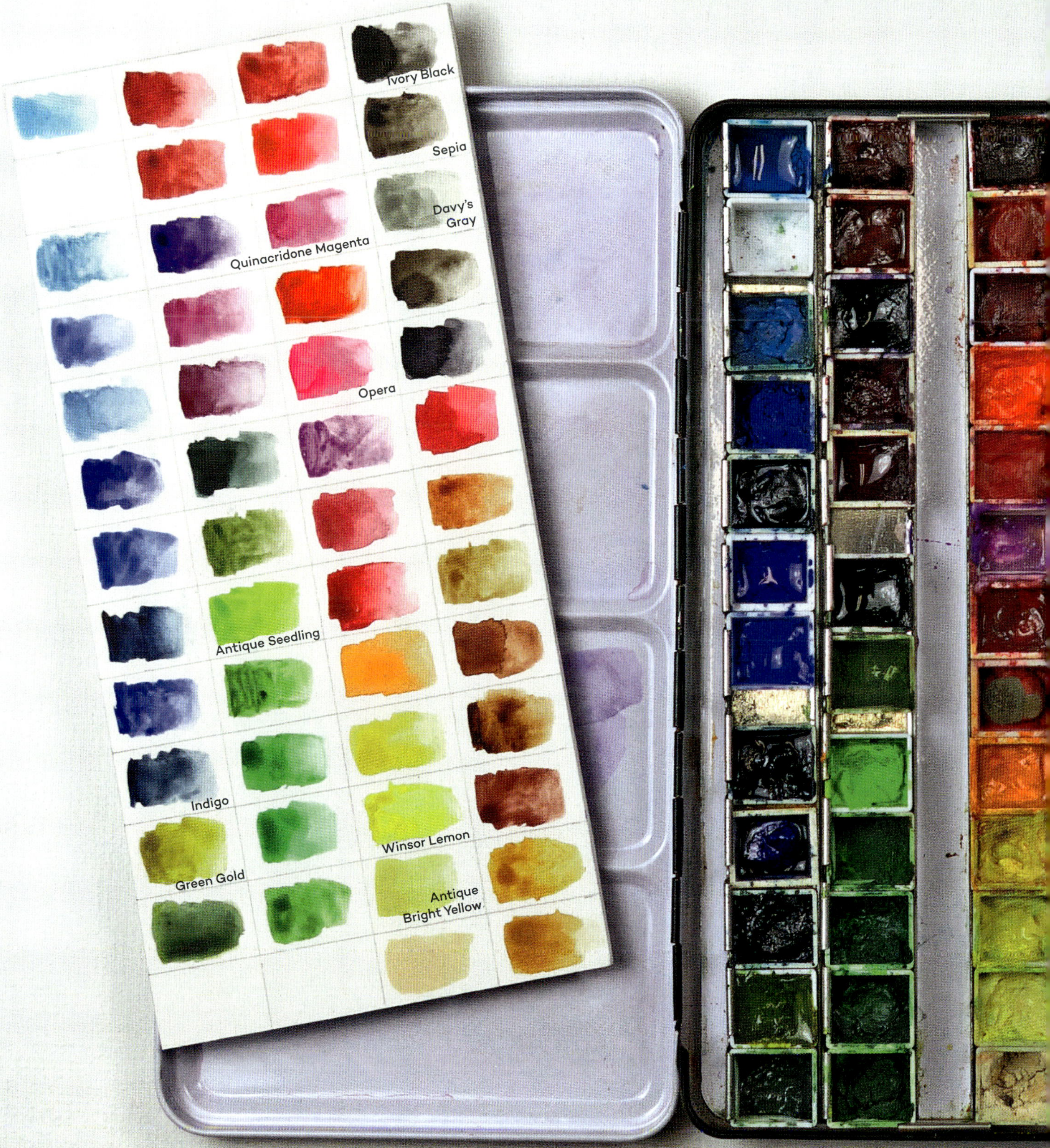

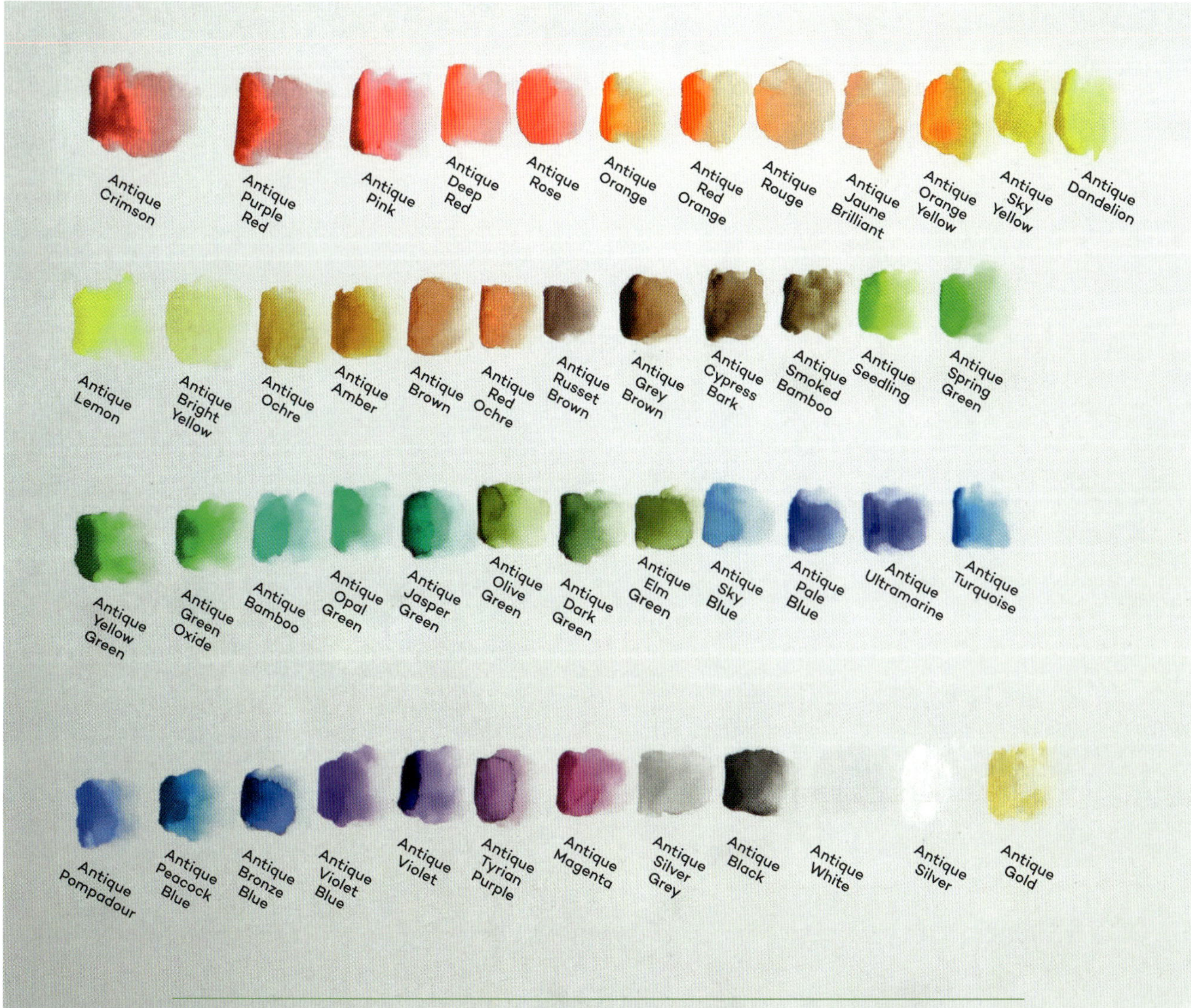

Holbein "Irodori" Antique Watercolor

Make your own color chart using the paints you own. You may want to make a separate chart for each brand of paints.

Making a Color Chart

To make your chart, line up all of your paints, grouping like colors together. On a piece of illustration board or heavy weight watercolor paper, make a small swatch of paint going from an intense thicker area to a lighter wash. This will help you envision both the dark and light values of that particular color. Write the name and brand of paint next to each swatch. When you've completed this color chart, it will be much easier to color match your subject to your paints. Once your eye becomes accustomed to choosing colors in this way, you can hold your chart up to an object and make an educated assessment about which colors mixed together will be the most accurate to your subject!

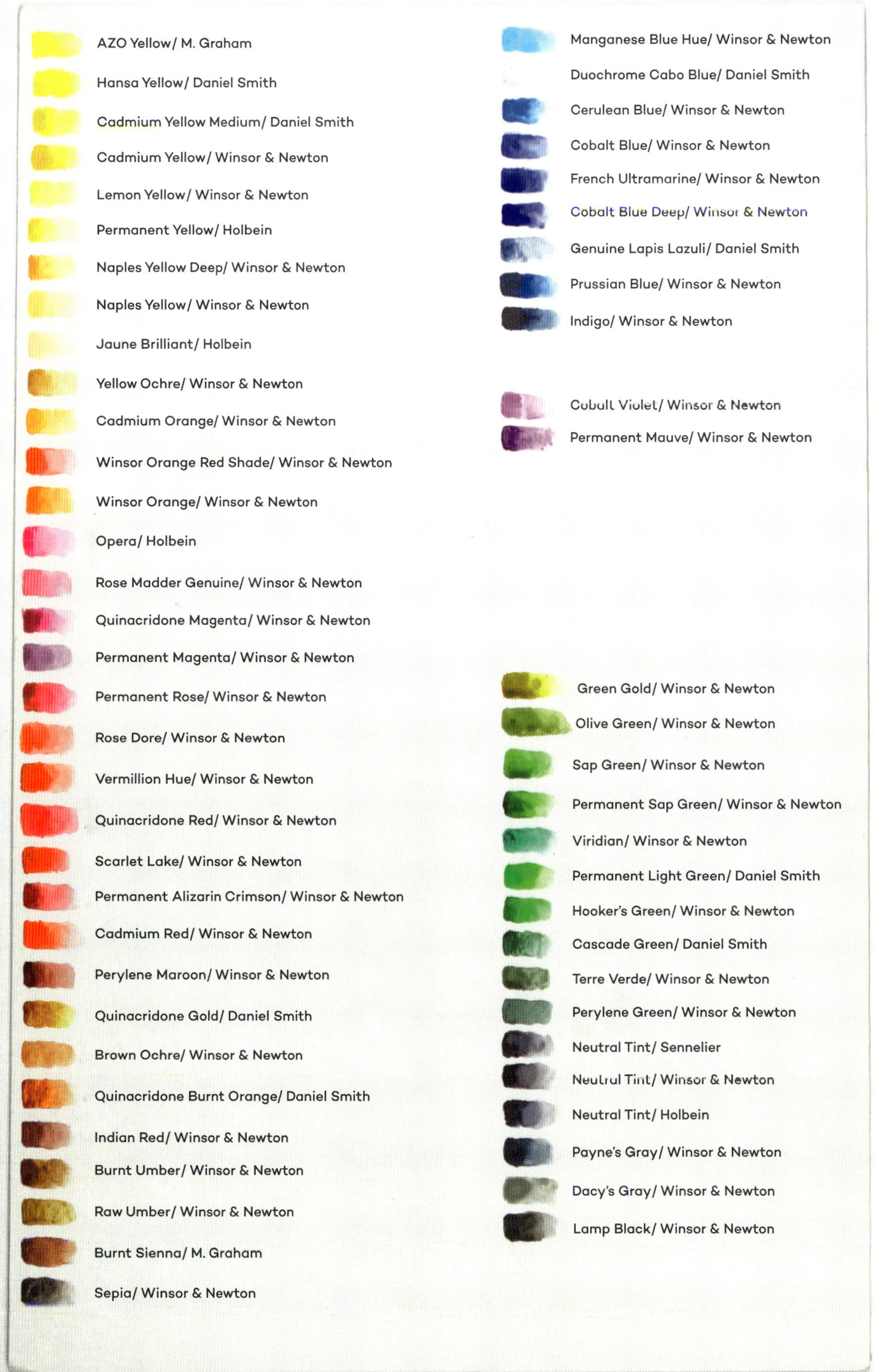
AZO Yellow/ M. Graham
Hansa Yellow/ Daniel Smith
Cadmium Yellow Medium/ Daniel Smith
Cadmium Yellow/ Winsor & Newton
Lemon Yellow/ Winsor & Newton
Permanent Yellow/ Holbein
Naples Yellow Deep/ Winsor & Newton
Naples Yellow/ Winsor & Newton
Jaune Brilliant/ Holbein
Yellow Ochre/ Winsor & Newton
Cadmium Orange/ Winsor & Newton
Winsor Orange Red Shade/ Winsor & Newton
Winsor Orange/ Winsor & Newton
Opera/ Holbein
Rose Madder Genuine/ Winsor & Newton
Quinacridone Magenta/ Winsor & Newton
Permanent Magenta/ Winsor & Newton
Permanent Rose/ Winsor & Newton
Rose Dore/ Winsor & Newton
Vermillion Hue/ Winsor & Newton
Quinacridone Red/ Winsor & Newton
Scarlet Lake/ Winsor & Newton
Permanent Alizarin Crimson/ Winsor & Newton
Cadmium Red/ Winsor & Newton
Perylene Maroon/ Winsor & Newton
Quinacridone Gold/ Daniel Smith
Brown Ochre/ Winsor & Newton
Quinacridone Burnt Orange/ Daniel Smith
Indian Red/ Winsor & Newton
Burnt Umber/ Winsor & Newton
Raw Umber/ Winsor & Newton
Burnt Sienna/ M. Graham
Sepia/ Winsor & Newton
Manganese Blue Hue/ Winsor & Newton
Duochrome Cabo Blue/ Daniel Smith
Cerulean Blue/ Winsor & Newton
Cobalt Blue/ Winsor & Newton
French Ultramarine/ Winsor & Newton
Cobalt Blue Deep/ Winsor & Newton
Genuine Lapis Lazuli/ Daniel Smith
Prussian Blue/ Winsor & Newton
Indigo/ Winsor & Newton
Cobalt Violet/ Winsor & Newton
Permanent Mauve/ Winsor & Newton
Green Gold/ Winsor & Newton
Olive Green/ Winsor & Newton
Sap Green/ Winsor & Newton
Permanent Sap Green/ Winsor & Newton
Viridian/ Winsor & Newton
Permanent Light Green/ Daniel Smith
Hooker's Green/ Winsor & Newton
Cascade Green/ Daniel Smith
Terre Verde/ Winsor & Newton
Perylene Green/ Winsor & Newton
Neutral Tint/ Sennelier
Neutral Tint/ Winsor & Newton
Neutral Tint/ Holbein
Payne's Gray/ Winsor & Newton
Dacy's Gray/ Winsor & Newton
Lamp Black/ Winsor & Newton

Make each little swatch (like this Winsor Orange one) fade from dark to light.

It's important to know the basics of color and how colors work together. There are some basics to know for botanical painting.

First, understand the colors you're seeing in your subject:

- **Local color** is the color of the object itself. It's the intrinsic color that isn't changed by light, shadow, or reflections.
- **Tonal color** is the color that's lighter or darker than the local color. They are the colors that have changed as a result of light hitting the subject.
- **Ambient color** is reflected color from what surrounds the subject. For example, a red apple that has a green leaf next to it may have green reflected onto the apple's surface.

By careful observation, you'll naturally see these shifts of color in the subject you're painting.

In painting flowers with watercolor, I like to begin with pure, clean, light colors. Pink or peach-colored flowers are best painted starting with a color that most matches the local color in the petal without trying to mix it.

The shadows in pale colored flowers will have other colors, often something with a blue tone, added to it. When the flower is a very pale color, use a light touch when adding blue or it can easily be too noticeable. Shifts in color in a pale flower should be subtle.

Shadow is created three ways:

1. Adding a blue color to the area.
2. Using the local color with a darker tone. In watercolor, this is done by layering the local color.
3. Adding a little bit of the color's complementary color; for example, adding red to a green leaf's dark shadows.

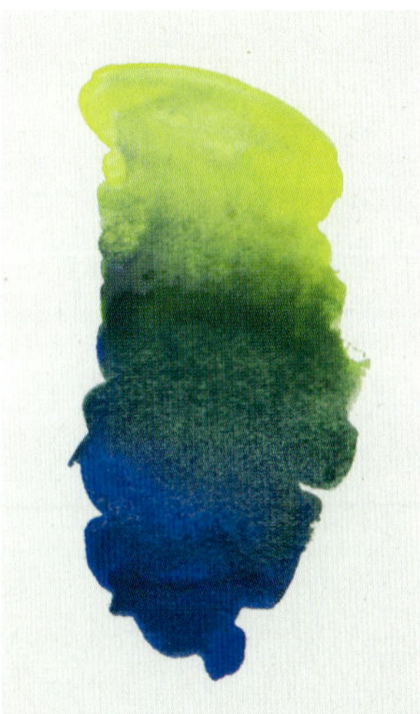

Color and Color Mixing

Mixing color is easiest done by looking carefully at your subject and then at your color chart. See what color most similarly matches the subject. In most cases, it won't be an exact match, and you'll have to make an educated guess as to what color or colors should be added. Let's say your subject is a leaf that looks most like Sap Green but it has more yellow in it. You might try adding a Winsor Yellow and testing the mix on your scrap paper. Do this mixing and testing no matter what colors you're matching. Some color mixes can get muddy or dull. By trial and error, you'll get a feel for it and get quicker at making informed decisions as to what colors to add to your mix to match your subject.

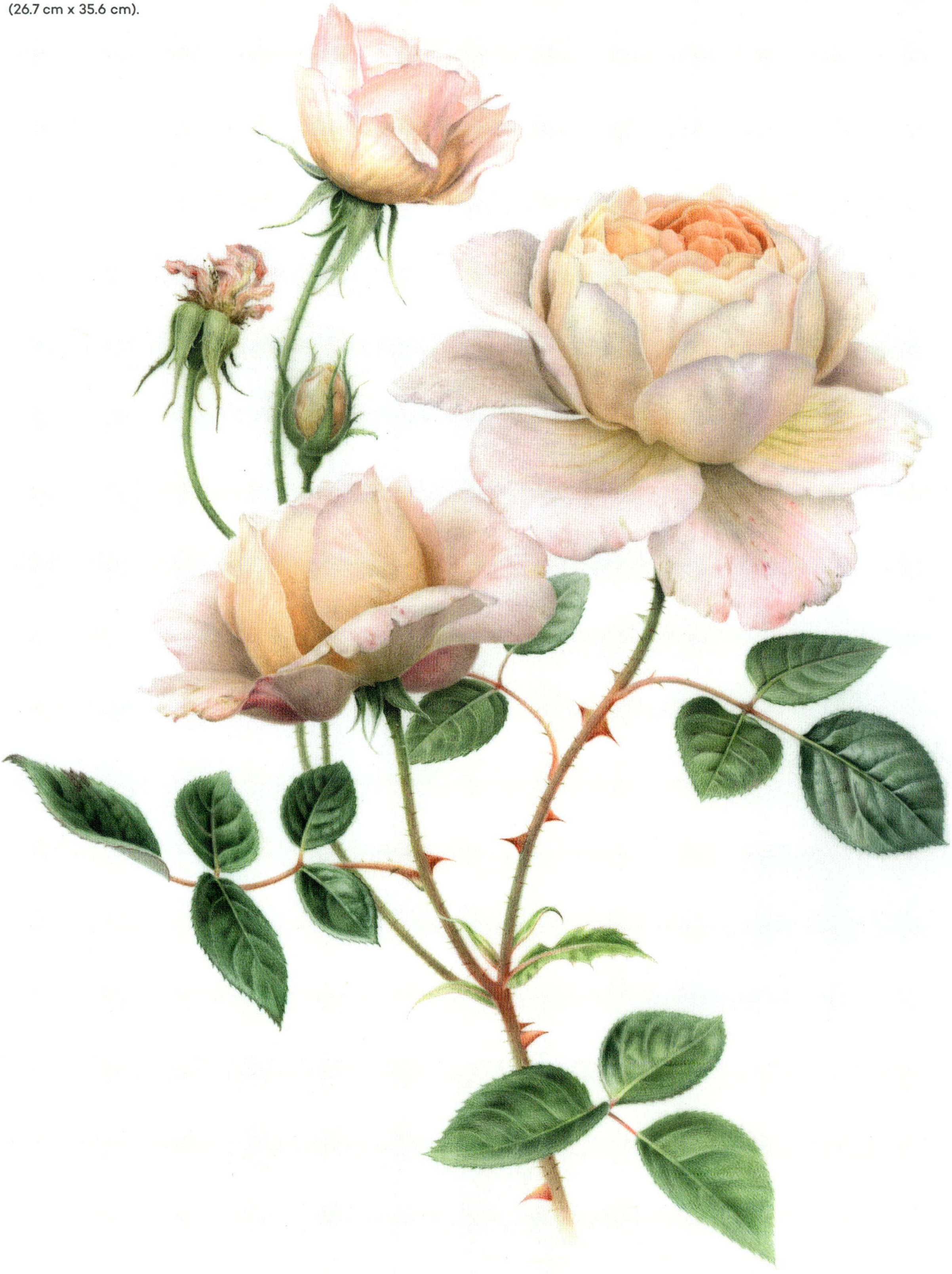

"Tamora Rose" (*Rosa 'Tamora'*) watercolor on vellum 10.5" x 14" (26.7 cm x 35.6 cm).

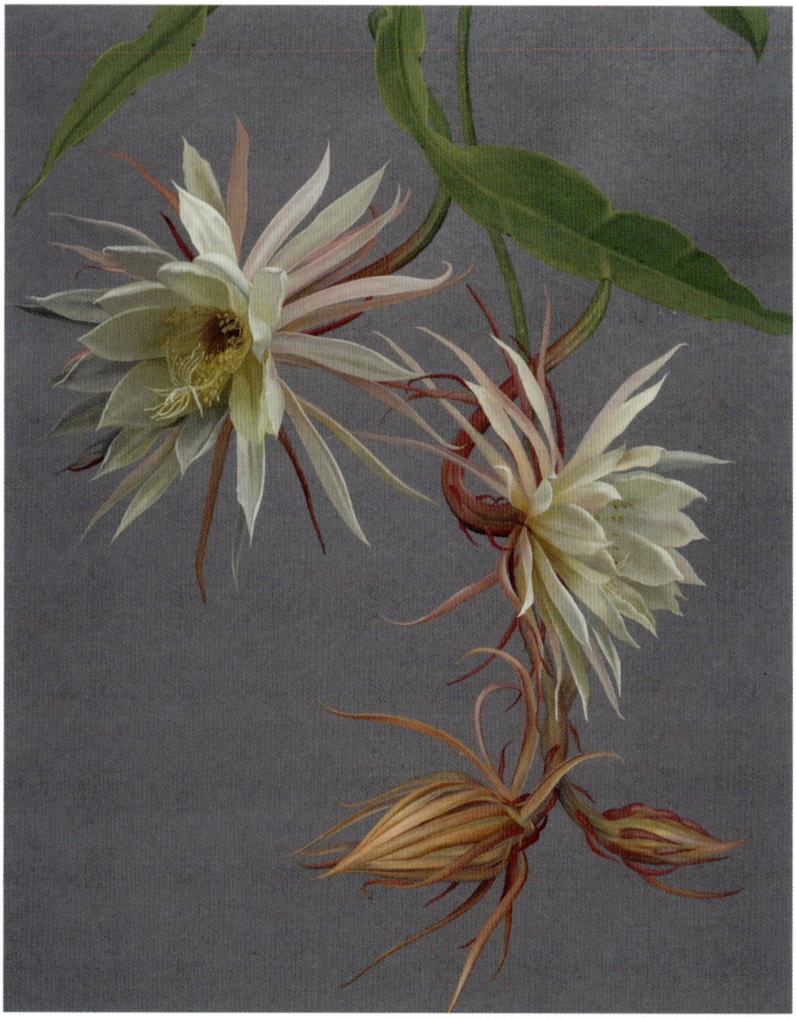

Gouache is very similar to watercolor, but it's thicker and more opaque. "Queen of the Night" E*piphyllum oxypetalum* night-blooming cereus flower gouache on paper 16.5" x 19" (41.9 cm x 48.3 cm)

GOUACHE

The primary difference between gouache and watercolor is that gouache has a white chalk in the pigment. Both mediums are water soluble and have similarities and differences.

Because of the added chalk, gouache is thicker, heavier, more opaque, and not as translucent as watercolor. For this reason, gouache can be used on a dark paper and watercolor cannot. Watercolor would fade away on a dark paper, whereas the pigment in gouache sits on top of the paper's surface. When using gouache on a dark background, you'll need to do many layers of paint, especially when building up light colors and whites. When painting with gouache on a white paper, begin with dark colors and add lighter colors on top. The consistency of the paint should be like cream. If it's too thick, it can crack when dry, and if it's too thin, it can flake off. Gouache is similar to watercolor in that the paint can be rewetted with a damp brush and lifted. When layering gouache, make sure the bottom layer is completely dry. Overworking an area can make the paint lift off completely. This is another similarity gouache has to watercolor.

Any white highlights in a gouache painting would contain white paint, whereas in traditional watercolor, white paint is rarely used. Instead, highlights are indicated with the white of the paper showing through.

Gouache dries a different color than when wet, so it can be tricky to use and takes practice! A finished gouache painting will have a matte finish with rich and vibrant color.

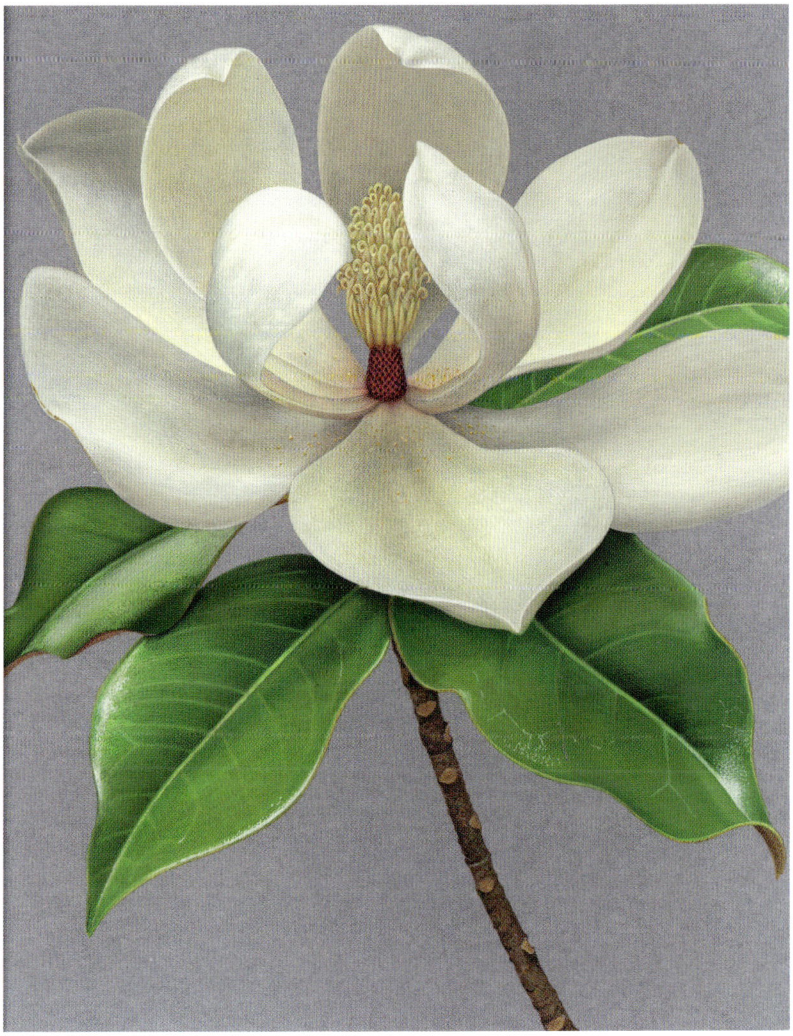

"Magnolia Grandiflora" gouache on colored paper 12" x 15" (30.5 cm x 38.1 cm)

Working with Acrylic Paints

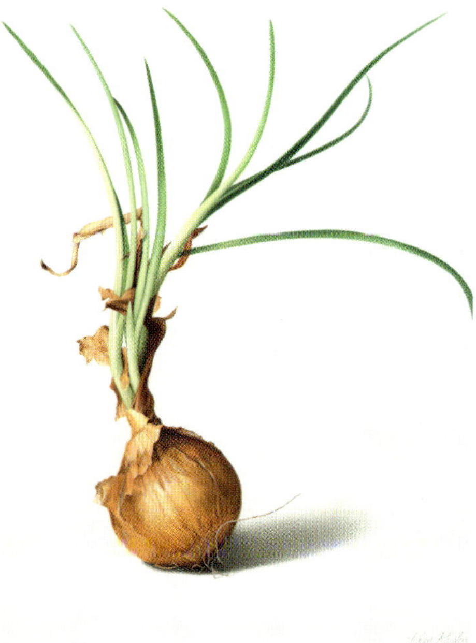

I chose to paint this onion with acrylics as an experiment to see if I could use acrylics thinned down with water to make the painting look like watercolor. White paint was not used so the thinned acrylic was more like a glaze of washes built up the same way as watercolor. This was tricky because if it got too dark I would not be able to remove paint. The painting was successful in that it does look like a watercolor but I did not find using acrylic with this technique advantageous since I prefer to be able to adjust and manipulate the paint if need be.

"Onion" acrylic on paper 8" x 10" (20.3 cm x 25.4 cm)

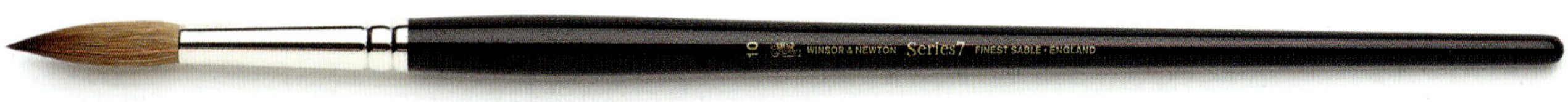

Winsor & Newton Series 7 natural Kolinsky sable brushes hold a lot of paint and keep a sharp point.

PAINTBRUSHES

Paintbrushes are an important tool for the botanical artist. They're made of different materials and are available in varying shapes. Brushes for acrylic paints need to be sturdier than brushes for watercolor. They're available in both natural (stiff hog or sable hair) and synthetic (nylon or polyester) bristles. Natural bristles won't last as long when using acrylics.

When painting with watercolor, I recommend using a natural sable brush. The hairs are soft and will hold a surprising amount of paint. I only use round brushes for acrylic and watercolor. Though it's tempting when looking at all the available brushes of different shapes, a round brush can always do the trick. Brushes come in various sizes, ranging from No. 000, No. 00, No. 0, No. 1, and up. When painting small areas, such as in petals or leaves, smaller brushes are needed. A No. 1 or No. 2 quality brush will be a good investment.

Always rinse your brushes when you're finished painting and reshape them into a fine point.

The miniature Series 7 brushes have shorter hairs and the standard brushes have longer hairs. Both are available in a range of sizes.

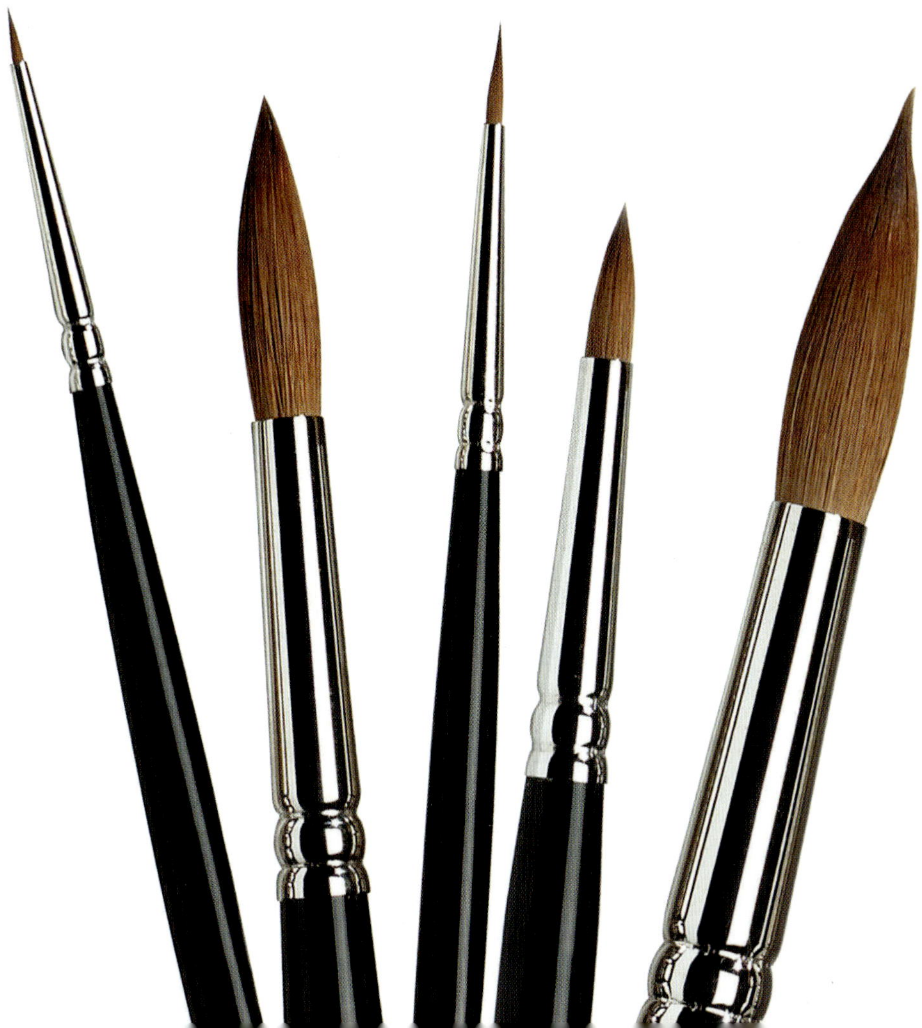

PAINTING SURFACES

The surfaces used to paint botanicals are most often very smooth in order to facilitate the even flow of paint and create exacting detail. Acrylics may be painted on a smooth paper or wood or composite board. The smoothest papers for both acrylic and watercolor are hot-pressed or hot-pressed with a plate finish. These may be a paper or a paper surface on board often called *illustration board*. A paper's thickness is indicated by weight. A heavier, thicker paper will have a higher number. For example, a 400 lb. (850 gsm) paper is thicker than a 200 lb. (540 gsm) paper. A heavier weight paper will resist buckling when wet and will be easier to handle. It's important that your paper is archival or acid free so that it won't yellow over time.

Many accomplished botanical artists also use vellum, which is a natural calfskin material. It's archival and gives the work an additional translucence, but it can't get too wet, which can be tricky when using watercolor!

Note that I use the same techniques for layering and drybrush on paper as I do when working on vellum. The important thing with vellum is not to let puddles of water sit on the surface, which causes buckling; this should be avoided on paper as well. When layering on vellum, move around the painting, letting each brushstroke dry before adding another. The single most important thing to remember when painting on vellum is to not let it get too wet!

Note that I use the same techniques for layering and drybrush on paper as I do when working on vellum. The important thing with vellum is to not let puddles of water sit on the surface, which causes buckling; this should be avoided on paper as well. When layering on vellum, move around the painting, letting each brushstroke dry before adding another. The single most important thing to remember when painting on vellum is to not let it get too wet.

Various surfaces to paint on include paper, illustration board, and masonite.

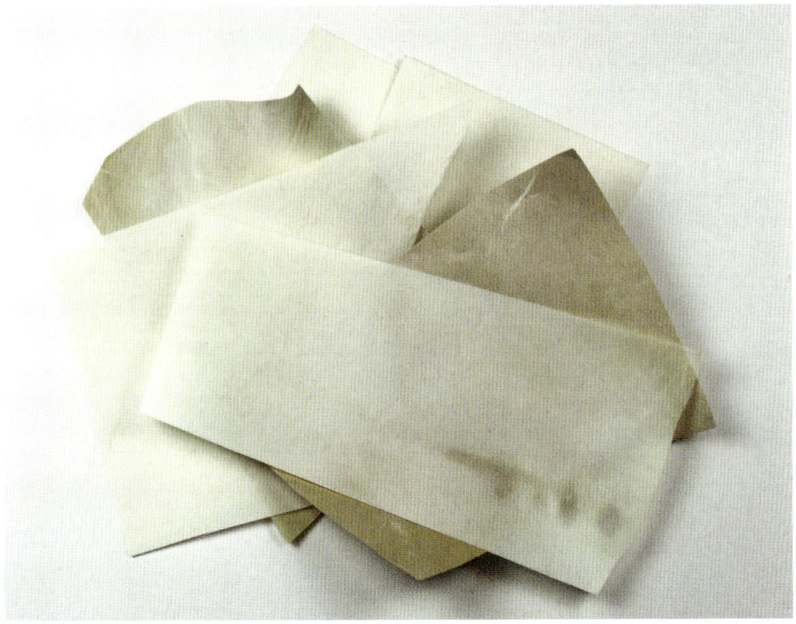

Usually a pale cream color, vellum is translucent.

ESSENTIAL PAINTING TECHNIQUES

What makes watercolor and gouache unique is that we are able to move and manipulate the paint on the surface unlike oil or acrylic paint which, once dry, cannot be moved.

Layering washes, making even gradations, lifting paint and drybrush are all techniques used to manipulate the paint.

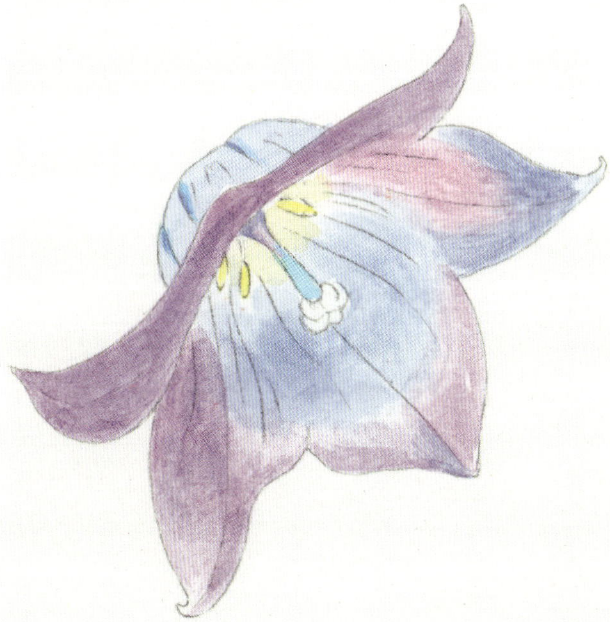

Mapping a subject's separate, yet often subtly distinct, areas of color should be done before you begin painting.

COLOR MAPPING

Color mapping is an expression used to describe the technique of placing different colors in different areas of your drawing or painting. Some subjects won't need as many diverse colors as others. An autumn leaf may have many colors, while a solid green leaf might have less. Using distinct colors in your piece will create interest, and your subject won't look *flat*. This mapping is especially important with watercolor because it's a transparent medium. If you cover the entire surface of a leaf with green and then decide you need to add red at the edges on top of the existing green, you'll end up with more of a brown color. So mapping is important to create clean, pure color (such as the red edges of the leaf). As layers of color are added, the edges of these mapped areas get overlapped and gradually blurred so that they don't end up looking too distinct or like sections of a patchwork quilt.

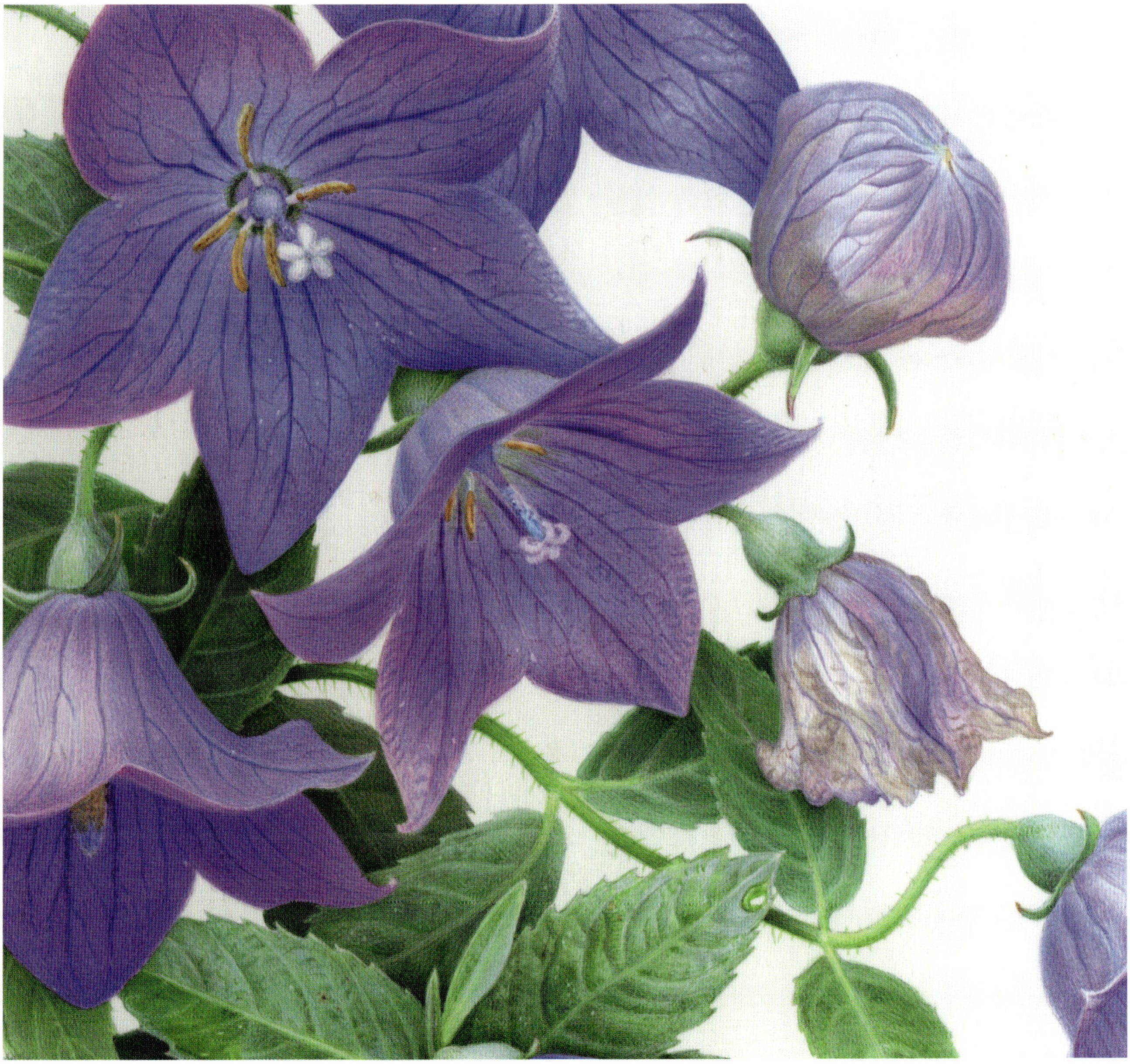

"Balloon Flower" (*Platycodon grandiflorus*)
The finished artwork, with the edges of the mapped colors softly blended

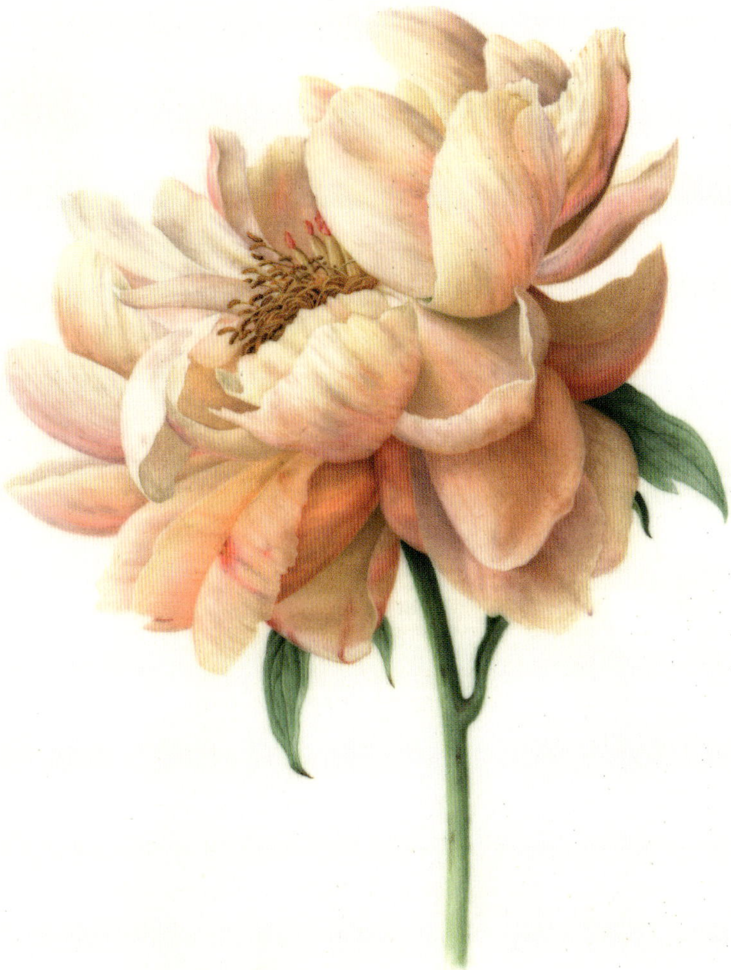

"Fading Coral Charm" (genus *Paeonia*); watercolor on vellum.

WASHES

Washes are made by diluting your paint with water. Touch your wet brush to paint and make a little puddle with water in your palette. Do the same again with a different amount of paint and water. The mix that has a higher concentration of paint to water will make a darker wash of color on your paper. Play around with this and get a feel for how much paint and water is needed for the value you want. This is something you'll do continuously as you paint. I always keep a scrap paper next to my palette to test the color and value before applying it to the painting.

One thing I should mention here is that this technique can differ depending on each artist's individual style of painting. Some artists are very timid with their paint and washes, which makes them barely visible on the paper, and other artists are too generous, which means some paint may need to be removed, or lifted. It takes practice to get a feel for the mix of paint needed for the value you want. This is an important procedure to master because it will save you time and help to avoid mistakes, such as needing to add more paint layers because the color is too light or removing and correcting paint when the area is too dark.

Some watercolorists prefer to wet their watercolor paper with plain water before applying paint. By doing this, the paint feathers and diffuses into the wet area and can create beautiful effects. Because I use a hot-pressed very smooth paper, I don't do this, but instead begin with a light wash and then I layer on top of it.

LAYERING

After your initial wash has completely dried, you can apply a second wash on top of it. This consecutive wash should not be too wet or it can move and remove the paint below it. The best way to ensure that you don't apply a wash that is too wet is to blot the side of your brush on a paper towel before applying the wash. This way, you have the correct value loaded in your brush but excess water is removed. Pass the brush quickly over the first, then dry wash and don't go over that area again. You might want to soften an edge, but avoid the temptation to fuss with an area that's wet. Once it's completely dry, you can apply another layer in the same way by blotting and applying quickly. Apply layers in different areas of your painting so that you can keep working while other layers dry. If the value you're trying to achieve is dark, the layers you apply should have a dense concentration of paint. Make a mix and test it on your scrap paper. Keep applying layers until it's almost but not quite the value you want. You'll be adding more paint when you smooth these layers by drybrushing.

Washes of Scarlet Lake were layered one on top of another to show how layering increases value and depth. The top section has one layer of paint, and it progresses to the bottom section, which has seven layers of the same mix of paint.

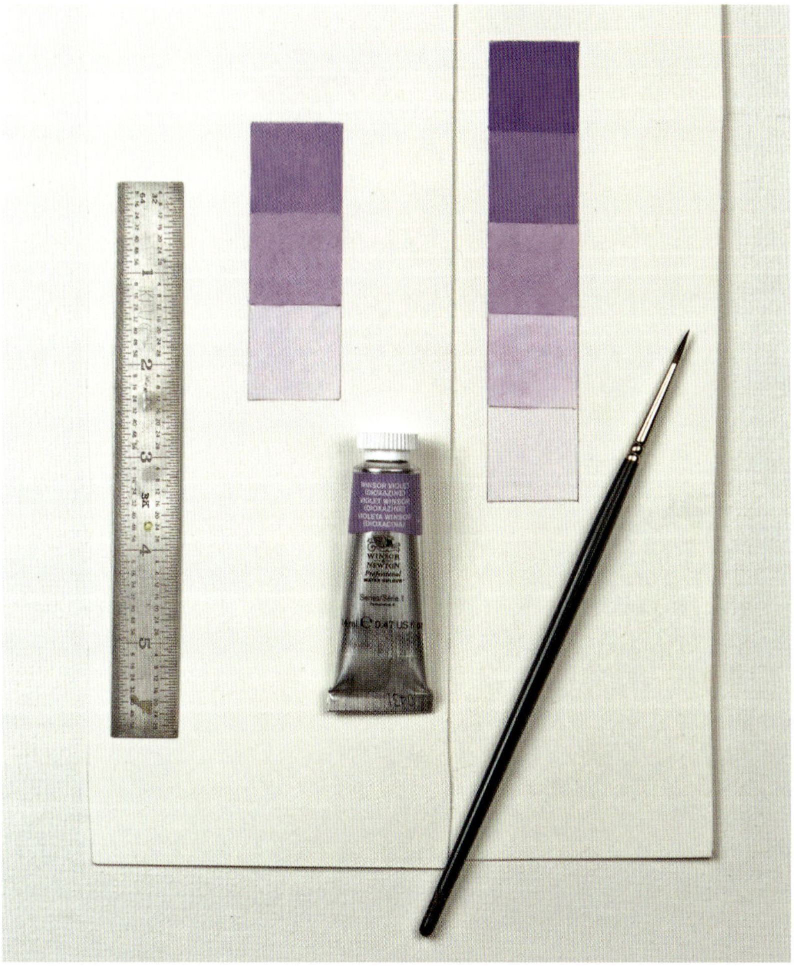

One beginning exercise is to draw a series of 1-inch (2.5 cm) squares that you'll fill in from dark to light.

GRADATIONS

When making a gradation with watercolor, it's best to have a few wells of paint premixed because we want to apply the paint quickly. In one well, make a mix of paint and water that has a good amount of paint the consistency of a light cream. Take your paint-filled brush, dip it in water, and make a second well of paint. Add another brushful of water to it. Your third well of paint should be mostly water with a hint of your paint color. The dark well of paint should give you a dark wash, the medium mix a medium wash, and the light mix a light wash. Test these mixes on scrap paper and adjust them by adding more or less paint and water as needed.

Prop the paper you're going to paint on at a 45-degree angle. Gravity will help the wash to pool at the bottom edge of your brushstroke. Load the brush and make a horizontal stroke left to right. For the second brushstroke, begin at the lower-left side of the previous brushstroke, catching the bottom edge with your brush and making another left to right stroke, allowing the paint to flow down from one stroke into the next. After a few strokes with the dark mix of paint, change to the medium mix of paint, catching the bottom edge and once again moving left to right. After a few strokes with the medium mix, change to the light mix for a few strokes. Don't be concerned if this does not look neat; instead, just let it dry completely.

Once dry, you may repeat this same process on top of what you've already done. In this way, the values are intensified until they are where you want them. You can keep adding layers until you have the darkest value that you want in your gradation. With watercolor, remember that it's always easier to add paint than to remove it. Layering the paint builds darker values to bring out shape and form in your painting. After you've added layers of paint to your gradation, it will still be uneven. This is where the technique of drybrushing comes in to even out and make your gradation smooth.

Gradation Exercise

An essential practice exercise for painters is learning how to make gradations.

Supplies

- HB pencil
- Hot-pressed watercolor paper
- No. 1 sable watercolor brush
- Paper towel
- Scrap paper
- Water
- Paint palette
- Winsor Violet (Dioxazine) watercolor paint

1

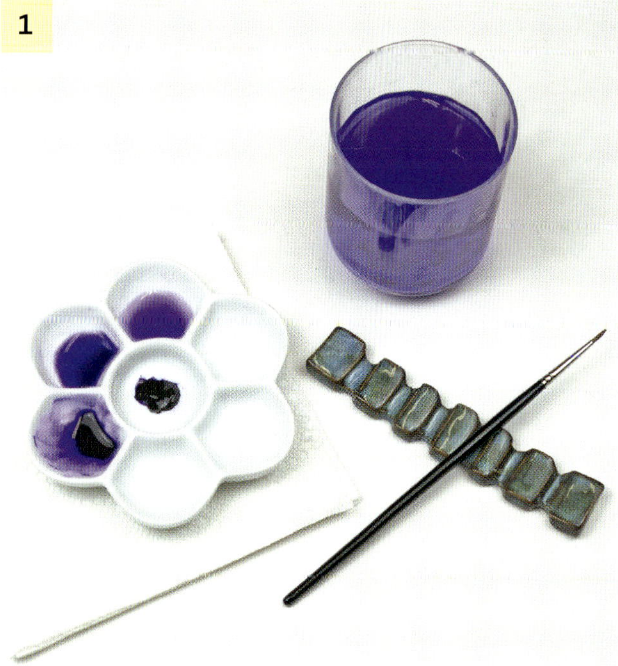

1. Make three wells of paint with different concentrations of dark, medium, and light pigment.

2. Begin with the paint from the well with the darkest value and move to the medium and then lightest value.

2A: Dark

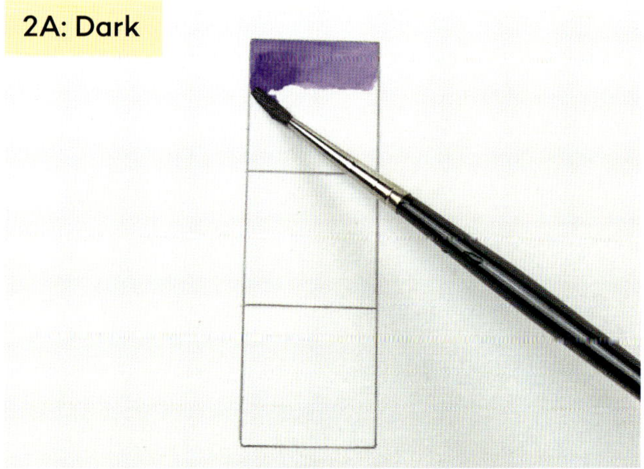

2B: Medium

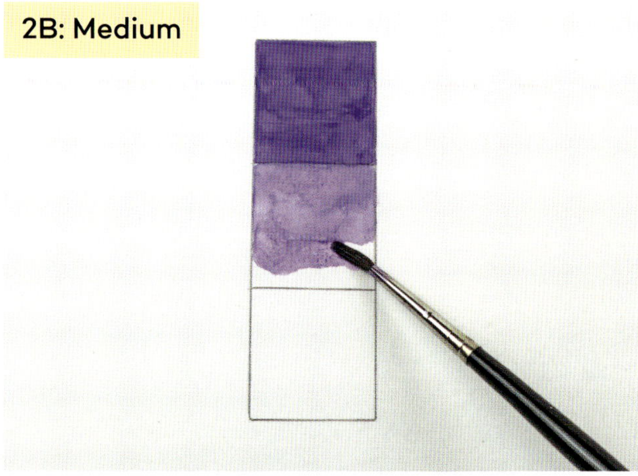

2A: Light

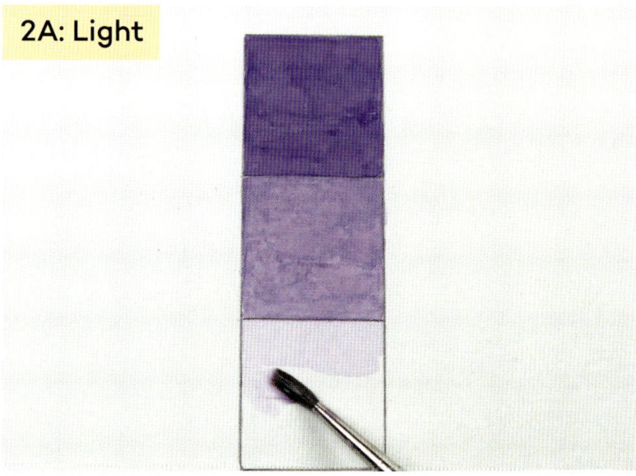

Values in Watercolor

In watercolor, highlights are created with barely any paint in your mix so that only a hint of color shows and the light is created by the white paper beneath. The darkest shadows are created with many layers of paint. To create a full range of tonal values, differing amounts of paint and layering are applied in different areas.

3

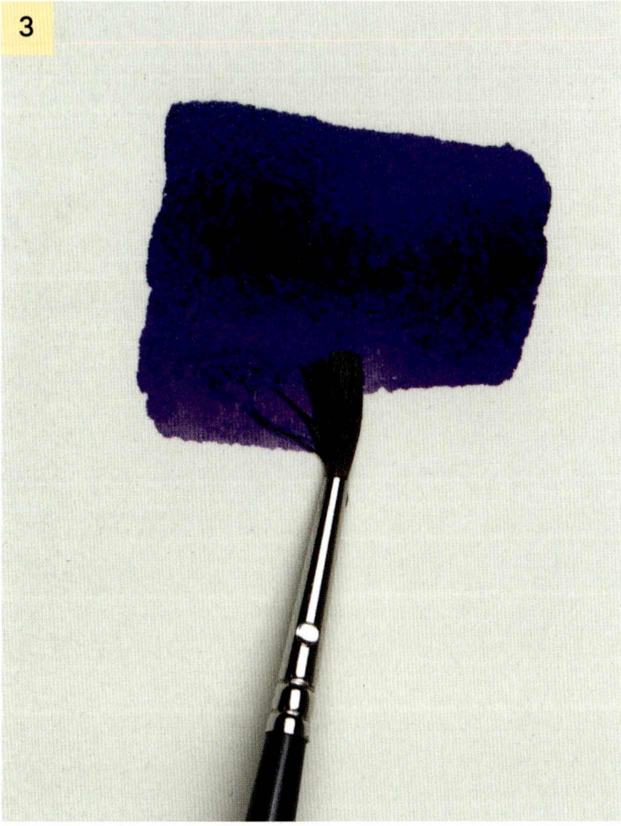

3. Next, do this without the squares and move quickly, dipping your paint from one well to another, touching the bottom edge and drawing the paint down.

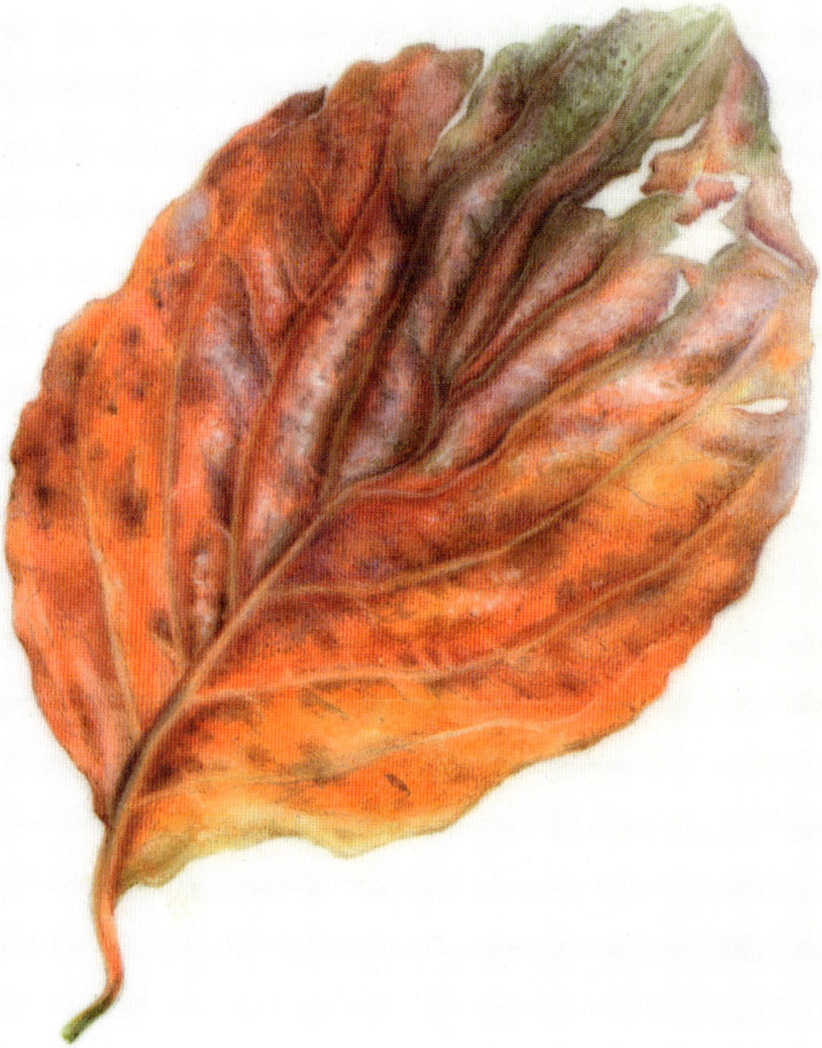

DRYBRUSH IN WATERCOLOR

After you've applied layered washes and the value is almost to where you want it to be, a *drybrush* technique is used to even the tone. Drybrush is important because it can give you a deep saturation of color as well as minute detail. This is important especially in botanical painting since our subject is often small, and a large brush using a wash of color won't work. To have control of the paint in a small space, it's important not to use too much water. The amount of water and pigment in your brush will be trial and error at first, but with practice, this will come naturally.

You'll want to have enough pigment in your brush to make a slight difference when painting over your already dry painting. By dipping your brush in the paint solution and blotting the side of the brush on paper towel, you'll remove most of the liquid and be able to draw with the tip of the brush. With a good quality brush, you'll be able to *draw* like this for several minutes before having to go back for more paint.

If the paint has the right consistency, it will lie flat on the surface and dry within seconds. If there's too much water in the brush, the paint will form a wet bead, which can dissolve paint already on your surface. If this happens, you can

"Autumn Dogwood Leaf"
watercolor on vellum
6" x 7" (15.2 cm x 17.8 cm)

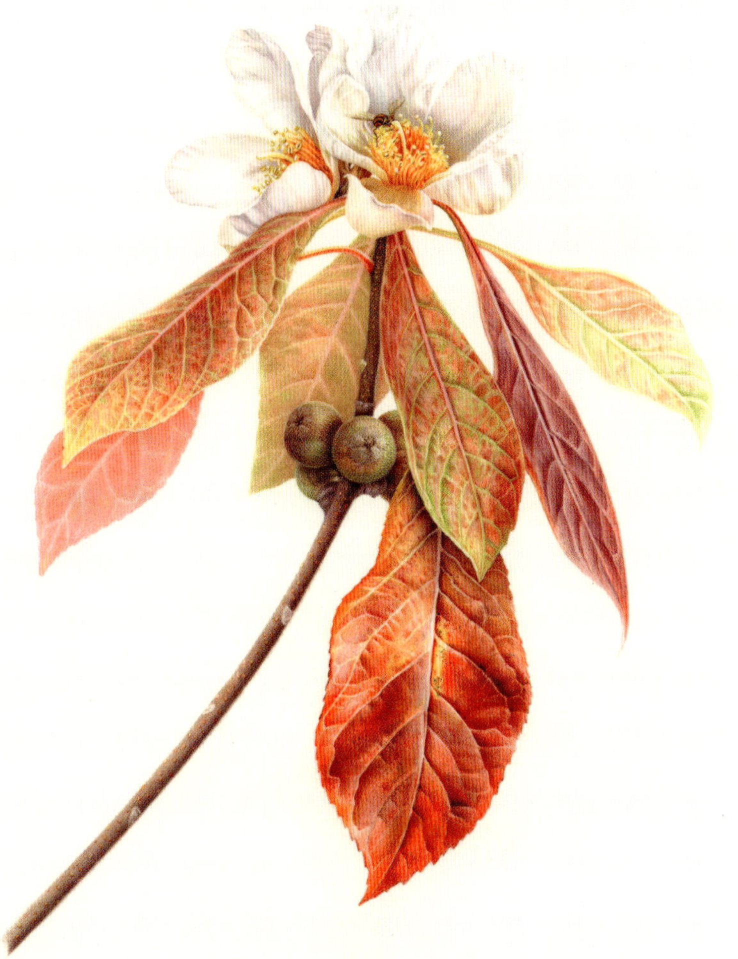

"Bartram's Franklinia"
(*Franklinia alatamaha*)
watercolor on vellum
10.5" x 12.5"
(26.7 cm x 31.8 cm)

remove the excess by touching the tip of a blotted brush to the bead of water to soak it up. Apply the second stroke only after the first stroke has completely dried. Because so little water is used, it will dry almost immediately and you'll feel like you're drawing with the paint. In the beginning, strokes can be made a little bit wider, but as the brush dries, it feels like you're barely tickling the surface of the paper with the tip of the brush.

It's better to have too little pigment on the brush than too much. You can reach the correct saturation of paint by layering. This is what is so time consuming because there are MANY layers, but these layers are also what gives you so much control and depth of color. You're building up saturation of color slowly, while defining contours. Thick paint and heavy brushstrokes are avoided because they can be too obvious and might need to be removed. When you're looking to achieve a deep saturation of color, apply the paint in small quick strokes and change the direction of the brush. To even out an area, use lines, crosshatching, or dots. For example, if you have a series of vertical brushstrokes with a lighter area between the strokes, a series of vertical strokes should be used to fill in those lighter spaces. Similarly, if there are small round areas that should go darker to even a flat tone, small dots can be used to fill in this space. Notice the lighter space you need to fill to even out the tone and apply the size and shape brushstroke to fill it.

Drybrush is also used when making minute detail after washes and gradations are completed. Small imperfections in a leaf, texture in a branch, or a flower's filaments all need a drybrush technique to be created. Once again, after testing the paint's value on scrap, detail is drawn with the point of your brush.

Drybrush is the opposite of traditional watercolor, with repeated washes of paint and where speed is a desirable quality. Above all, this technique takes practice and patience, but you'll find it relaxing and meditative.

Drybrush Exercise: Sphere

This sphere, using a single color (French Ultramarine), demonstrates light and shadow, gradations, and drybrush.

Supplies

- HB pencil
- Hot-pressed watercolor paper
- No. 1 sable watercolor brush
- Kneaded eraser
- Paper towel
- Scrap paper
- Water
- Paint palette
- French Ultramarine watercolor paint

1. First, cover the entire surface with a light wash.

2. Place a second crescent-shaped wash where the darkest values are.

1

2

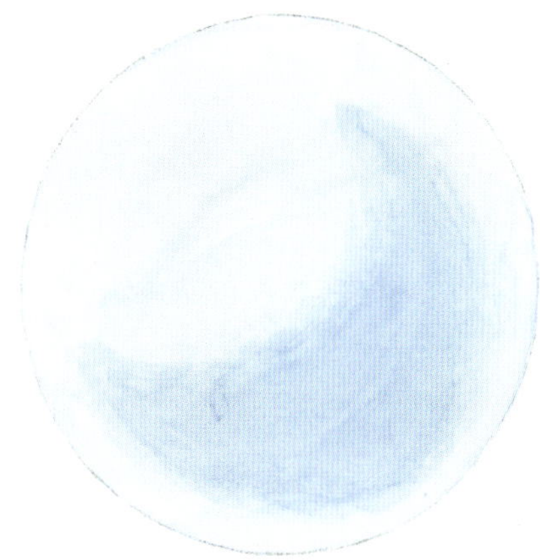

3

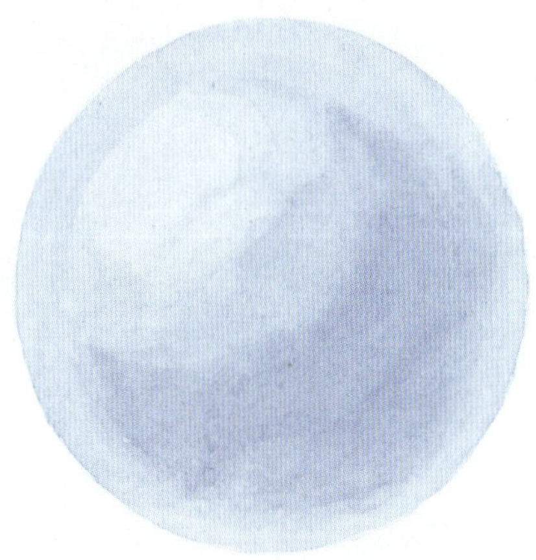

4

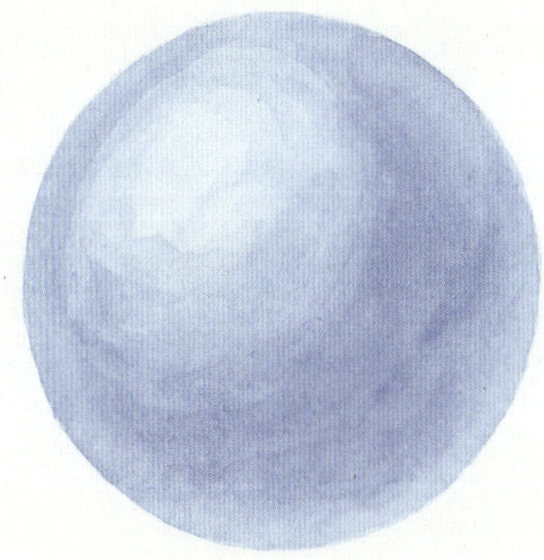

5

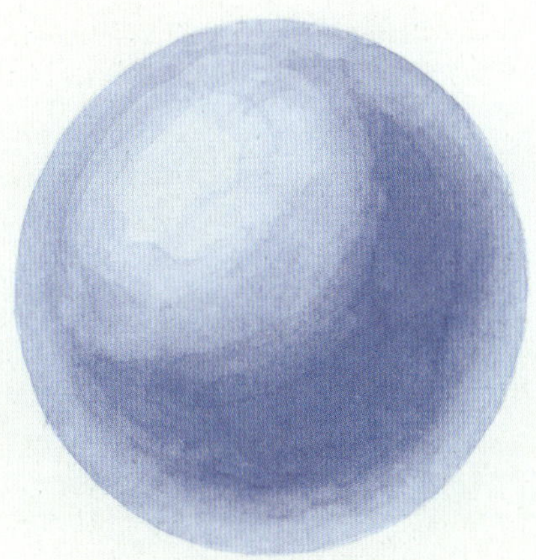

6

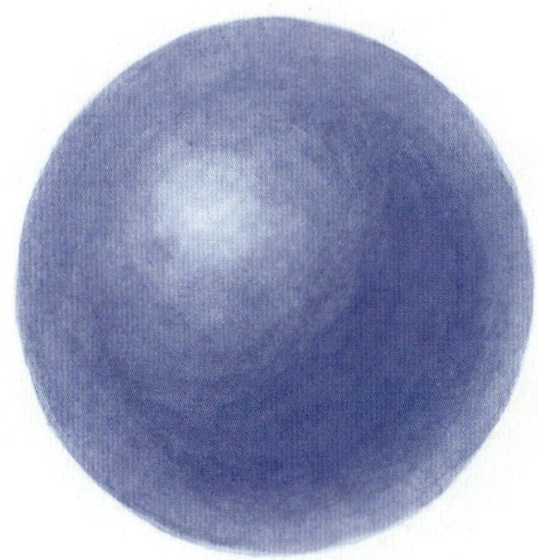

3. Erase the pencil line around the edge with the kneaded eraser before too much paint is placed on top of it. Then, place another wash over the entire sphere, avoiding the highlight area.

4. Quickly apply another layer to the entire surface, except the areas with the highlights. Use a clean wet brush to go around the hard edge that's surrounding the highlight and quickly diffuse it. Everything is done with quick motions to avoid leaving rigid edges.

5. Add and soften another crescent-shaped layer.

6. Add a few more layers and crescent shapes to define the highlight. At this point, smooth the gradations and even the tone using the drybrushing technique. Start drybrushing when the value is *almost* to where you want it to be.

7

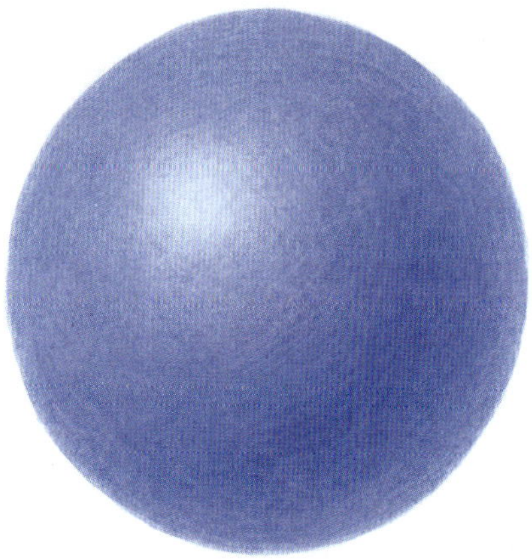

8

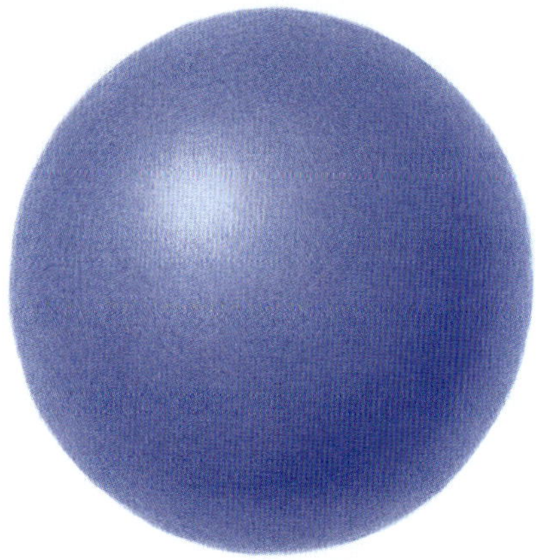

9

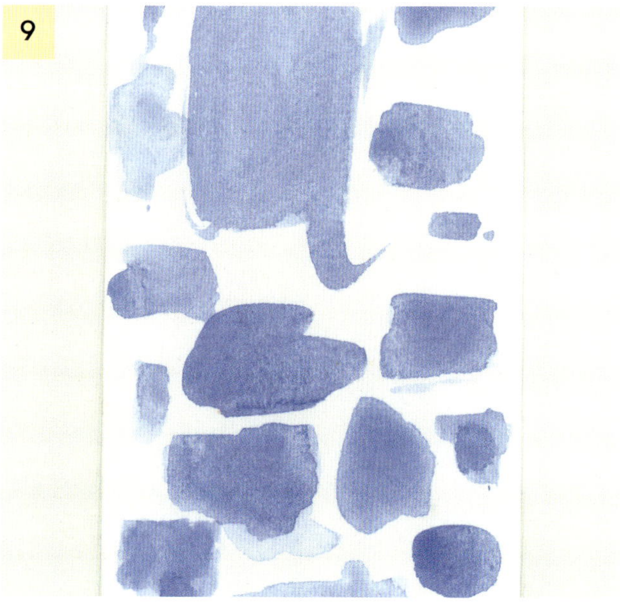

10

7. Add lots of curving lines, working around the sphere to even the gradations. Use a thinner mix of paint near the highlight; use a thicker mix in the shadows.

8. To determine whether the tone is even, look at what you're painting in different ways. Perhaps take off your glasses off, put it up to a mirror, or look at it from a distance. Use a No. 0 brush to fill in the little lighter dots of the texture of the paper.

9. Test the value of the color on scrap paper and blot on a paper towel before tickling the surface with the tip of your brush.

10. When using drybrush to make a gradation smooth, think of it as though you're filling in lighter spaces with lines or dots to fill the required shape. The goal is to have an even value and smooth gradation so that the surface looks smooth.

Drybrush Exercise: Columns

On these two pages are some additional practice exercises that can help you perfect your drybrush technique.

In the example for the Columns exercise, note that the gradation on the left isn't yet smoothed with drybrush, and the one on the right has been smoothed. The more even you can get your washes, the less time will be needed to smooth with drybrush.

Supplies

- HB pencil
- Hot-pressed watercolor paper
- No. 1 sable watercolor brush
- Kneaded eraser
- Paper towel
- Scrap paper
- Water
- Paint palette
- Sap Green watercolor paint

Drybrush Exercise: One-Color Leaf

This practice leaf uses only one color (Sap Green) and shows small gradations going in all different directions.

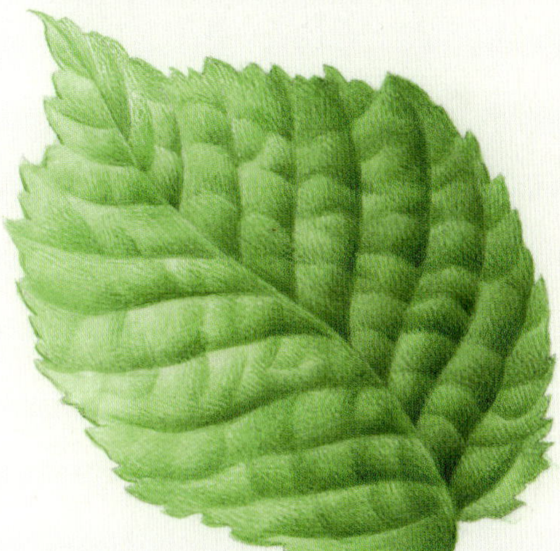

Supplies

- HB pencil
- Hot-pressed watercolor paper
- No. 1 sable watercolor brush
- Kneaded eraser
- Paper towel
- Scrap paper
- Water
- Paint palette
- Sap Green watercolor paint

Drybrush Exercise: One-Color Berry

The berry shape uses only Scarlet Lake to bring out this smooth form.

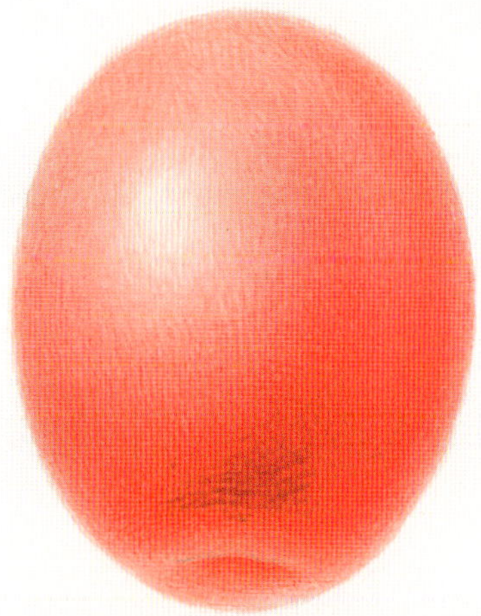

Supplies

- HB pencil
- Hot-pressed watercolor paper
- No. 1 sable watercolor brush
- Kneaded eraser
- Paper towel
- Scrap paper
- Water
- Paint palette
- Scarlet Lake watercolor paint

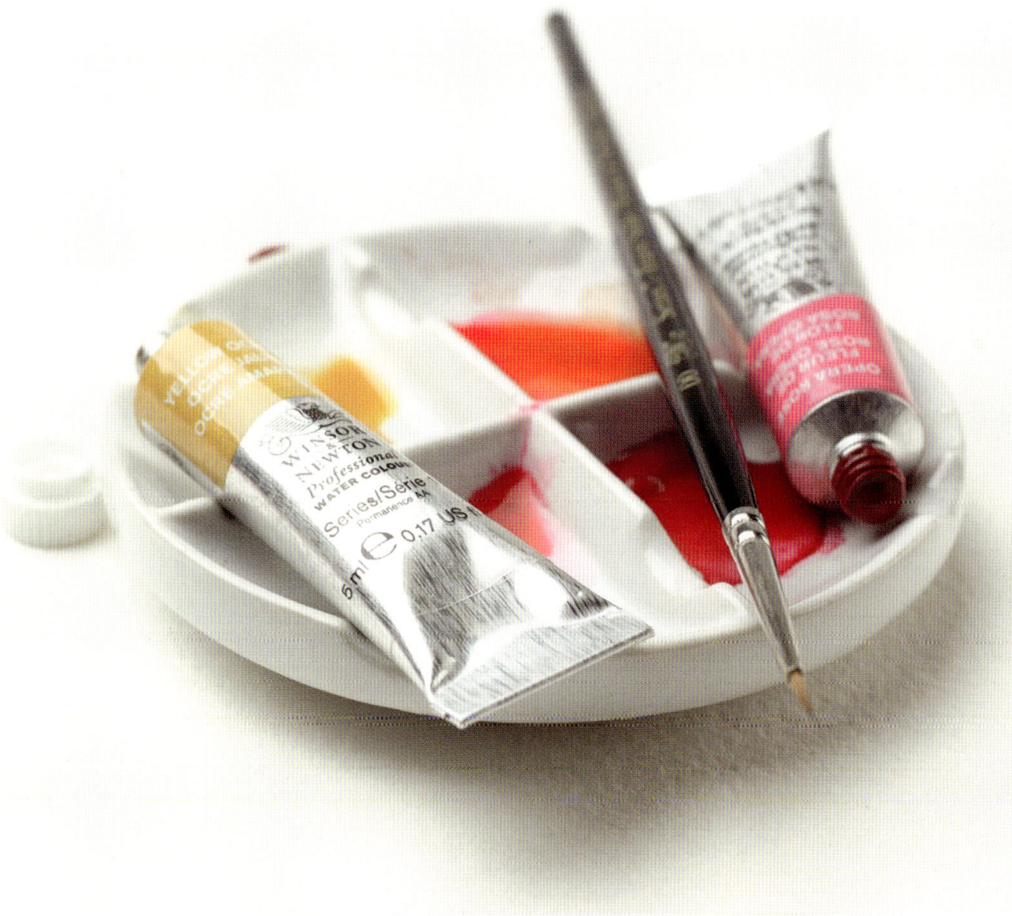

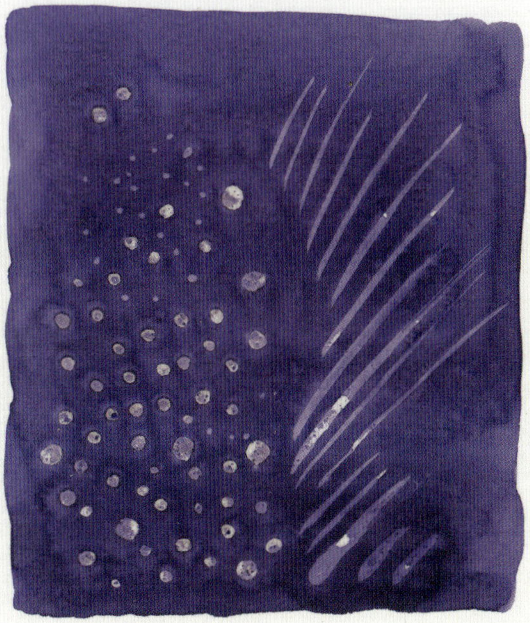

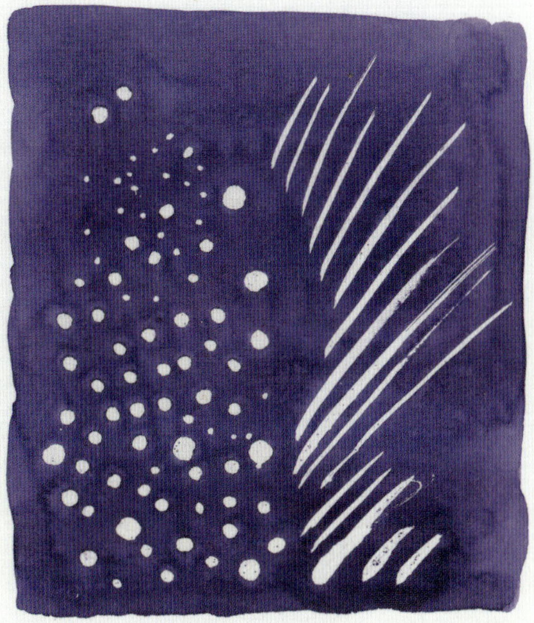

Masking fluid is applied, left to dry, and then painted over. When the paint is dry, the masking fluid is rubbed off to reveal the white paper beneath.

LIFTING

Supplies

- Hot-pressed watercolor paper (preferably plate finish)
- No. 1 sable brush
- Paper towel
- Eraser: electric or Tombow MONO precision

Paint can be lifted and manipulated at any stage, although it's preferable to add paint gradually and avoid having to lift it, unless in small areas. Whenever lifting watercolor, the surface will become uneven and need repair. This creates unnecessary steps for you, which is why it's best instead to add the paint gradually as you go.

It should be noted here that the success of lifting paint is very much dependent on the paper you're painting on as well as the color of paint you're using. Some color paints are staining and will be more difficult to lift. A traditional watercolor paper is absorbent, and it can be difficult to lift paint from the surface. A paper with a very smooth surface where the paint sits more on top and isn't absorbed into it will be easier to lift paint from. That said, the process is the same with all papers.

To lift, use either a damp brush, paper towel, or erasers. The size of the brush used depends on the size of the area you want to lift. To remove a very tiny dot, use the point of a small brush that has been dipped in water and the excess blotted on a paper towel. Move the tip of the damp brush in the small area to loosen the paint and quickly press down with the paper towel to blot up the paint. Don't swipe the paper towel to the side or it can pull the softened fibers in the paper. Usually, this process will have to be repeated frequently in the same area, wetting and blotting until enough paint is removed and the spot is light enough.

Many artists use a masking fluid when they want to keep small areas white. It's not something I use often, but it's another tool that's available and worth mentioning. Masking fluid is a product applied with a brush before paint is applied to the surface. When dry, you can paint over it and later remove it with your finger to reveal the white paper beneath.

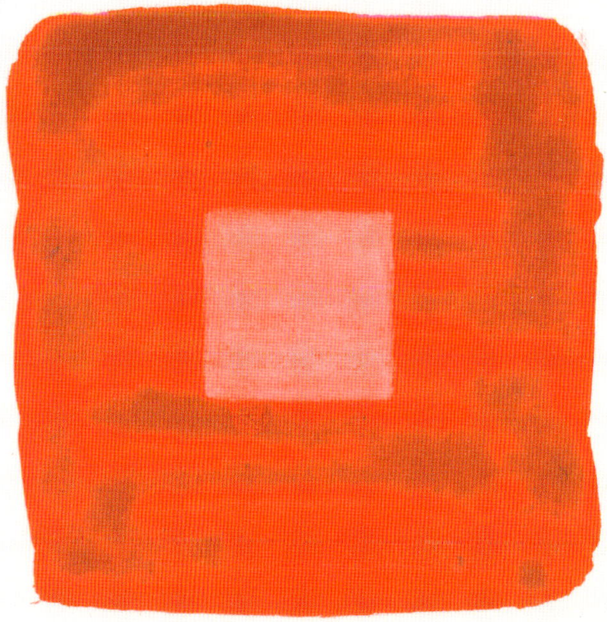

An area of paint can be lifted by wetting the desired shape and blotting it with a paper towel.

Paint is also lifted by lightly scrubbing with a damp brush and blotting with a paper towel. This can be done in spaces both large and small. Wet the area with a damp brush. Quickly blot down with a clean paper towel. Try to do this in one swift step. If more paint needs to be removed, repeat this process. You don't need to let it dry between blottings, but remember not to swipe sideways with the paper towel or work on it so much that the paper tears. Once this area is the value you wish, let it dry completely, and any evening of tone will be done with drybrush.

If the area you want to remove paint If you want to remove paint from a large area, a larger brush would be used. Generally, removing paint from a large area is something we want to avoid, but it can be done. Gauge the size of the area you want to pick up and choose the brush accordingly. The same wetting and blotting with paper towel is done, although with a large size area, more water will be needed in your brush. Turn the paper towel as you blot. If you're using a heavy weight tough watercolor paper, you may be able to gently scrub the surface with a stiff bristled brush to remove paint until it's the desired value.

Erasers are another way to lift paint. At all times, this should only be done when the surface is completely dry. Erasers are most helpful when you've already done the wetting and blotting method and have lifted as much as you can but would still like the area to be lighter. When the paper is completely dry, the electric eraser can lift tiny spots, often removing the paint to the white of the paper. A Tombow MONO zero precision eraser can also lift a small area. A kneaded eraser will lift a wider area and will probably not lift as much paint, but will be more gentle to the paper's surface.

OVERLAPS

Often, students ask about how to make a leaf or petal look like it's overlapping another. This is done by defining the edge of the leaf or petal that's on top and often, but not always, making a shadow along the leaf or petal it overlaps. This is dependent upon how the flower or leaf is lit. To define the edge on top, you might lift a fine line of paint to highlight it and make it look lighter. Or, perhaps it's the petal on top that's darker. There should be enough contrast between the petal on top and below to show separation. When making the shadow on the petal beneath, the shadow should be darkest at the edge where it meets the petal on top, then it fades gradually away from it.

Supplies

- Hot-pressed watercolor paper
- No. 1 sable brush
- Paper towel
- Scrap paper
- Water
- Paint palette
- Sap Green watercolor paint

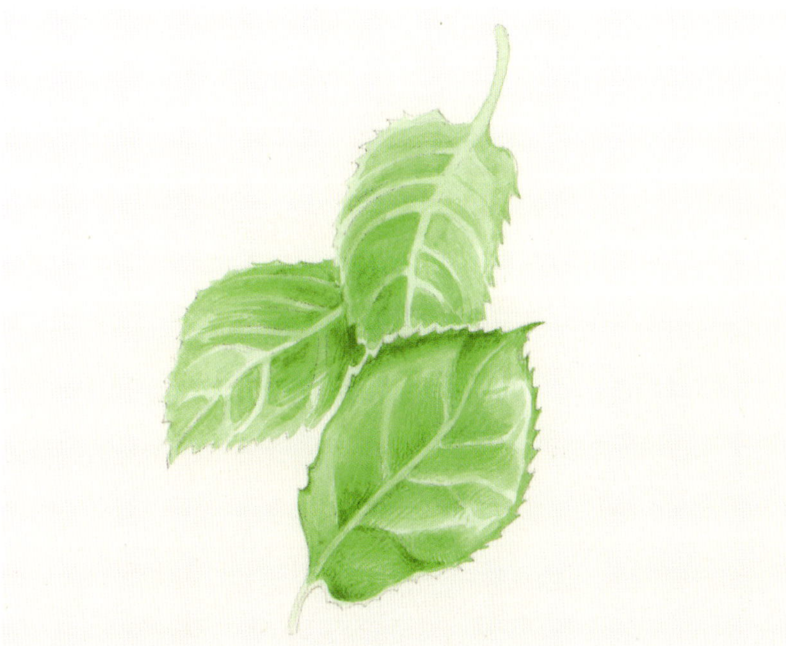

These are the same leaves painted only with Winsor & Newton Sap Green. Here are the first layers blocking in paint.

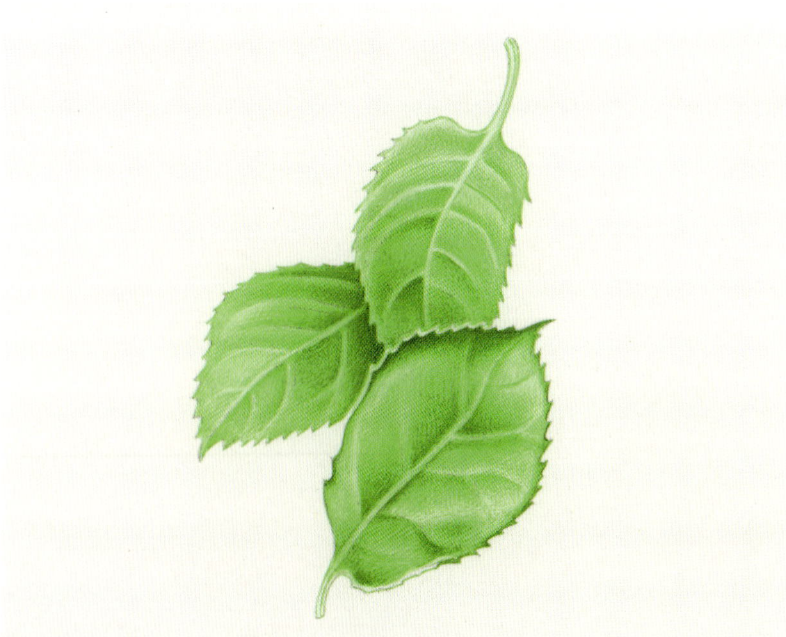

Differing values at the leaves' edges convey one leaf on top of another.

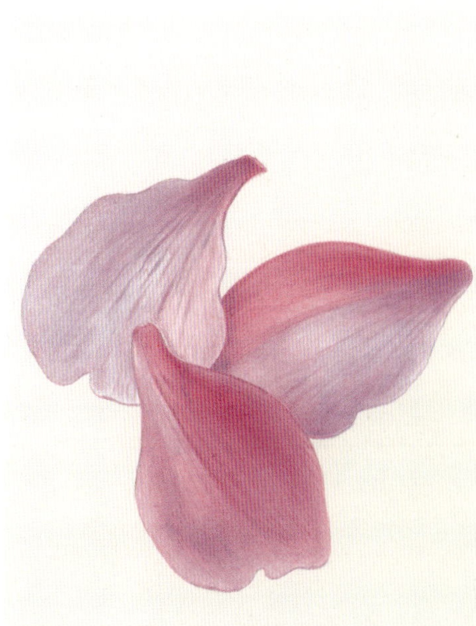

The illusion of depth can be created by overlapping one petal over another.

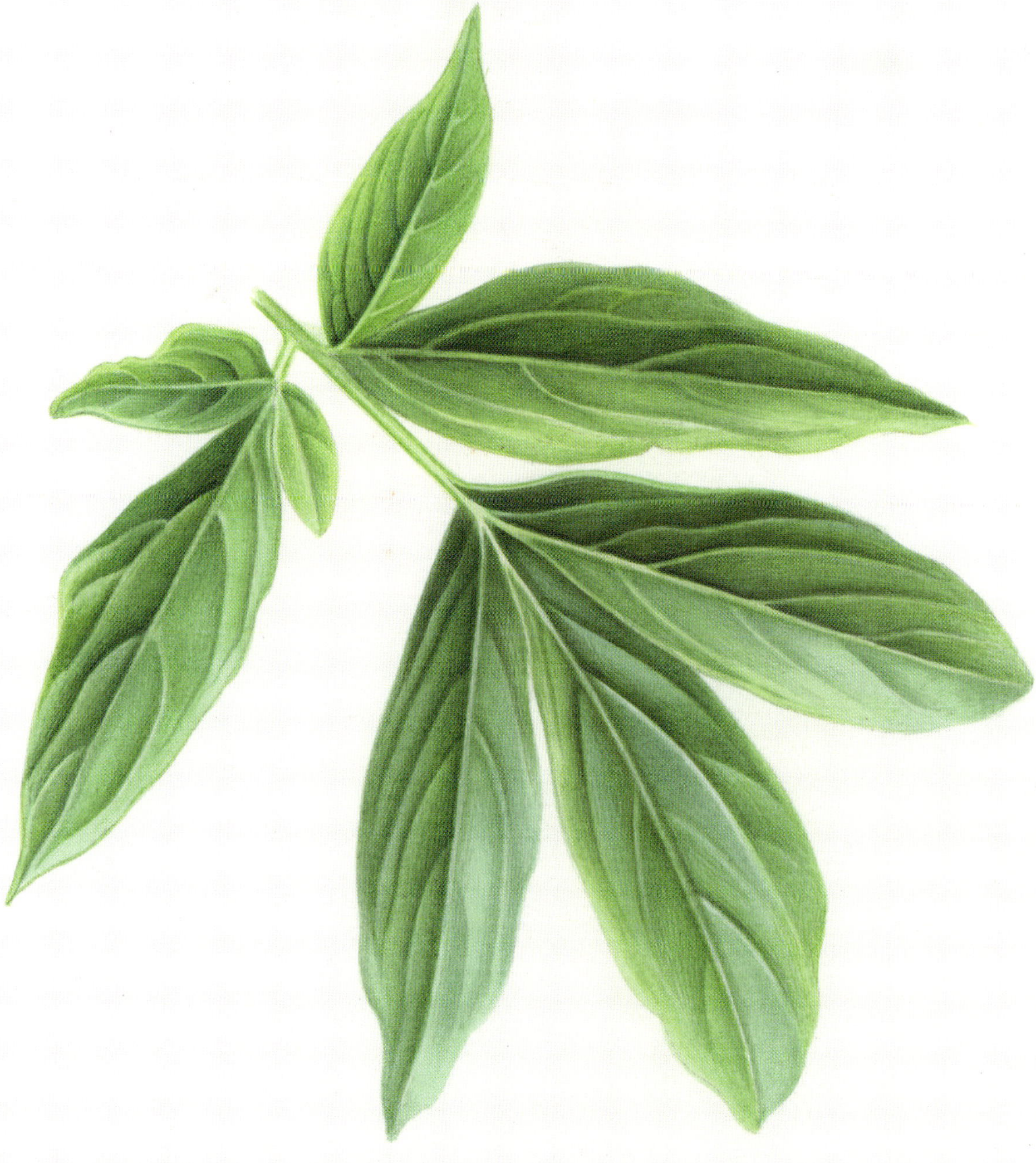

CORRECTING MISTAKES AND MAKING REVISIONS

Watercolor is very forgiving and adaptable. It can be pushed around, layered to adjust color, and lifted so correcting mistakes and making adjustments are easy once you get the feel for it. I would not recommend trying to remove the large areas you've already painted in—such as trying to completely remove a leaf and hoping to get back to the original white of the paper. Even if you were able to remove all the paint, the water and scrubbing will leave a mark. But other lesser mistakes can usually be corrected.

The original painting.

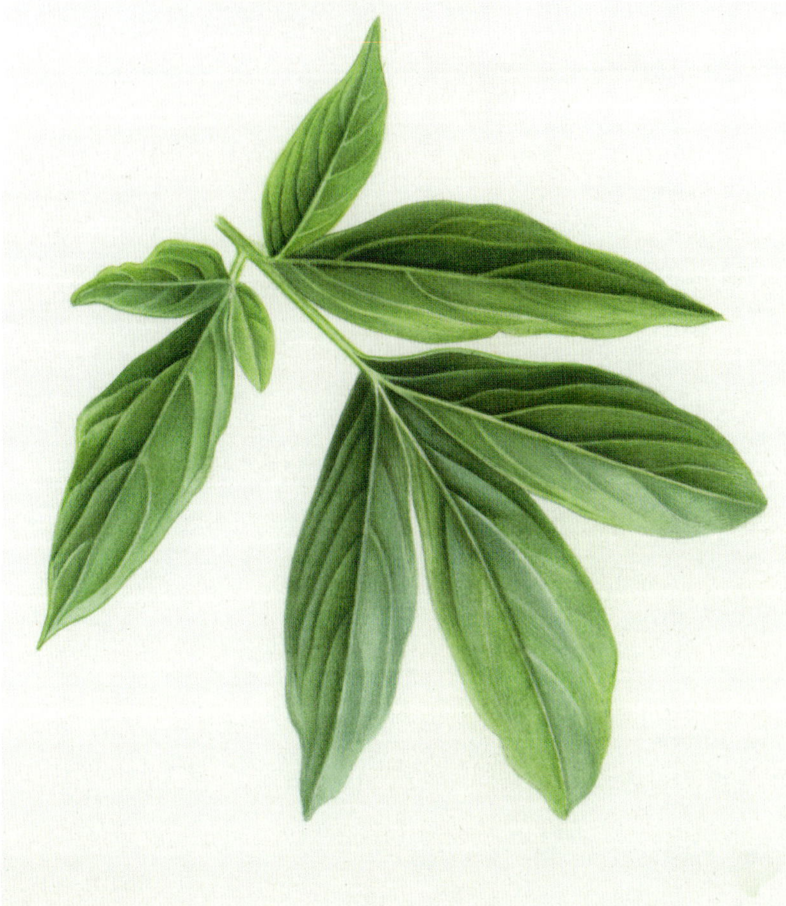

On the bottom middle leaf, veins and the surrounding area are removed by wetting and blotting.

A subtle shift in color can be made by adding a layer on top. If your leaf is too yellow, try adding a blue to your wash. This is best accomplished while you're building up layers early on, but subtle shifts can be done later too. Do a little test on your scrap paper where you have the color green you've already used in your leaf. Layer different blues on top and see which one you like before adding it to your finished piece.

Veins in a leaf can be lifted and new veins painted in. First, remove the vein by repeated gentle scrubbing and blotting along the vein. You may not be able to pick everything up using this technique, so be careful not to overdo it and end up damaging your paper. Next, fill in the old vein that you want to get rid of using drybrush. Go back into the new vein with a sharp point of a small brush and adjust the value and clean up the leaf's new vein. If the veins you wish to remove were made with dark lines, they can be picked up as well. These leaves are used as an example of how to move veins. The middle leaf has veins removed by repeated wetting and blotting.

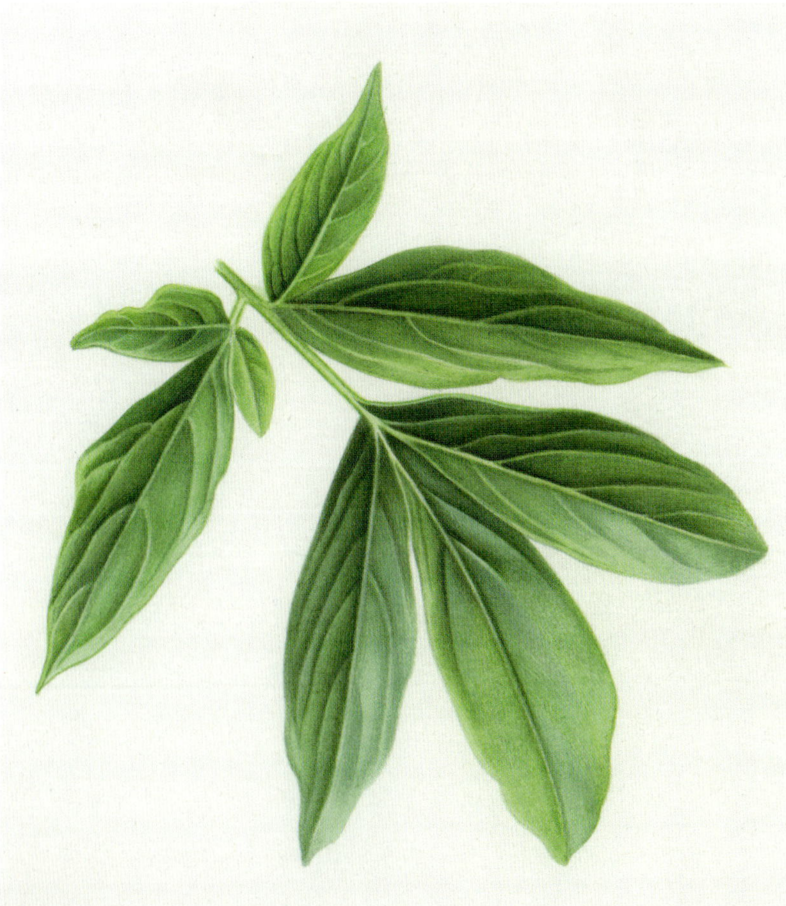

Drybrush is used to even the tone before adding the new veins.

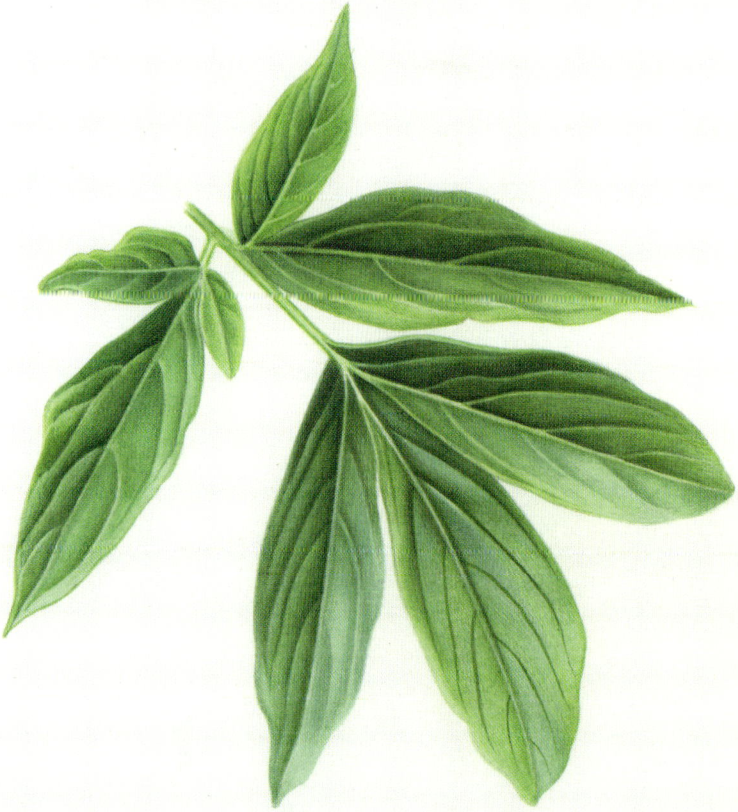

New vein placement is indicated with lines.

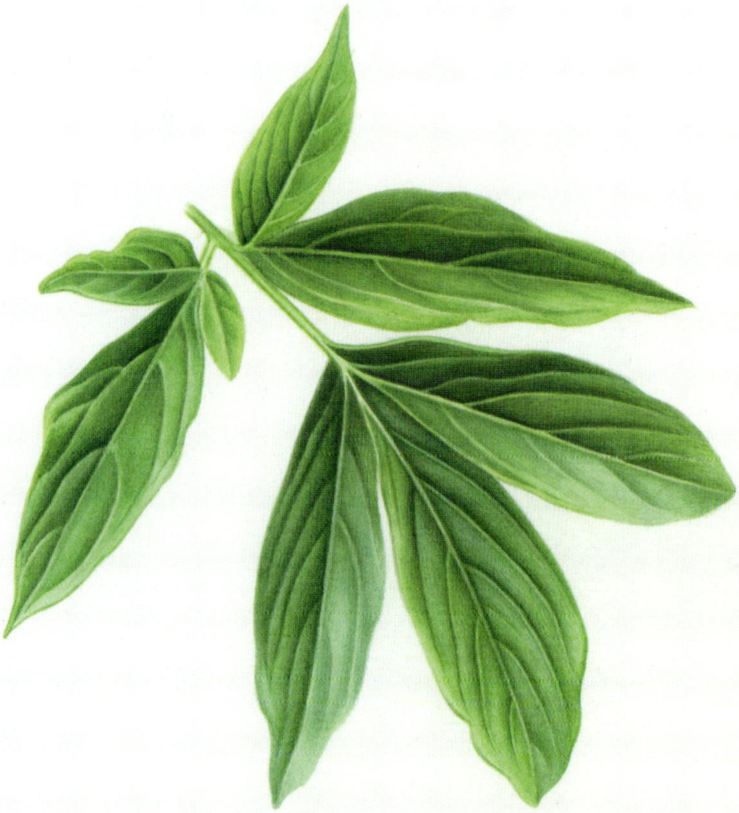

Gradations with drybrush are added, being mindful of how the contours are lighted.

How to Change a Petal's Shape

A blotted damp brush with a sharp point is applied over the line and a paper towel is pushed into it. Make sure when doing this that your clean paper towel is dry. I keep one folded paper towel next to my water cup to blot excess in the brush and a clean paper towel in my left hand to blot paint from the paper. After these small lines are picked up, the area can be smoothed with drybrush and new veins added.

Edges of petals can be moved and changed as well. It's easy to make the petal's edge larger when you're expanding it into a white background. With graphite, lightly draw the new petal's shape. Wet and blot the edge that's going to be expanded to soften if needed. Then, add washes and complete the petal in the new area. The contours of the expanded petal should flow seamlessly from old to new.

A petal's shape can be changed and expanded into a white background.

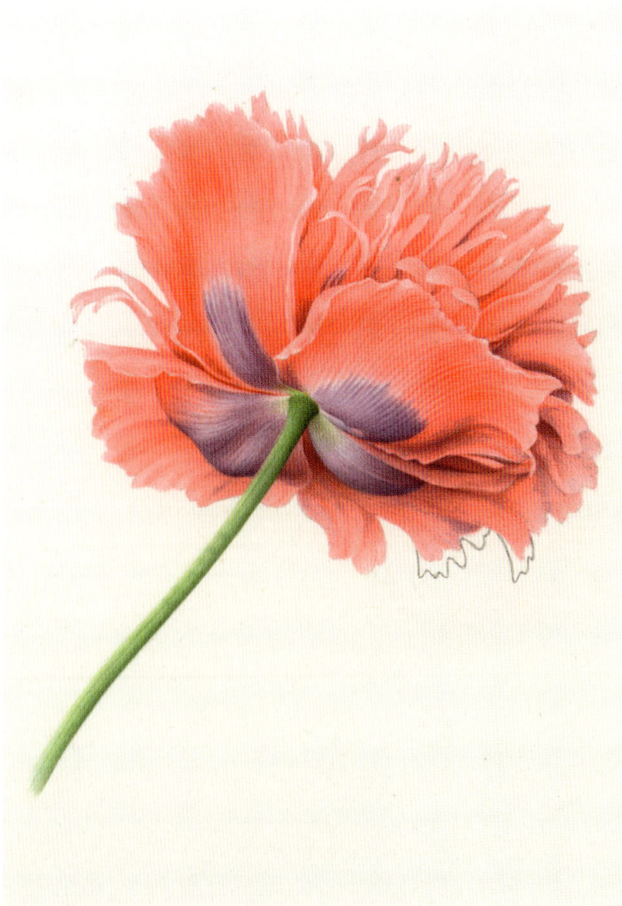

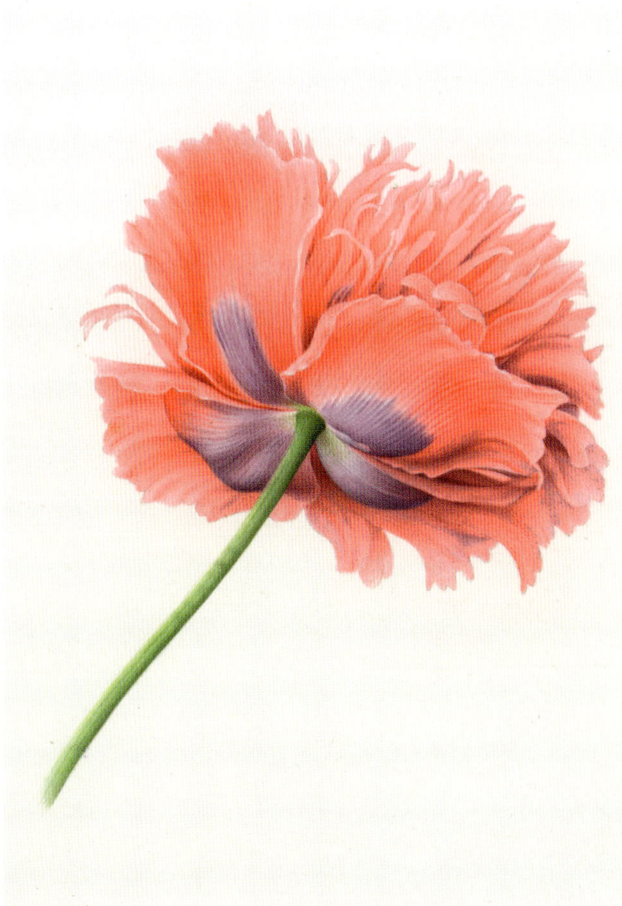

If the petal you wish to enlarge encroaches into a dark area, the paint in the dark area needs to be picked up. If you want to paint a pink petal where there had been a green leaf, you'll need to remove as much green as possible. The success of this depends on the paper and paints used, but it's possible to do. A color change from dark to light will be more successful in a small area than a large one. Wet the area you wish to pick up and blot with your paper towel. A dark color may need gentle scrubbing, blotting, and perhaps erasing when the surface is completely dry. Carefully paint in the new petal. Drybrush will be needed to make smooth gradations.

A petal's straight edge can be made more undulating by lifting and adding paint as needed.

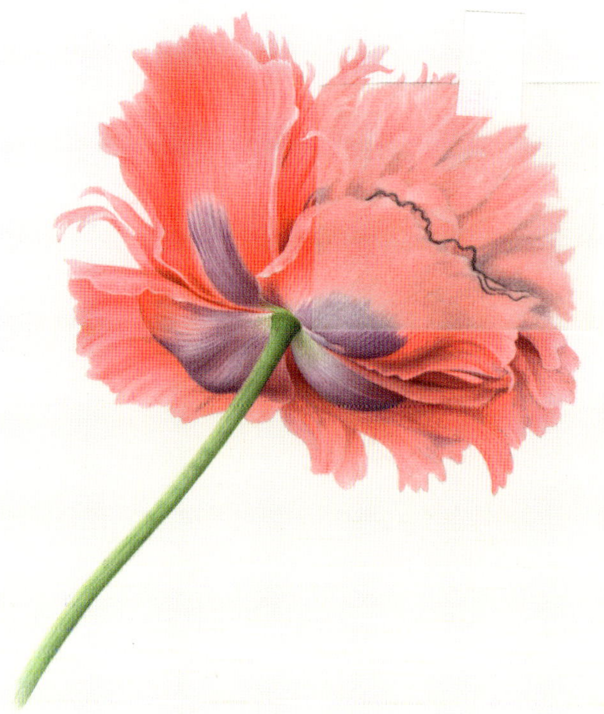

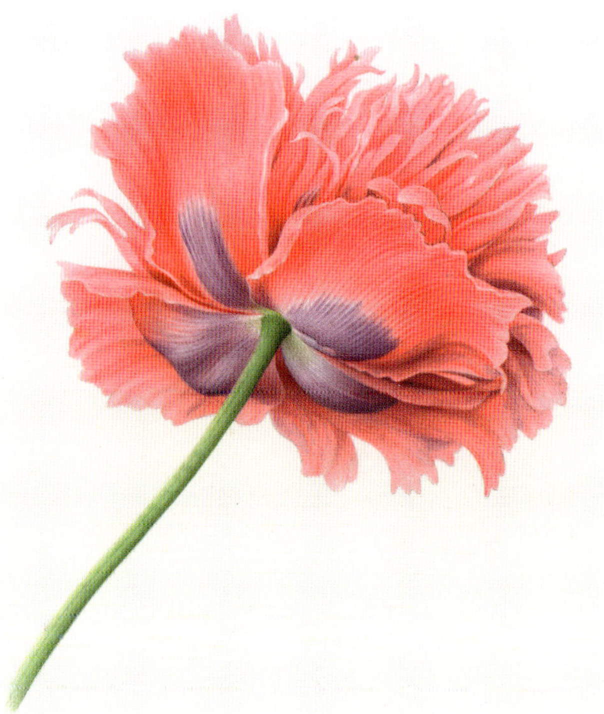

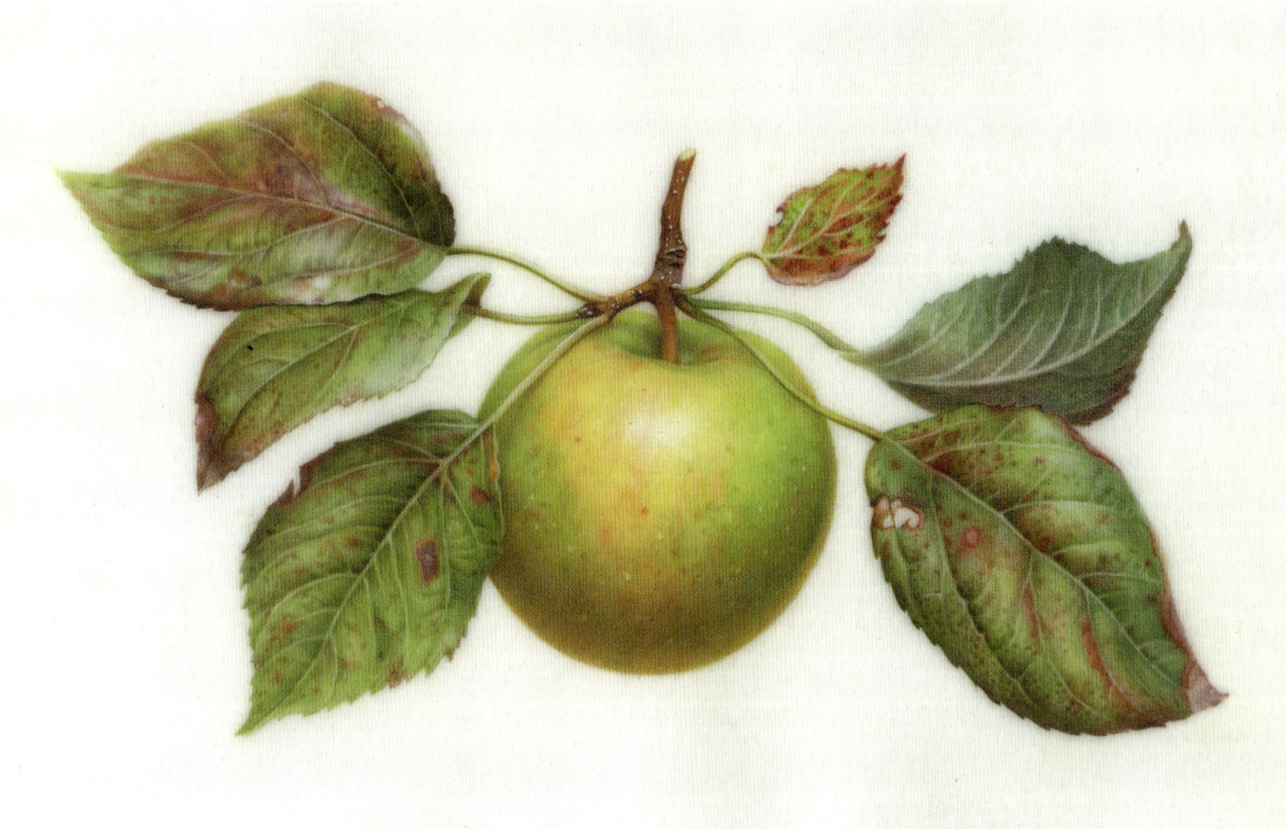

"Halsey Farm" Green Apple
watercolor on paper 9.5" x 10.5"
(24.1 cm x 26.7 cm)

DETAILS AND FINISHING

Details such as veining, spots, mottling, and texture are added at the end of your painting after gradations, contours, and values seem correct. They are done with smaller brushes (No. 000, No. 00, No. 0, and No. 1) with sharp points. Detail is added by either adding or taking away paint. The darkness of an added line is determined by how much paint is in the mix you're using, the same as for a wash.

Veining

Veining is found in both flowers and leaves and, depending on the subject, can be numerous, few, pronounced, or subtle. By observing the subject, you may need to either add lines of paint or lift and blot to take paint away.

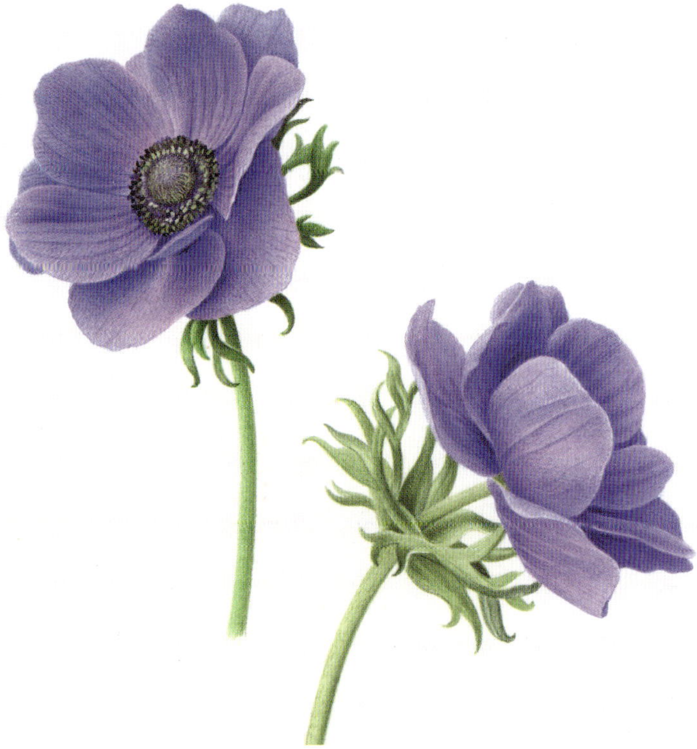

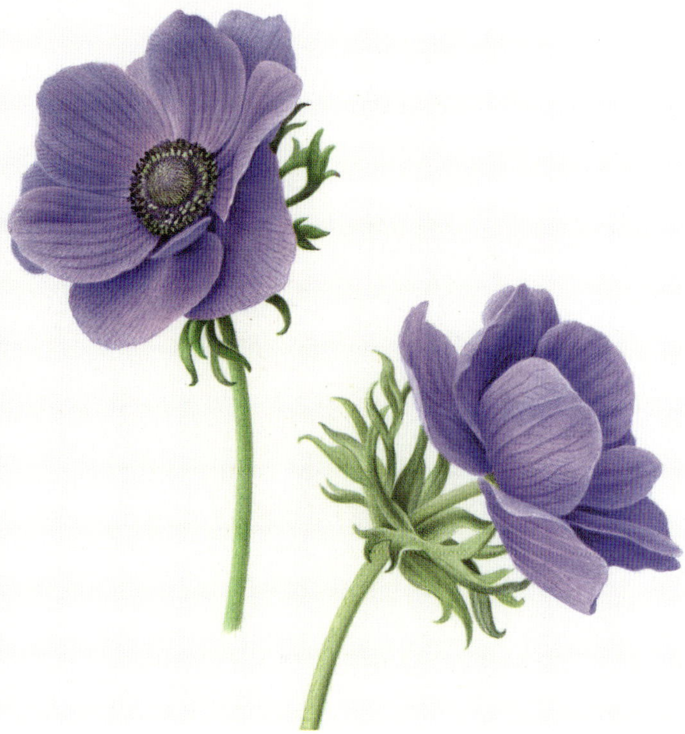

Here, veining is added by both lifting lines of paint by wetting and blotting or drawing lines in. Dots large and small may be added or taken away.

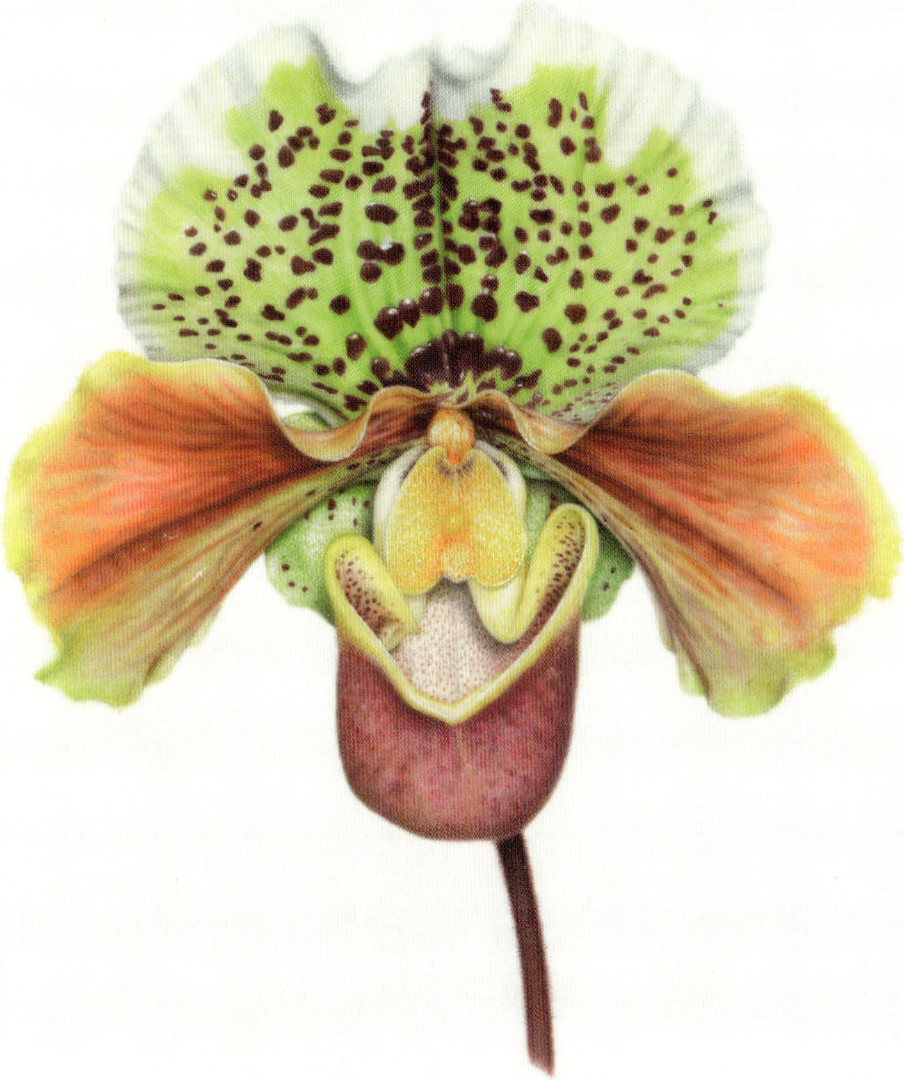

In the "*Toad Orchid*" (*Paphiopedilum henryanum*), some spots are raised while others lie flat on the surface.

Spots

Most often, plants will have small speckles that lie flat on the surface. They can be of varying sizes or uniform, depending on your specimen. They're created with the tip of a small brush without much water in it.

When spots curve around a surface, they should look as though they recede in space. The spots that come most toward you will be rounder and fuller. As they move towards the edge, they become more and narrow.

Occasionally, a spot is raised, as in the *Toad Orchid* above. You can portray this by the way the light falls across it. There will be a gradation and a highlight.

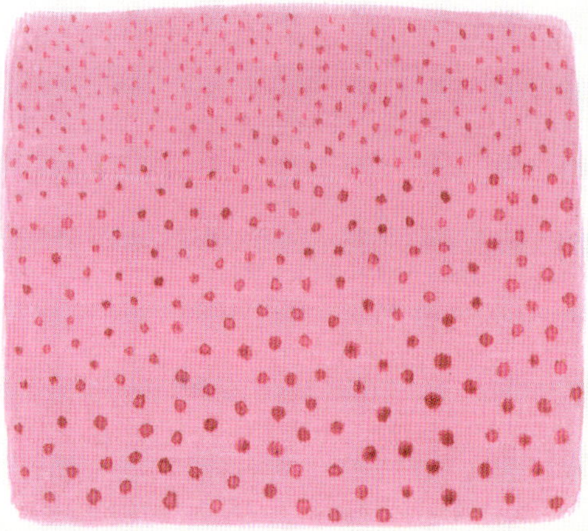

Little dots of varying sizes are made with the tip of a brush.

A raised spot's contour is shown with a gradation and highlight.

Splotches or areas of irregular patterns will probably have soft edges.

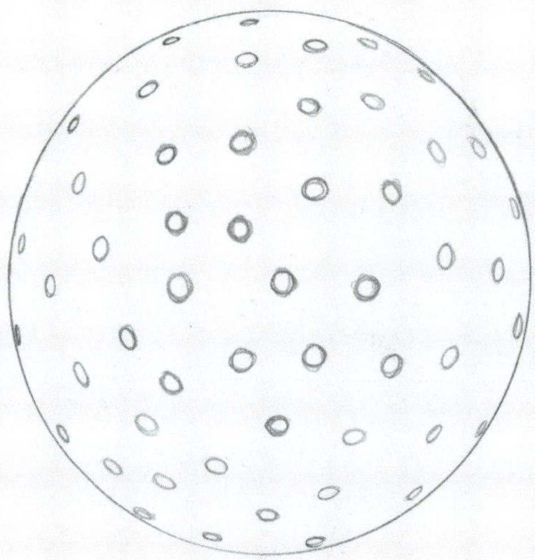

Spots or any markings curving back in space get smaller and narrower.

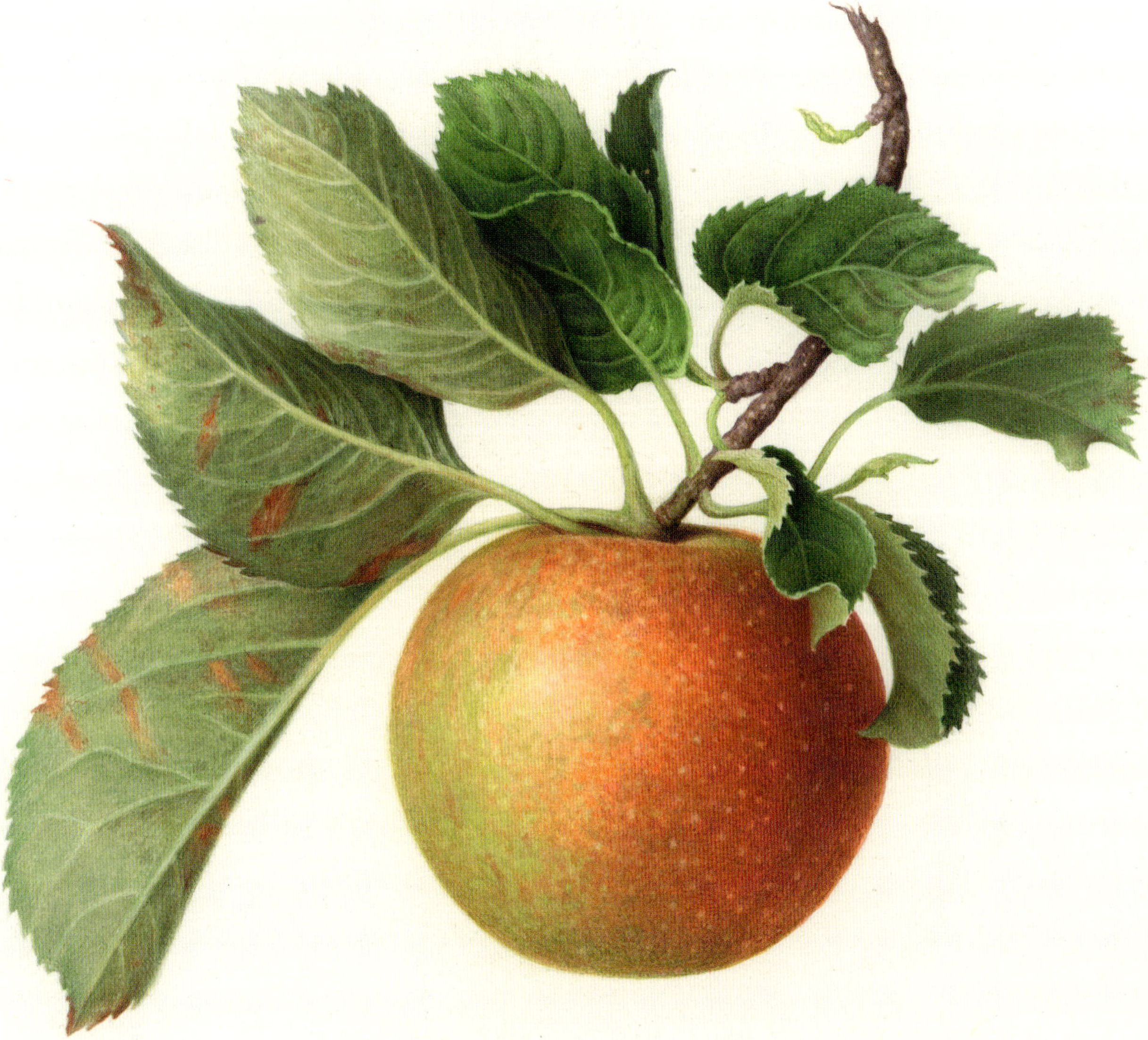

Since we're adding an orange tone first, green is lifted with blotting as well as the electric eraser.

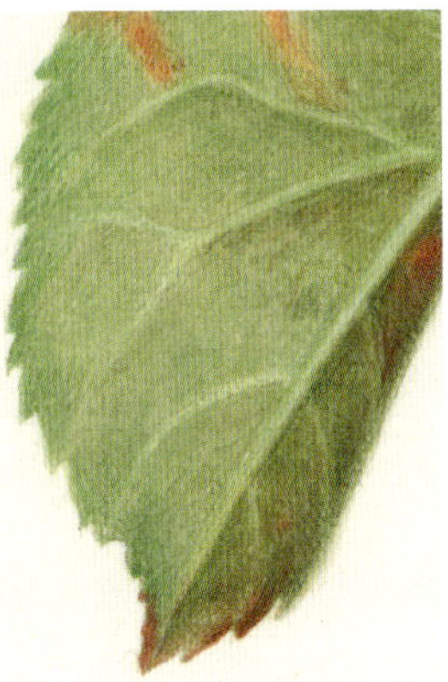

Mottling

You can also add and adjust mottling in a leaf towards the end of the painting. Here, additional splotches are painted into the leaves. Drybrush lines in different directions to build up color in an irregular pattern. This often has a messy look, so once again, mimic what you see and capture the unevenness of it.

A red/orange/brown mix was added with drybrush to create splotches of color where the green was lifted out. Spots in the apple were also adjusted and darkened to make them more subtle.

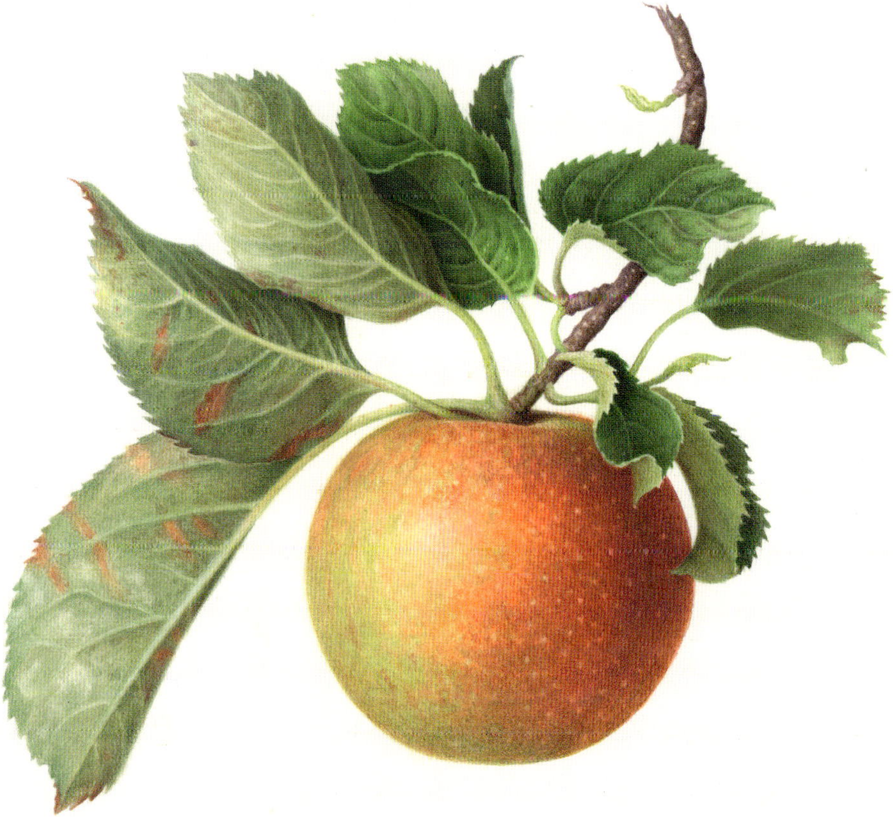

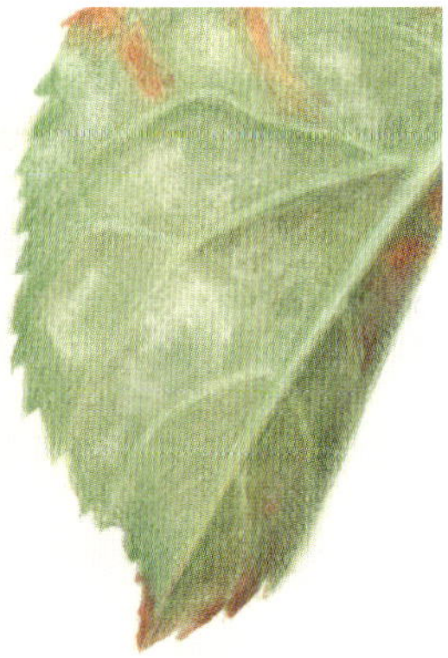

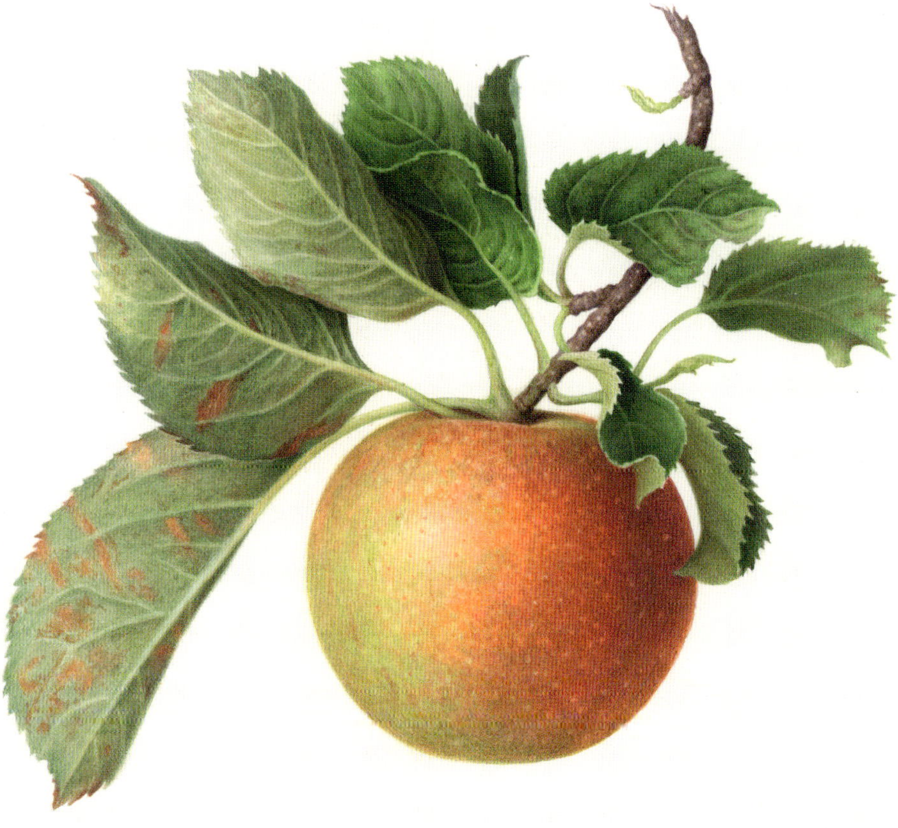

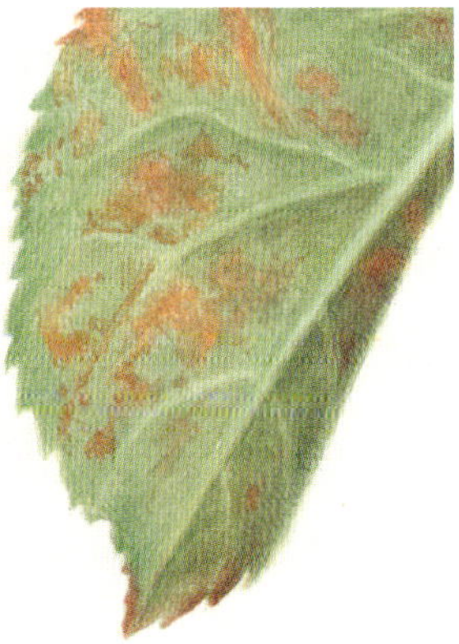

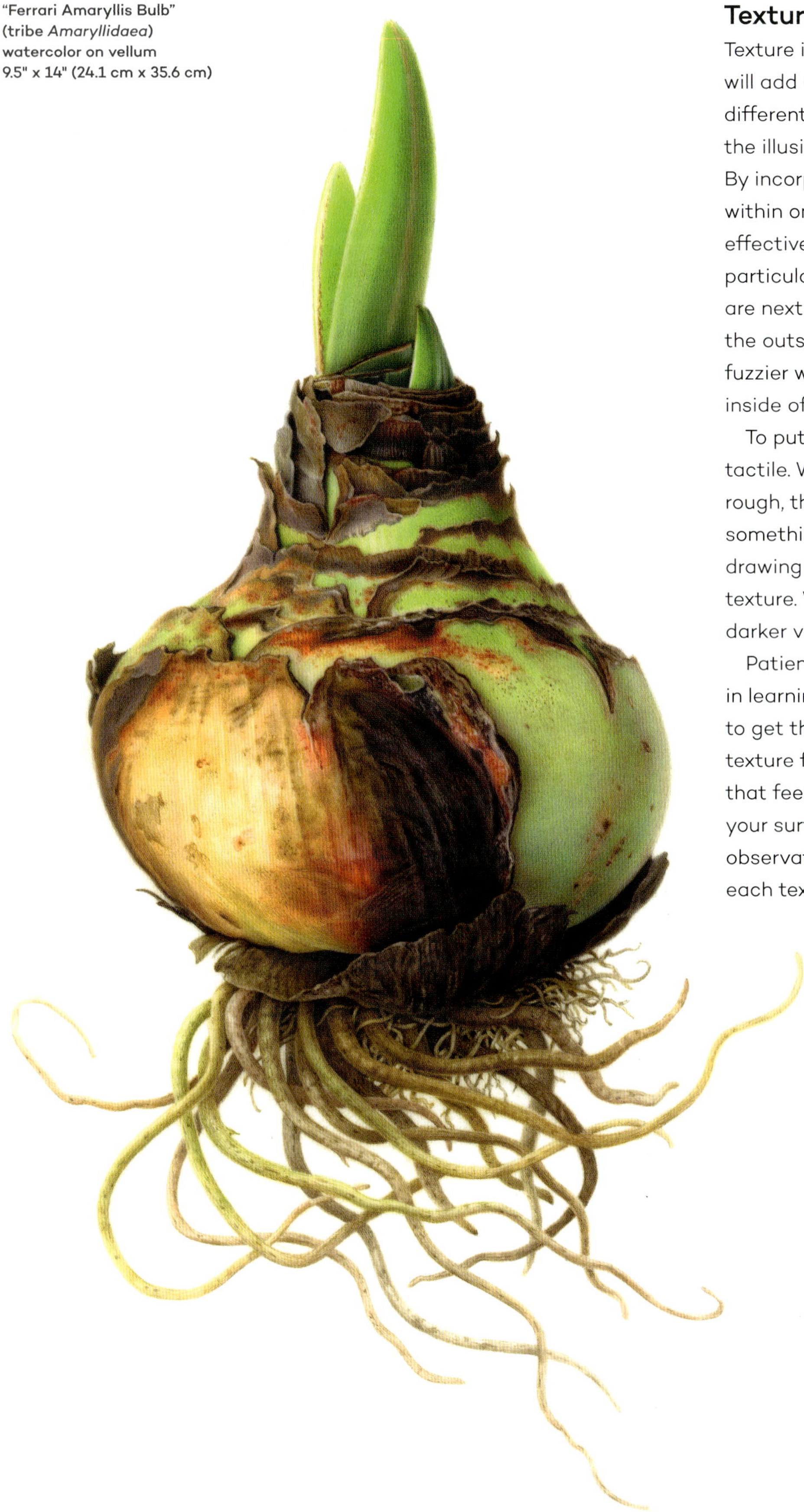

"Ferrari Amaryllis Bulb"
(tribe *Amaryllidaea*)
watercolor on vellum
9.5" x 14" (24.1 cm x 35.6 cm)

Texture

Texture is an important quality that will add realism to your work. By using different techniques, one can create the illusion of any surface texture. By incorporating a variety of textures within one piece, you can enhance the effectiveness of each by way of contrast, particularly when the different surfaces are next to each other. For example, the outside of a fuzzy peach will seem fuzzier when shown next to the wet juicy inside of the peach.

To put it simply, you have to think tactile. When painting something that's rough, think rough. When painting something smooth, think smooth. Avoid drawing all surfaces with the same texture. When the texture is rough, a darker value will be useful.

Patient observation goes a long way in learning to paint textures. You want to get the tactile sense of what that texture feels like and then translate that feeling through the paint onto your surface. This requires very close observation to determine what makes each texture unique.

The subtle texture of this leaf was created with many tiny spots of color, usually by adding paint but occasionally by lifting. In the close-up, you can see fine lines created by the No. 000 brush.

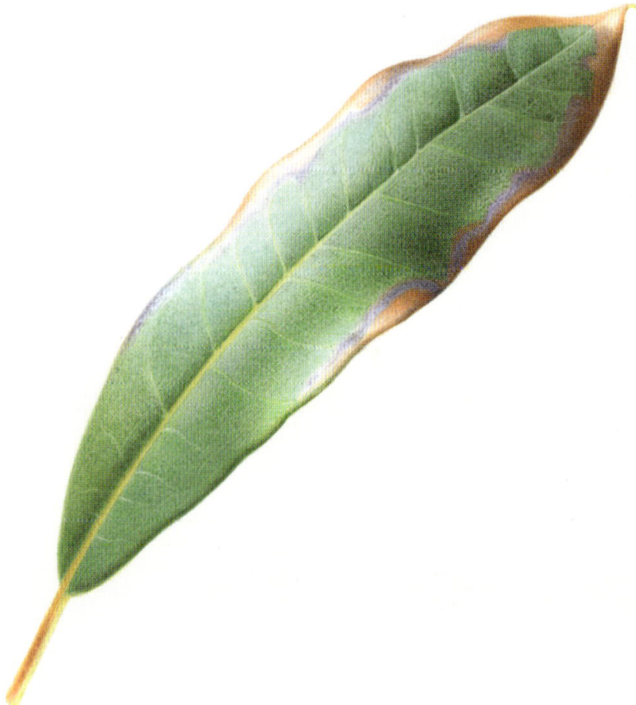

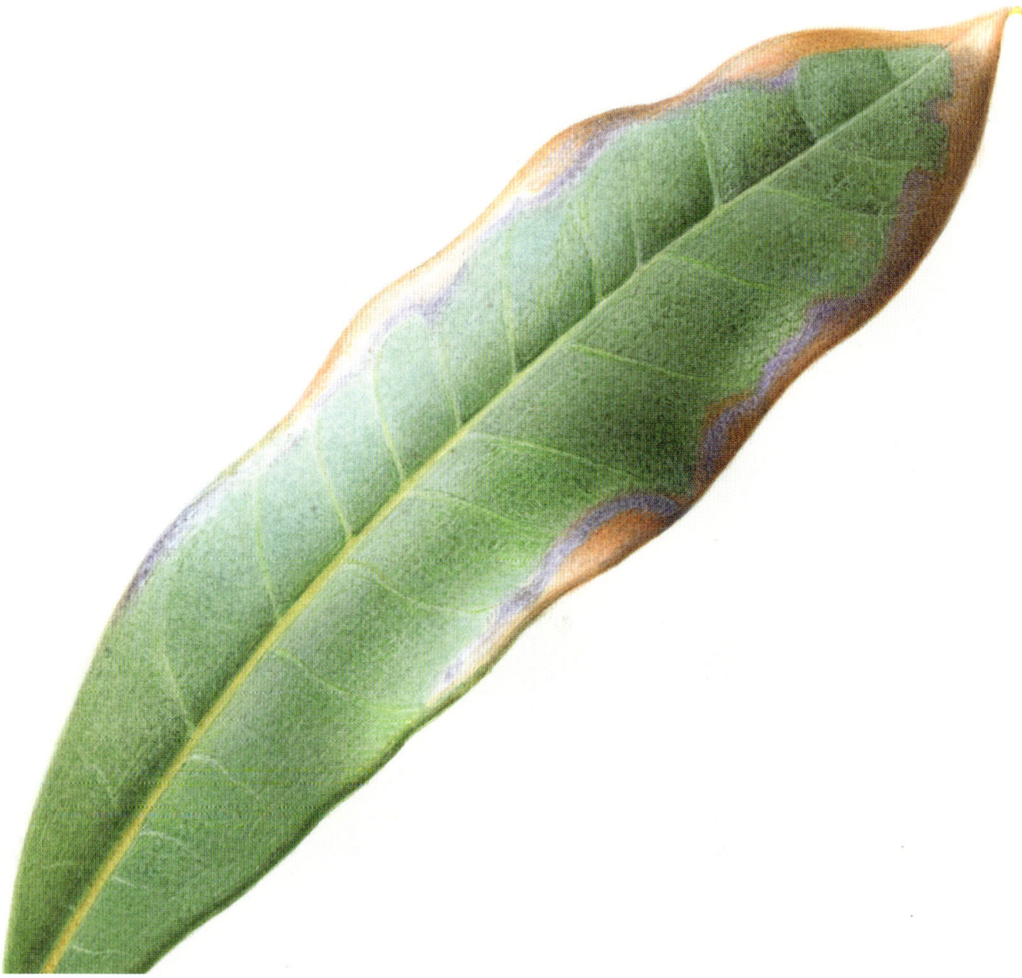

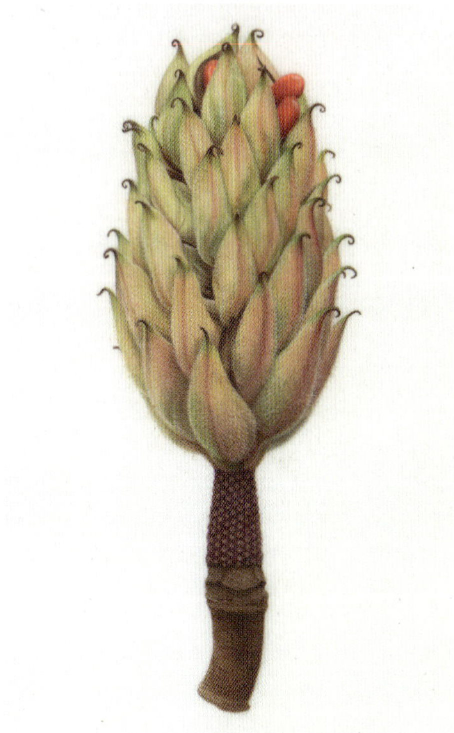

There are various textures in this magnolia pod.

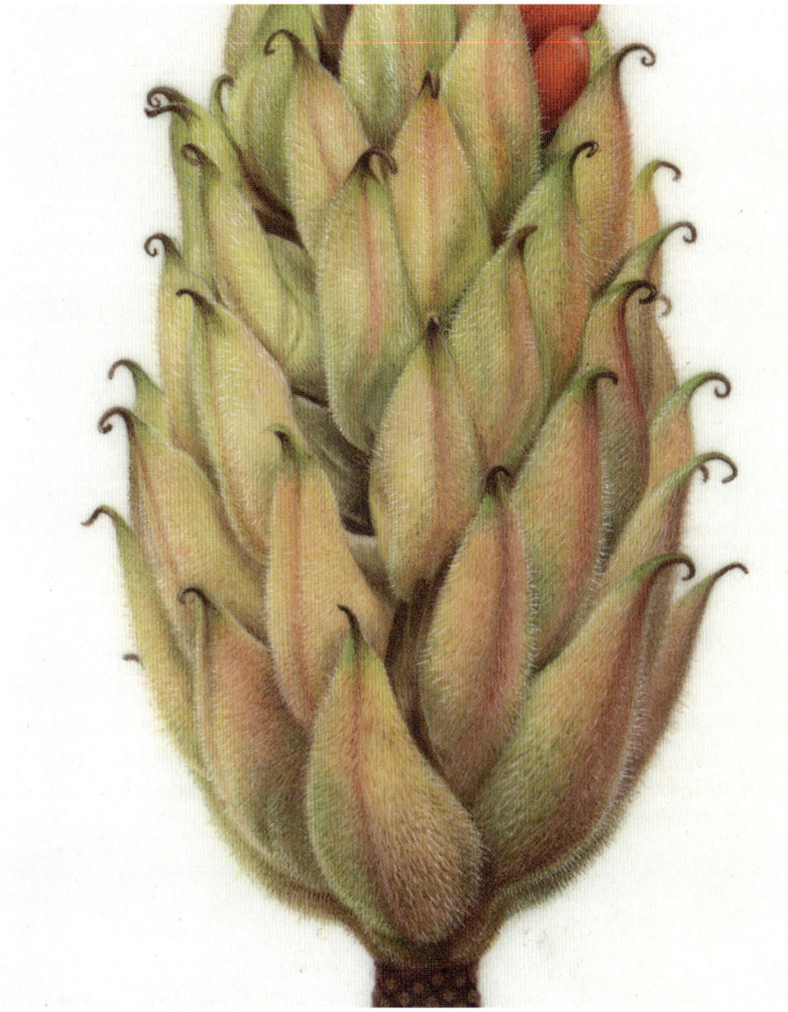

White paint with a No. 000 brush was used for the tiny hairs.

This magnolia pod (*Magnolia grandiflora*) uses different textures within the one image. The shiny red seeds are created by using contrast between the smooth red surface and the white highlight. The spirally arranged carpels have a fuzzy texture that's created with many little lines to indicate hairs. This was a rare instance where white paint was used to create the tiny hairs because the painting is so small at 7 inches (17.8 cm) high. It was more effective to add paint than to pick out and blot such minute lines.

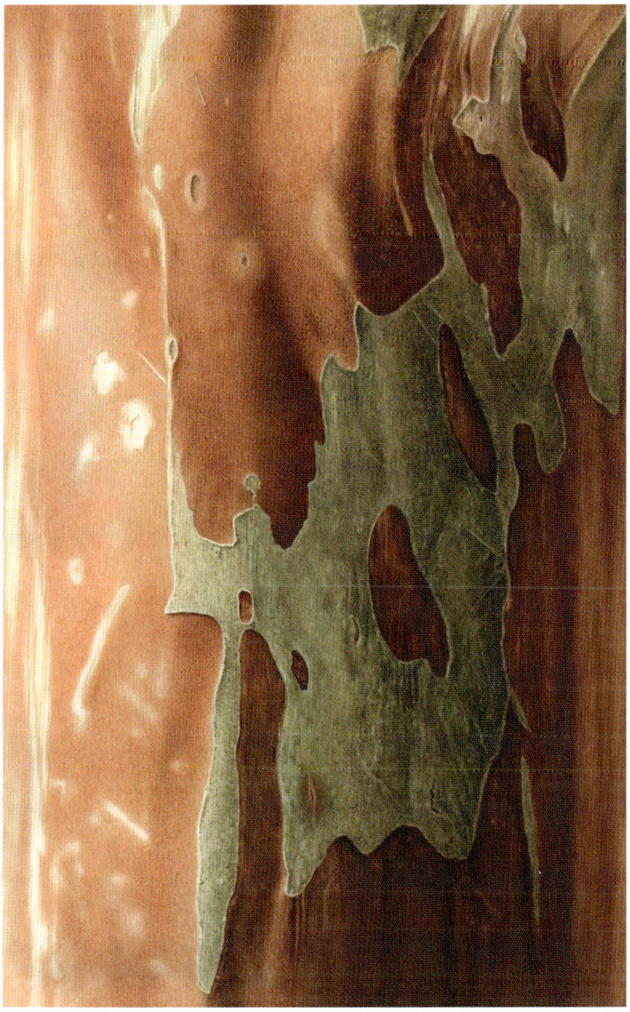

Crepe Myrtle Bark; watercolor on paper.

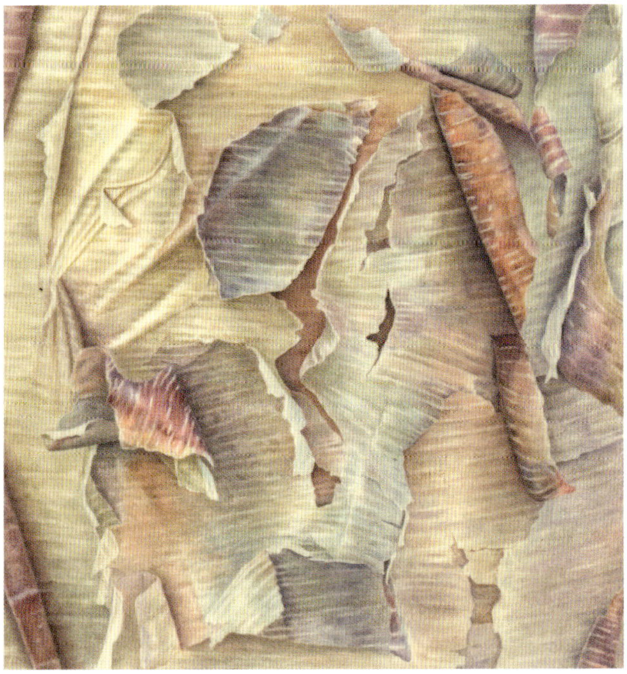

Birch Bark; watercolor on vellum.

The bark on these two trees, crepe myrtle (*Lagerstroemia indica*) and birch (*Betula alleghaniensis*), are good examples of differing textures and how they are created.

The birch has raised peeling and curved layers of bark. Sharp edges help to define one layer from another and make them look like one layer is on top of another. Special attention is paid to how each curl is lit to make it look three dimensional and create realism.

The crepe myrtle bark is much smoother, with an almost felt-like texture. Smooth gradations show the roundness of the trunk and its irregular markings and help to portray the bark's soft feel. The sharp edge around the green section of bark makes it look raised. This is created by a dark shadow behind the green bark and a lighter outline at the edge.

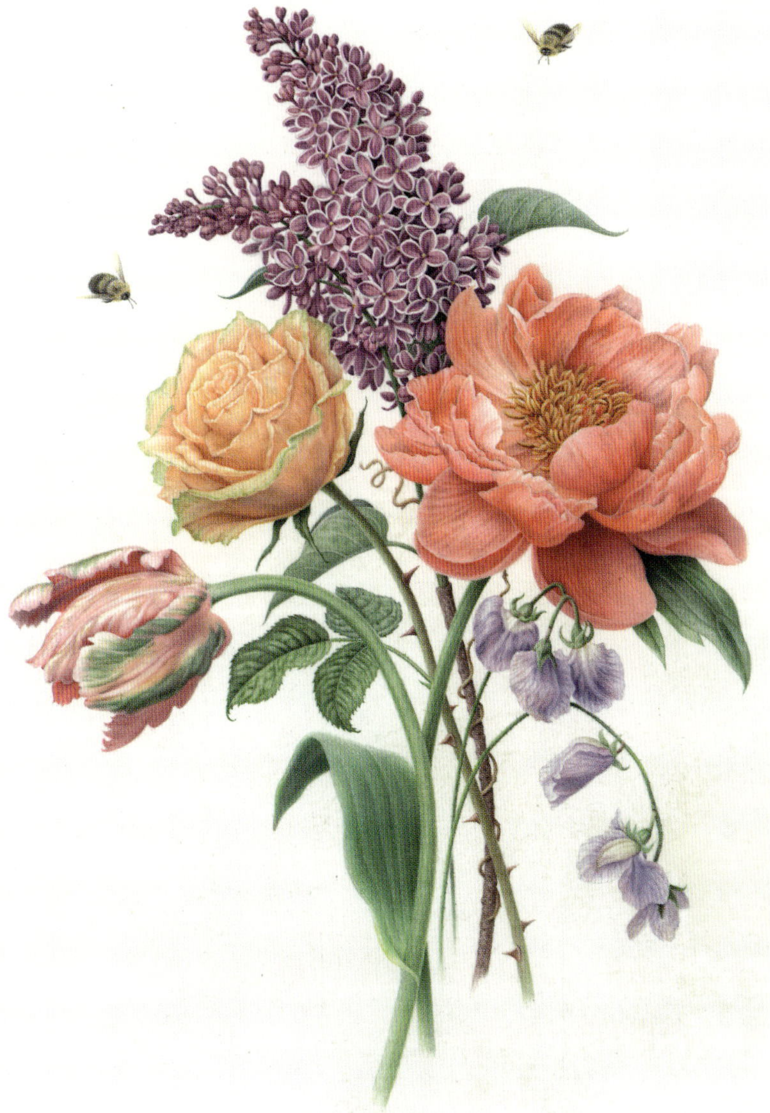

"Spring Bouquet" watercolor on vellum.

ADDING PERSONALITY

Every single one of us has our own artistic style.

It may seem surprising, but personal style is very evident in botanical painting. Even if a few artists are painting the exact same rose, they will look different and individual to the artist. They may all be realistic and scientifically accurate, but each artist has their own recognizable style.

From teaching classes, this has become very clear to me. After a couple of days, I can usually guess which student has done what. Someone may have a heavy or light touch, make lyrical curves, or include lots of detail.

One student I had always drew beautiful lyrical curves whether she was drawing stems, leaves, or petals. Of course, this only works if these shapes are similar to your subject, but she made it work. This student already had a beautiful style.

The key to having your own style is to recognize what comes naturally to you and work with it. Don't fight with your natural tendencies and try to imitate another artist. Build on your own natural strengths so that your style is visually pleasing, while also remembering to capture the necessary characteristics of botanical art: scientific accuracy, detail, good composition, and so on.

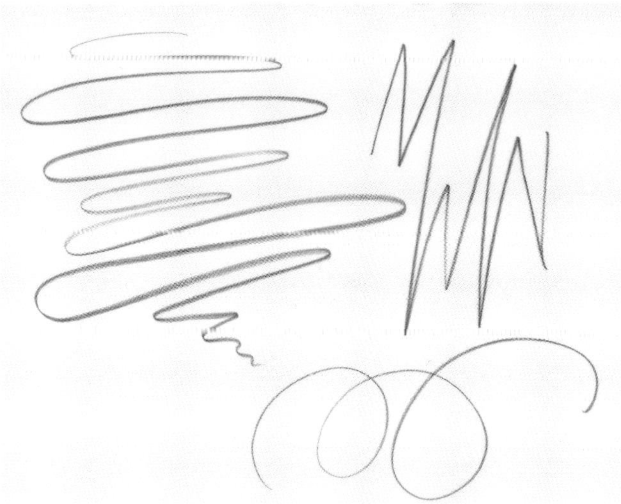

An artist's hand often shows distinct personality, which may be expressed in curves, sharp lines, and heavy or light pressure.

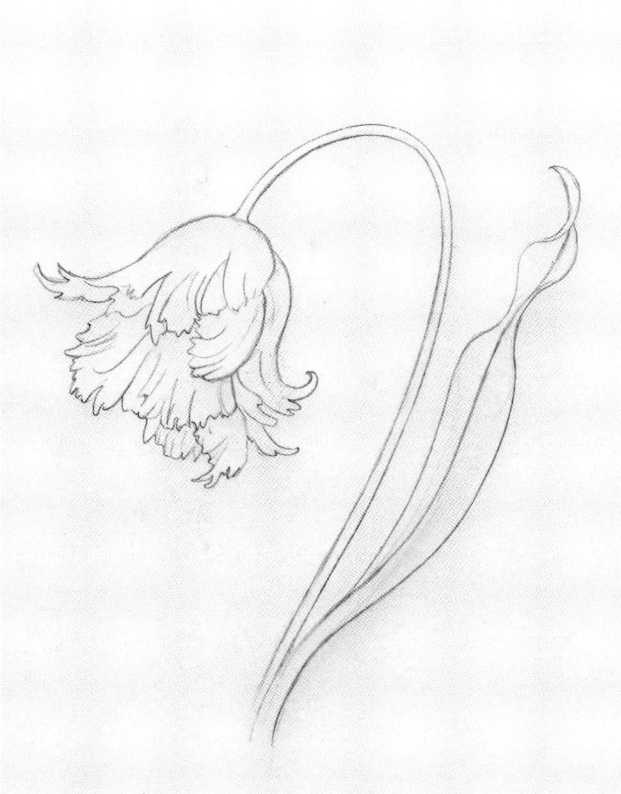

Curving stems, leaves, and petals can be worked out in the sketch stage.

Knowing When Your Painting Is Done

When finishing your painting, everything has to come together. Is the composition good? If something seems wrong, ask yourself, "Is there something that can be changed or added that will help it?" Notice if the values in the painting seem correct. Are there dark medium and light values that transition smoothly from one to another? Are gradations smooth where they should be? If not, spend more time with a drybrush and even them out. Make any adjustments to the edges. Remember, if your image has a line going around the edge, it will look like a cut out. Pick up some edges by wetting and blotting so that it looks like the edges go in and out of space. Do the highlights look correct? Do they look too white or do their edges look too defined? Is there enough detail in the focal points of the painting or where your eye goes to rest?

There are some tricks to help you to figure out what the painting needs. First, put it away for a day or two and don't look at it. When you take it out again, often something will stand out that needs to be changed. You can also ask someone, friend or family member, that has a good eye for a critique. My mother, also an artist, and I used to critique each other's work and it was very helpful. Another trick is to hold the painting up to a mirror and look at it in reverse. It's amazing how some glaring little thing will stand out. Go back to the drawing board, fix it, and check again in the mirror to see if it's better. Anything you can do to look at the painting in a new way will be helpful, even if it's just walking away and looking at it from a distance.

PAINTING SUBJECTS

If the flower is the "star" in the painting the leaves may be thought of as the "supporting role." They can be used to round out the composition and be an important element in the design. Many botanicals however may be mostly or all leaves, and it is important to know how to portray them.

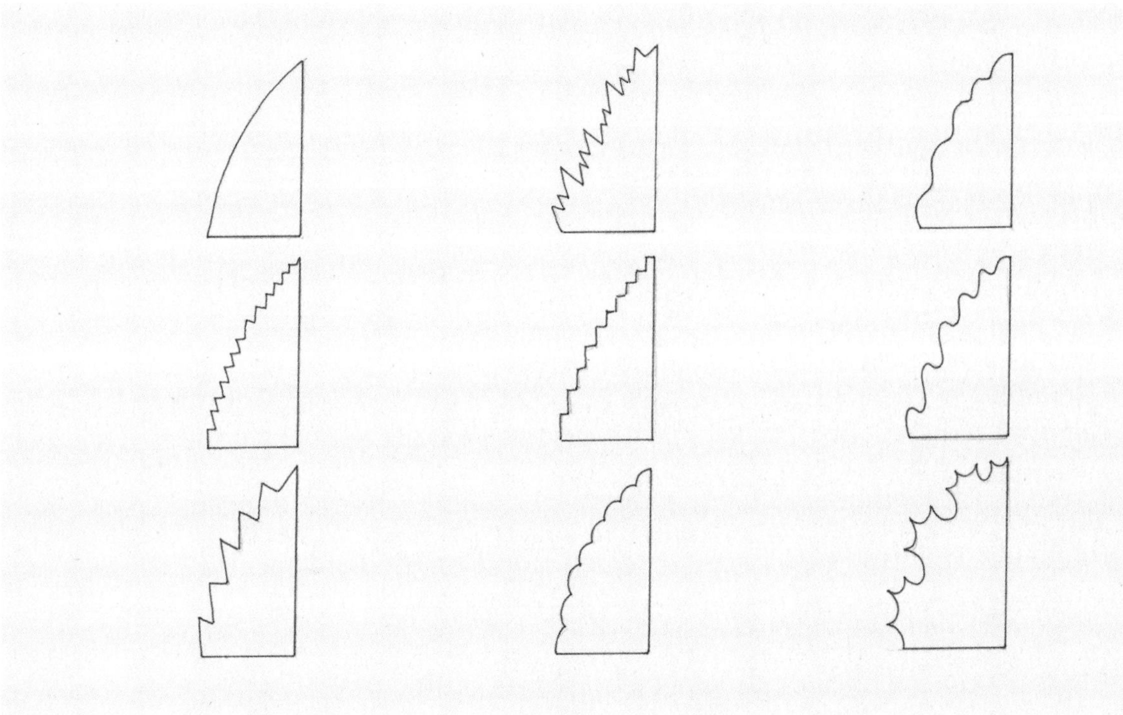

A leaf's edge may be smooth, toothed or serrated, or lobed.

PAINTING LEAVES

Before painting a leaf, be aware of the different variables that distinguish one leaf from another. Leaf shape and arrangement, edges or margins, and veins or venation patterns are all things to consider. Is the leaf shiny, dull, thick, or thin? We want to convey the feel of the leaf in the painting.

Because in botanical art we're being scientifically accurate, our initial sketch shouldn't stray from the leaf structure as we see it.

It's important to have the actual subject as reference in front of you and not only a photo, which may not show the important details you need to see.

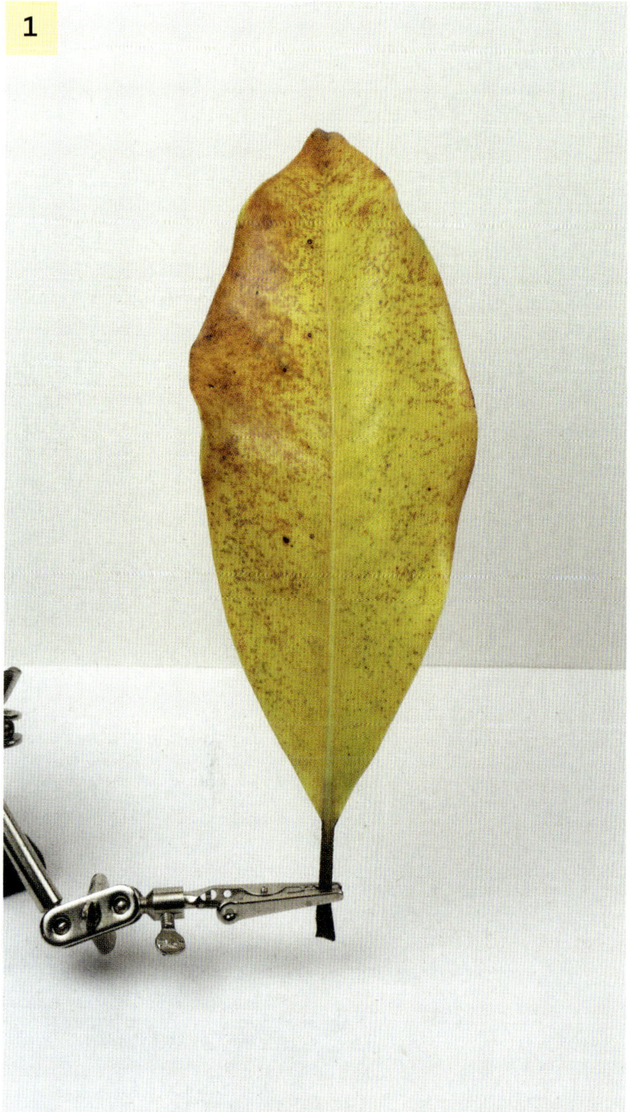

1

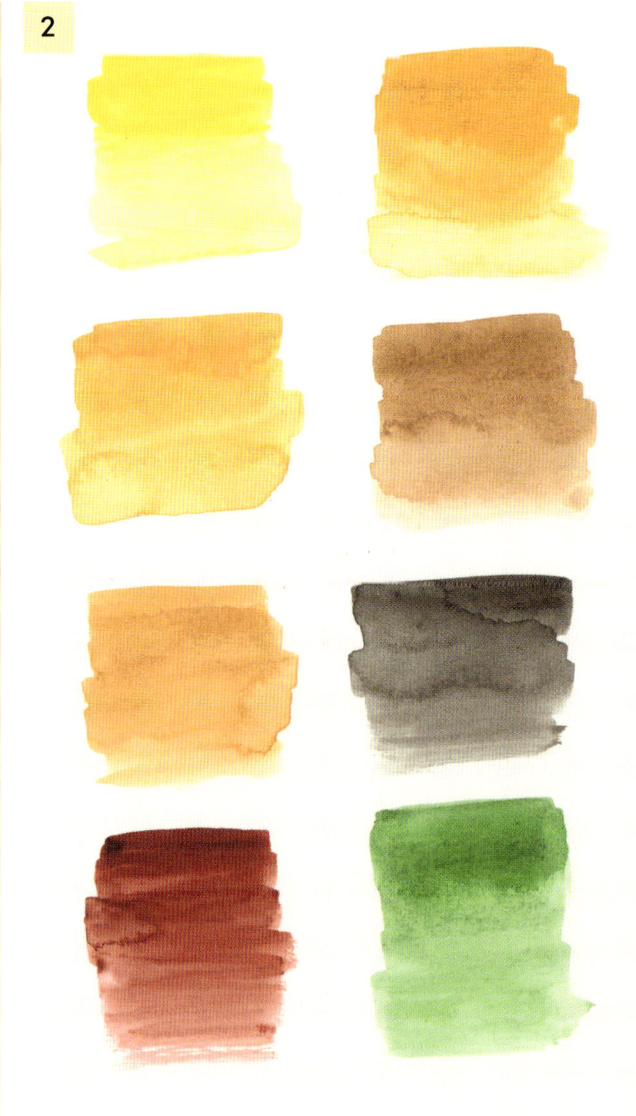

2

Magnolia Leaf in Watercolor

The shiny magnolia (*Magnolia grandiflora*) leaf has a white highlight, even gradations, and lots of spots.

Supplies

- Hot-pressed watercolor paper
- No. 1 and No. 2 sable watercolor brushes
- Paper towel
- Scrap paper
- Water
- Paint palette
- Watercolor paints in the following colors: Cadmium Yellow Medium, Naples Yellow Deep, Yellow Ochre, Quinacridone Gold (Daniel Smith), Burnt Umber, and Perylene Maroon

1. An autumn leaf won't wilt as quickly as a flower, but take a photo just the same.

2. Choose the colors for your leaf. For this exercise, use Cadmium Yellow Medium, Naples Yellow Deep, Yellow Ochre, Quinacridone Gold (Daniel Smith), Burnt Umber, and Perylene Maroon.

3

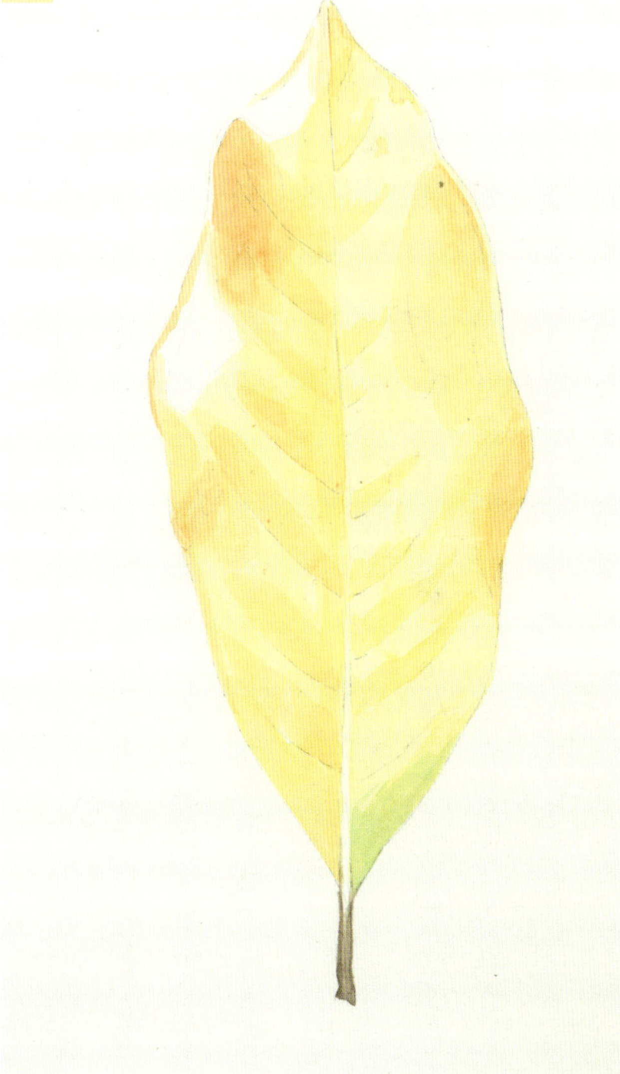

4

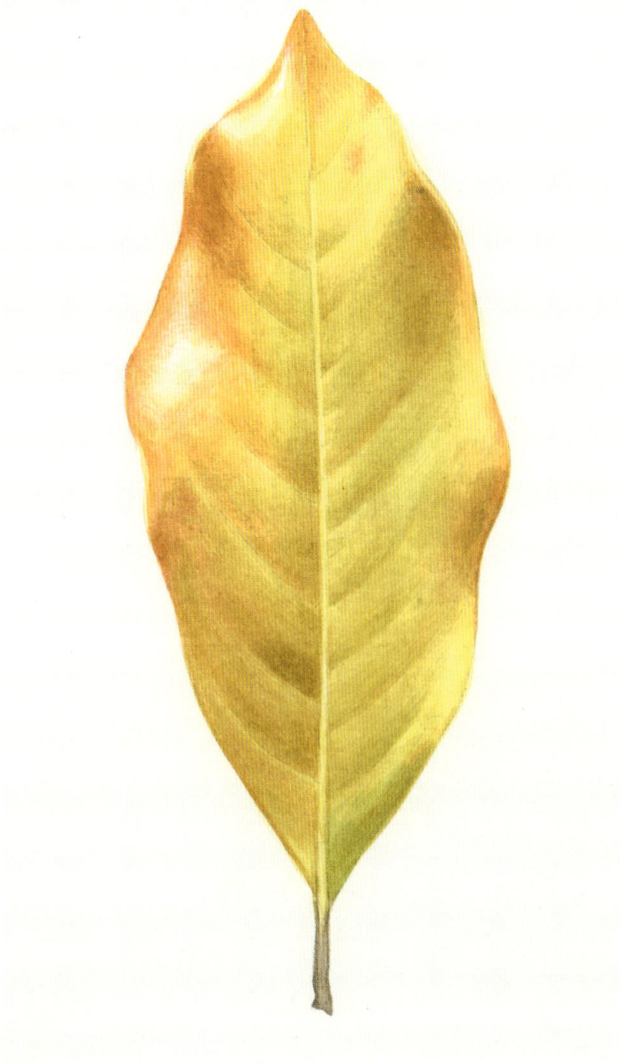

3. Apply the first washes, leaving highlight areas without any paint at all. Layer on color only in the areas you see colors in. As you define the edges, notice how some will be darker and sharper than others.

4. Soften the white highlights with a pale wash.

5

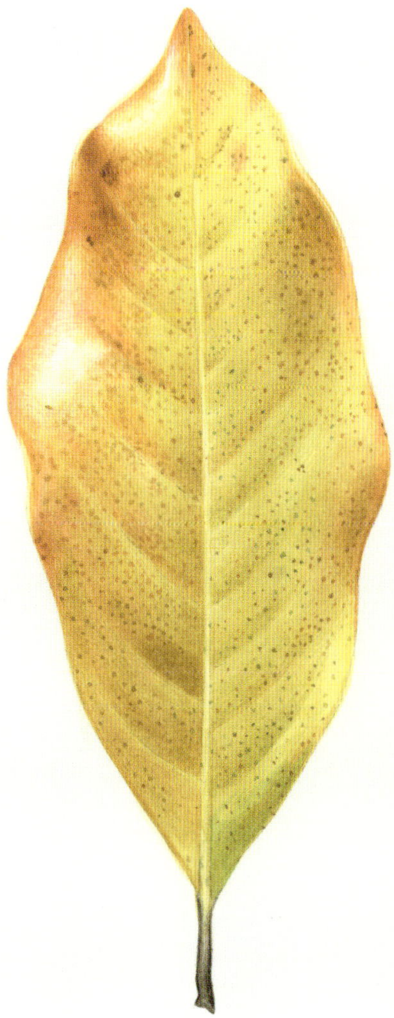

6

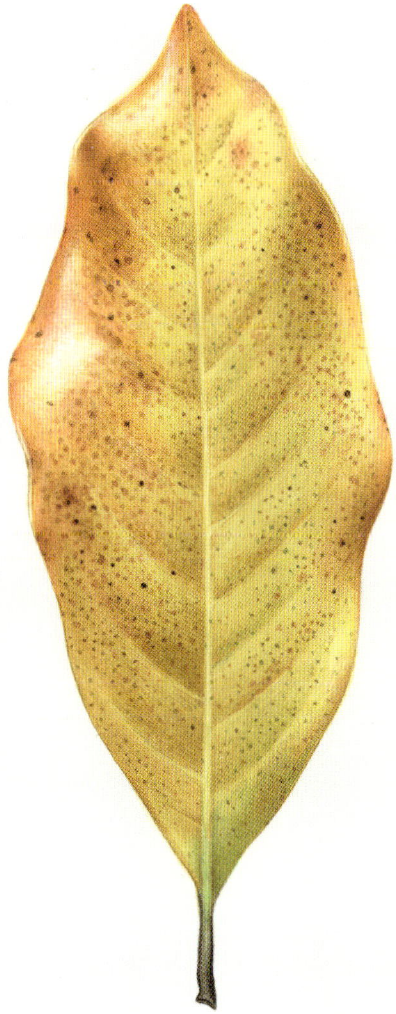

5. When a leaf has many speckles, you don't have to be too concerned with excessive smoothing of gradations because adding the spots will make it look mottled anyway. Add large speckles at the same time as the shadows and contrast with a No. 2 brush. Add these dotted areas with a drybrush. Emphasize the little dots by adding paint to the darker areas already there.

6. Add any additional spots and darken them and refine, soften, and deepen any shadows.

1

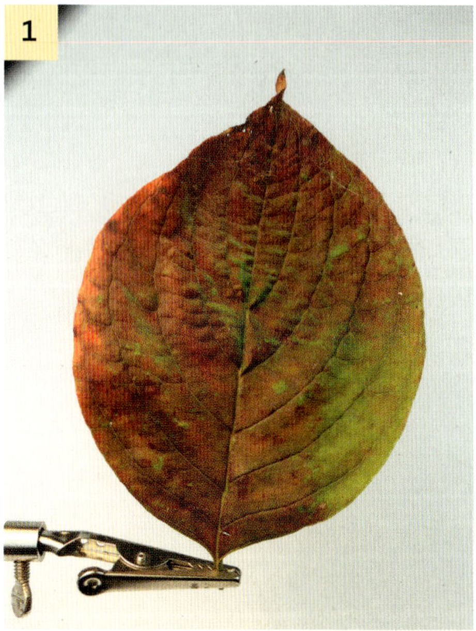

2

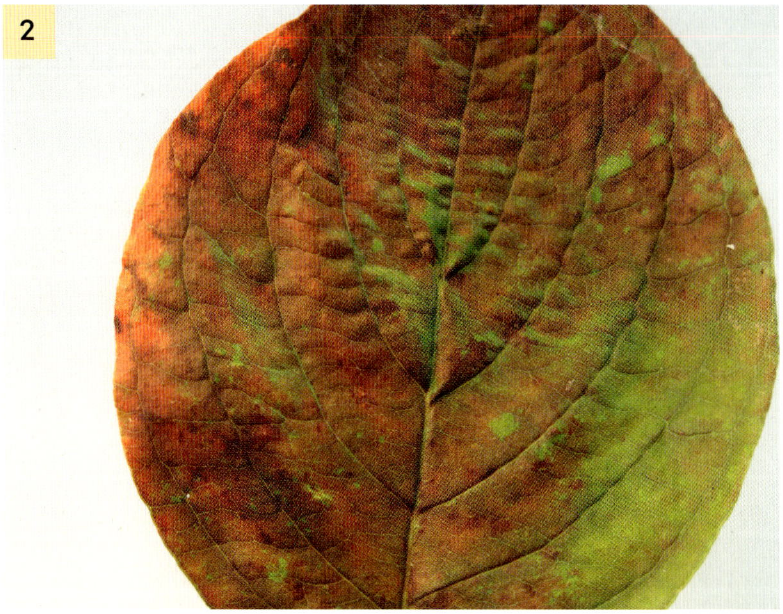

Autumn Dogwood Leaf in Gouache

The autumn dogwood (*Cornus florida*) leaf will make a good subject for practicing gouache techniques because it has so many colors in a small space. Obtaining a large even tone in gouache can be difficult.

Supplies

- HB pencil
- Hot-pressed drawing paper
- Canson Hot Press Illustration Art Board
- No. 1 and No. 2 sable watercolor brushes
- Paper towel
- Scrap paper
- Water
- Paint palette
- Gouache paints including Indigo, Permanent Alizarin Crimson, Primary Yellow, Olive Green, and Permanent Light Green

1. Take a photo before you start.

2. Make sure to take close-up photos to capture all the details.

3. Transfer the sketch to a Canson Hot Press Illustration Art Board. Keep the graphite lines very light because you ultimately don't want to see them.

4. Make a mix of your paint the consistency of cream. Be bold and begin *color mapping* (see page 74). Since this leaf has many of these small areas, use a No. 2 brush. A solid color leaf would need a larger brush. Applying where each area of red, yellow, green, or orange goes in the beginning will prevent you from losing your place when you begin painting. At first, it can be frustrating and like trying to solve a puzzle. But with practice, accurate color mapping will become quicker and easier.

5. When you're finished mapping the entire image, it may look messy or, as in this example, quite colorful. Don't let the temporary chaos discourage you—instead, continue on! I often find students want to give up too soon and don't realize their work is salvageable.

3

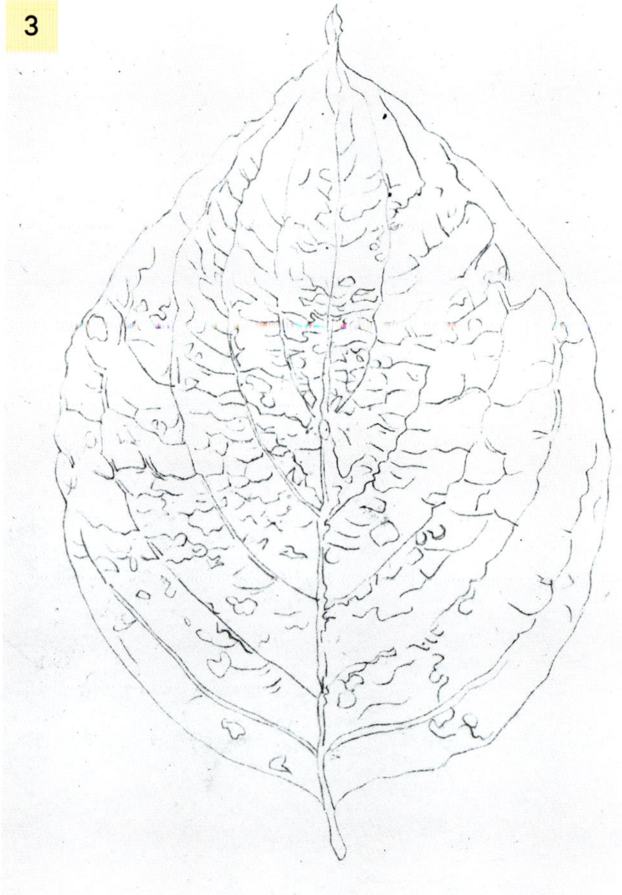

4

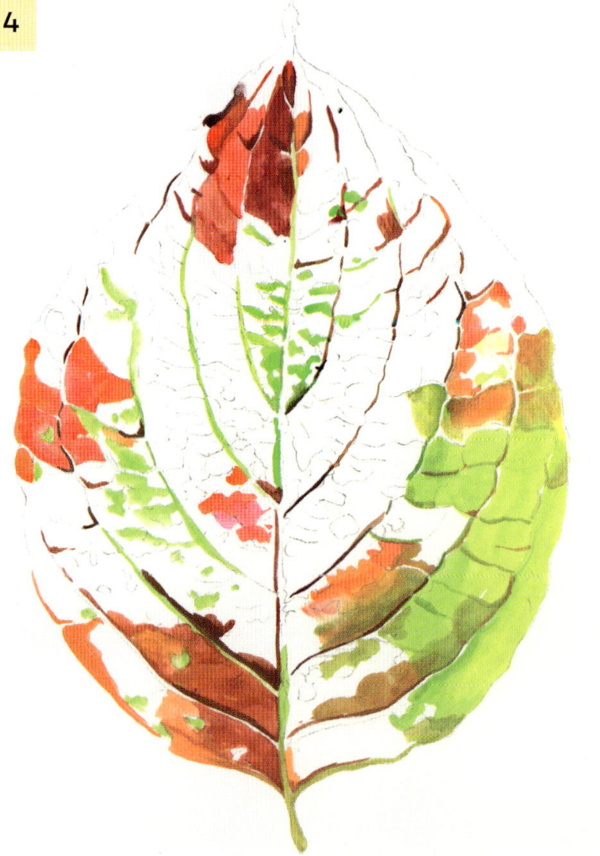

5

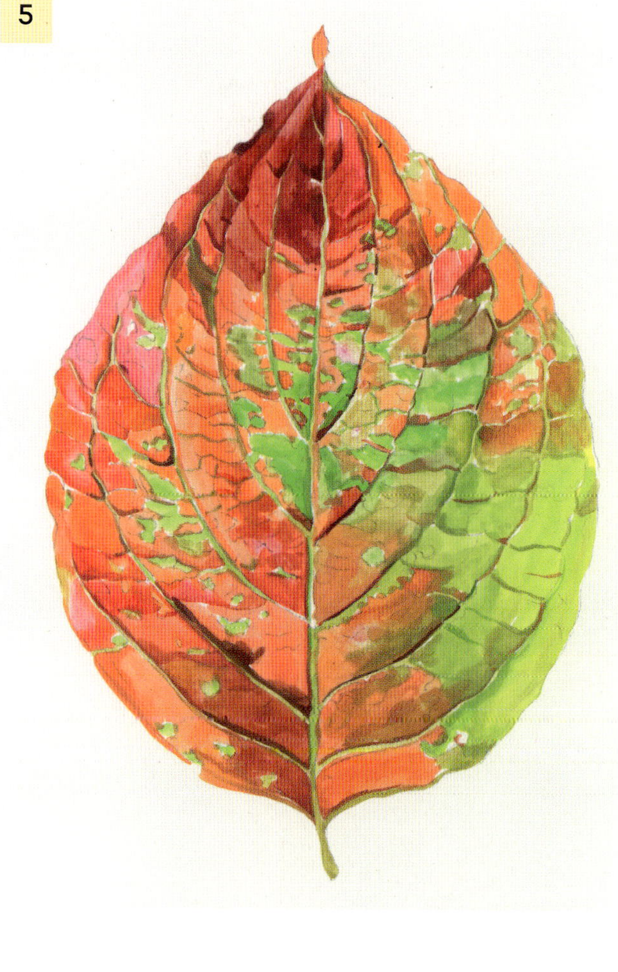

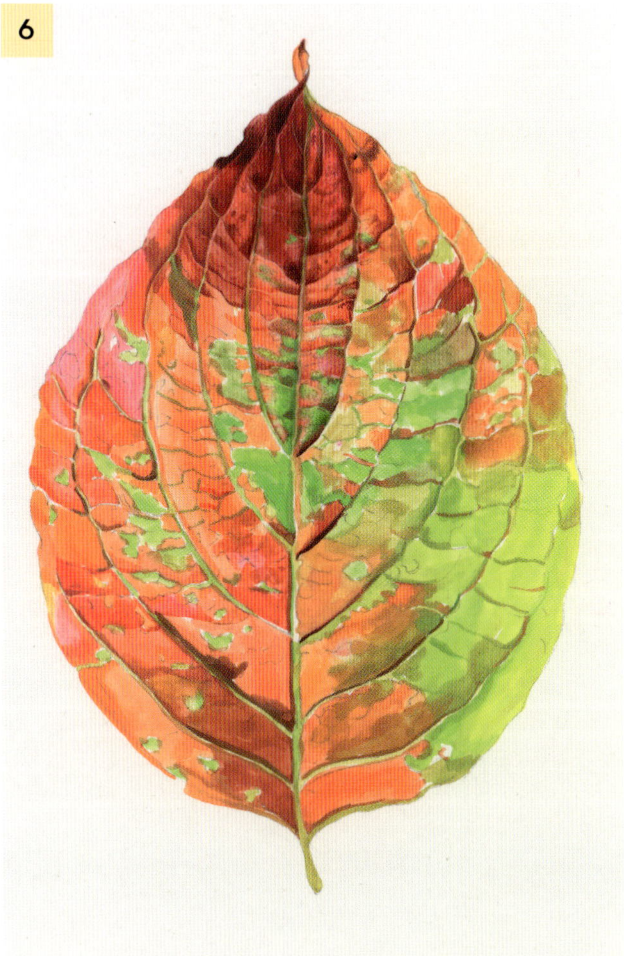

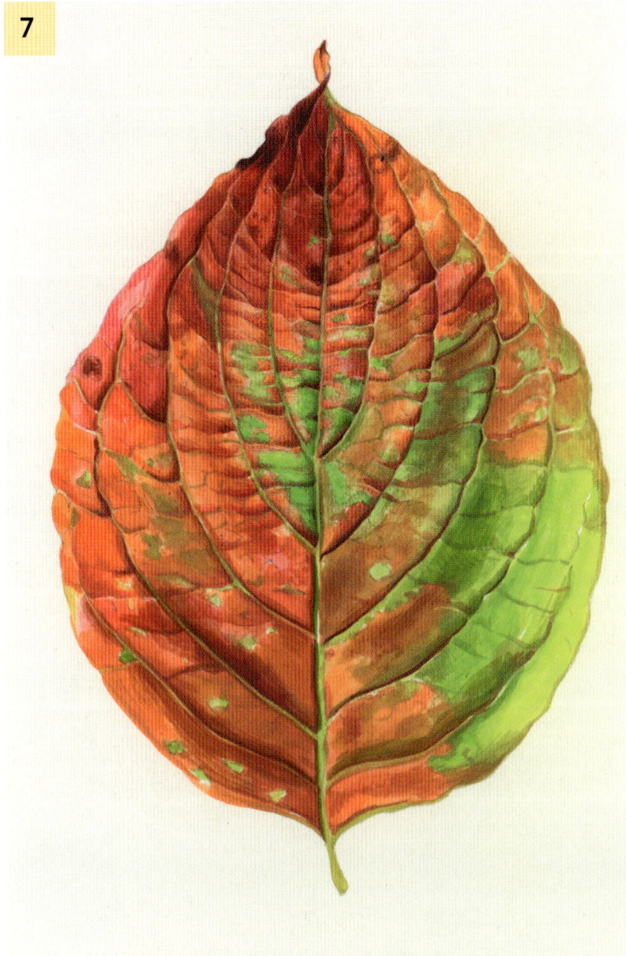

6. Make a mix of paint for the darkest of shadows. Mix Indigo with Permanent Alizarin Crimson (bluish-red) to add in the deepest veins. Use small dots of color and fine lines and go section by section, beginning at the top of the leaf.

7. Intensify the values and make the veining darker. With gouache, the colors don't blend together as easily as with watercolor, so there's more of a defined line between brushstrokes and it's more difficult to blend.

This leaf with its many colorful segments was a great specimen to practice attaining the deep rich colors that gouache offers.

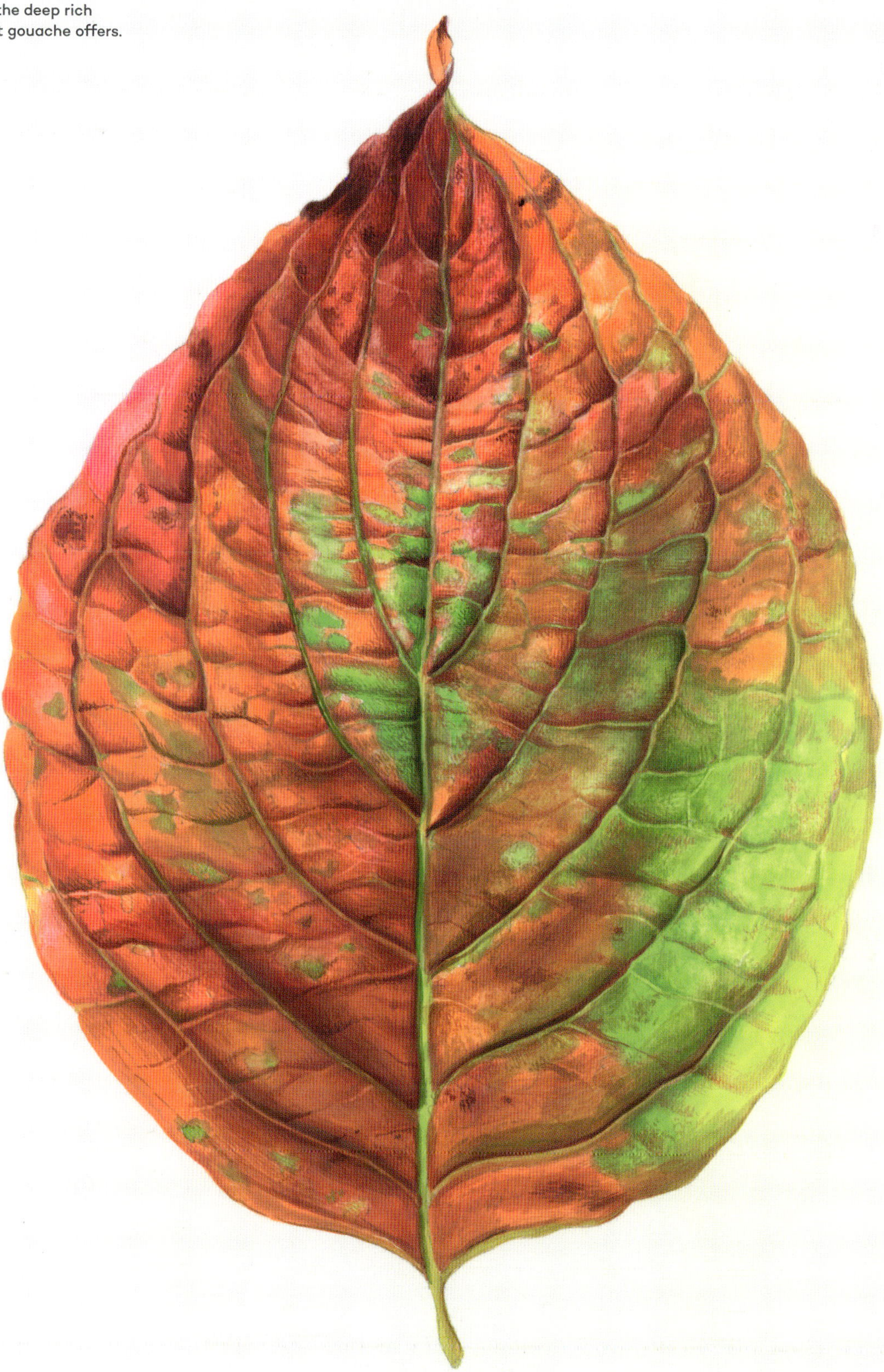

"Spring Orchids" watercolor
on vellum 9" x 14"
(22.9 cm x 35.6 cm)

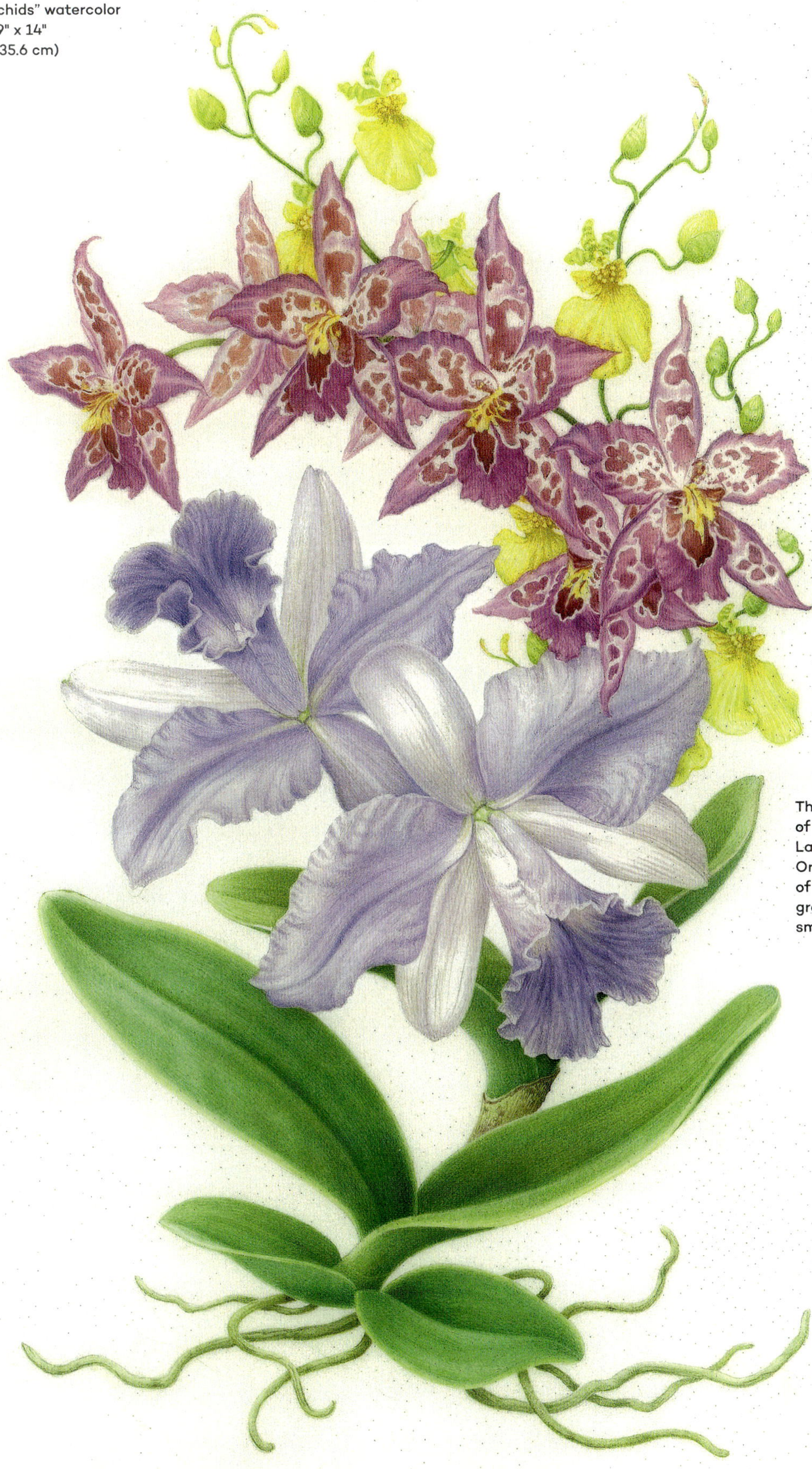

The ruffled lip of the showy Lavender Cattleya Orchid has lots of veining and gradations in a small area.

PAINTING FLOWERS AND PETALS

Flowers, often the "star" of a botanical painting, always need special attention, as they're usually what the viewer focuses on.

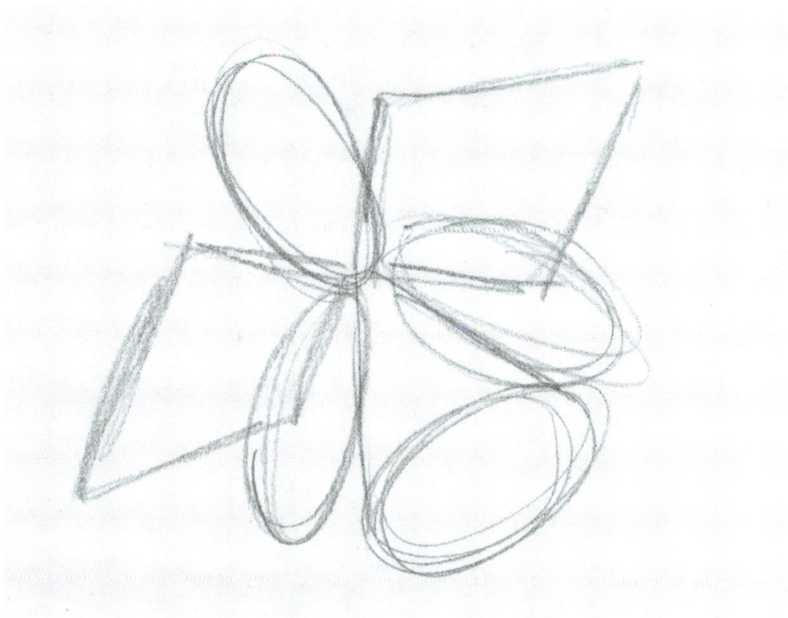

The symmetrical flower comprises basic cone and triangular shapes.

Painting Flowers: Lavender Cattleya Orchid in Watercolor

The Lavender Cattleya Orchid (*Cattleya mossiae*) in the painting *Spring Orchids*, opposite, is a good flower to recreate and practice gradations, layering, and drybrush. Form, shadows, and a rippled texture in the petals give us a bit to work with. And the ruffled edge of the central lip is just fun to paint!

The paper of choice for painting botanicals is a hot-pressed or very smooth, heavyweight paper. For this demonstration, I used Canson Hot Press Illustration Art Board.

Supplies

- 2B and 6H pencils
- Hot-pressed drawing paper
- Tracing paper (optional)
- Hot-pressed watercolor paper
- No. 1 and No. 2 sable watercolor brushes
- Paper towel
- Scrap paper
- Water
- Paint palette
- Watercolor paints in the following colors: Winsor Violet (Dioxazine), Cobalt Blue Deep, Permanent Rose, and Jaune Brilliant (Holbein)

1

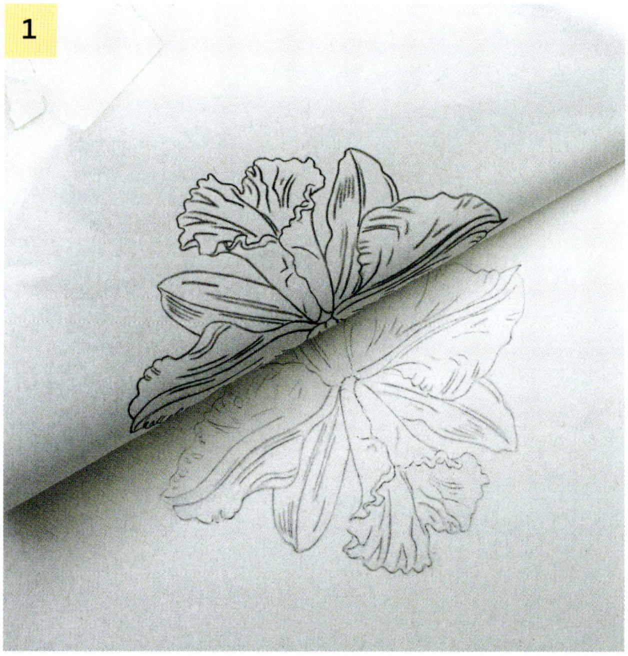

1. Use 2B and 6H pencils to lightly transfer a sketch to your paper in one of two ways: (1) outline the back of the drawing with the 2B pencil and then turn it over, place it on your paper, and trace over the front with the 6H pencil, or, (2) place a sheet of transfer paper (Saral) on your surface carbon-side down, place the drawing on top of it, and then trace. The transferred drawing should only be a light indication because we don't want it to show through the paint, and eventually, we'll be erasing them completely.

2

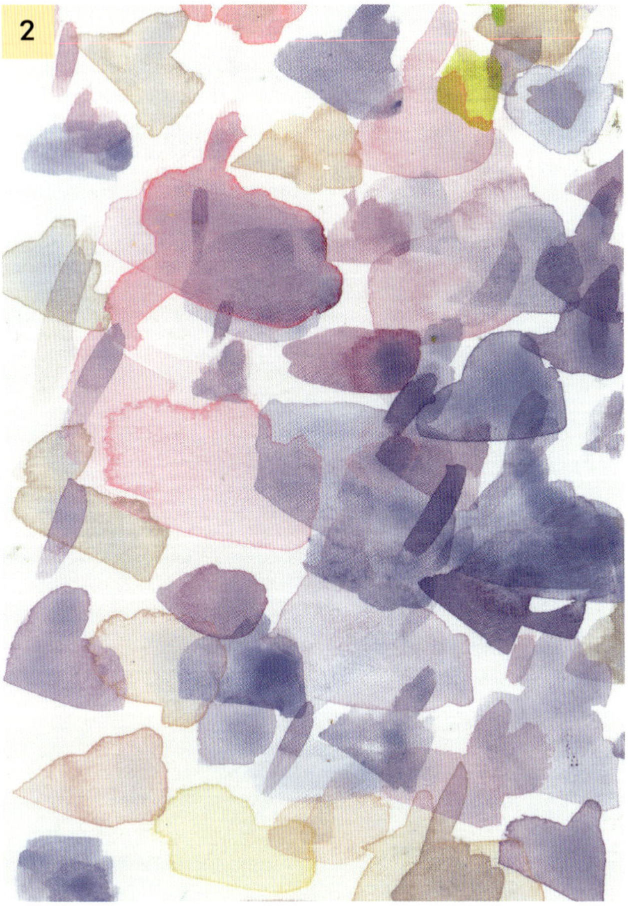

3

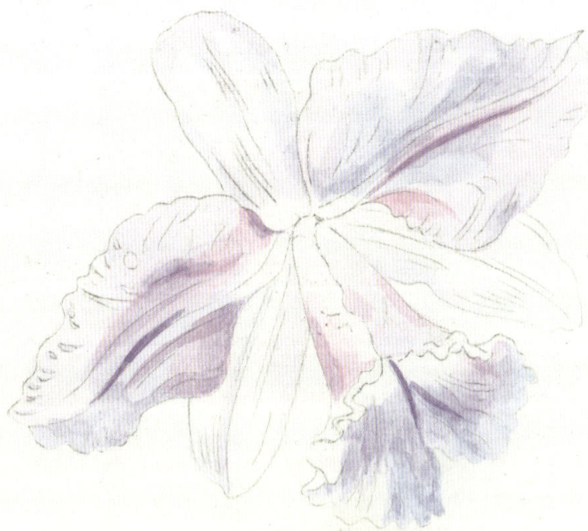

4

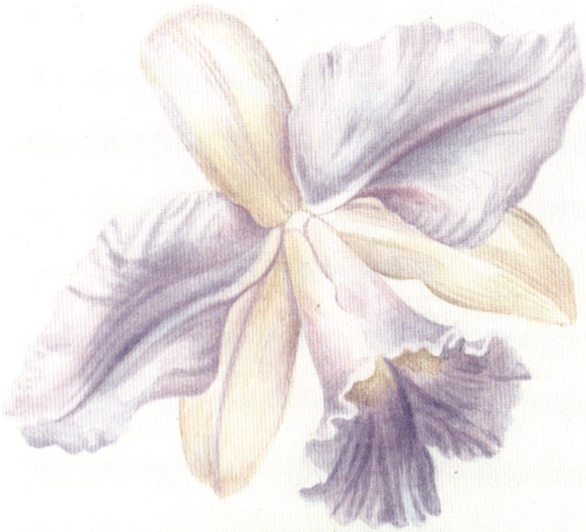

5

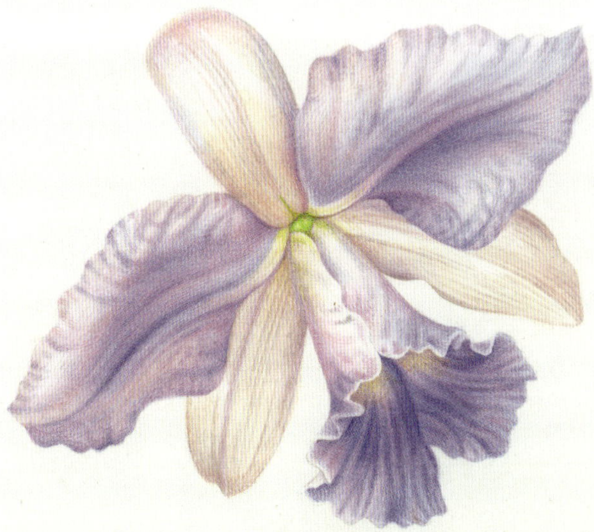

2. Test your paint mix on a scrap of the paper you're using.

3. Use a No. 1 sable brush to block in the variations of Winsor Violet (Dioxazine), Cobalt Blue Deep, and Permanent Rose. Alternate between applying wider washes and determining where the darker shadows are in the creases. This helps establish a color map, so you won't lose your way among the subtle changes in color and value. Load your brush with the color of water/paint mix that you think is the correct value needed for the area you're going to paint. Blot the tip of your brush on a paper towel to remove most of the water so you won't leave a puddle on your paper. After applying, move to another area while this area dries.

4. When the paint applied in the previous step is completely dry, gently erase the pencil lines. Add a pale yellow (Jaune Brilliant [Holbein]) to the blue and violet to create the shadows in the three sepals and center of the cone-shaped lip. Focus on the darkest shadow areas, such as the recesses of the lip, to enhance the form. Let dry.

5. Continue to layer and adjust colors while adding more detail. Small, soft gradations indicate indentations in the petals. Add a brighter yellow and green to the flower's center. Mix the creamy yellow of Jaune Brilliant into both the blue and purple to gray or dull down larger areas of the petals and help to soften the colors. This layering is done while also using the tip of the same No. 1 brush to make gradations smooth and add details.

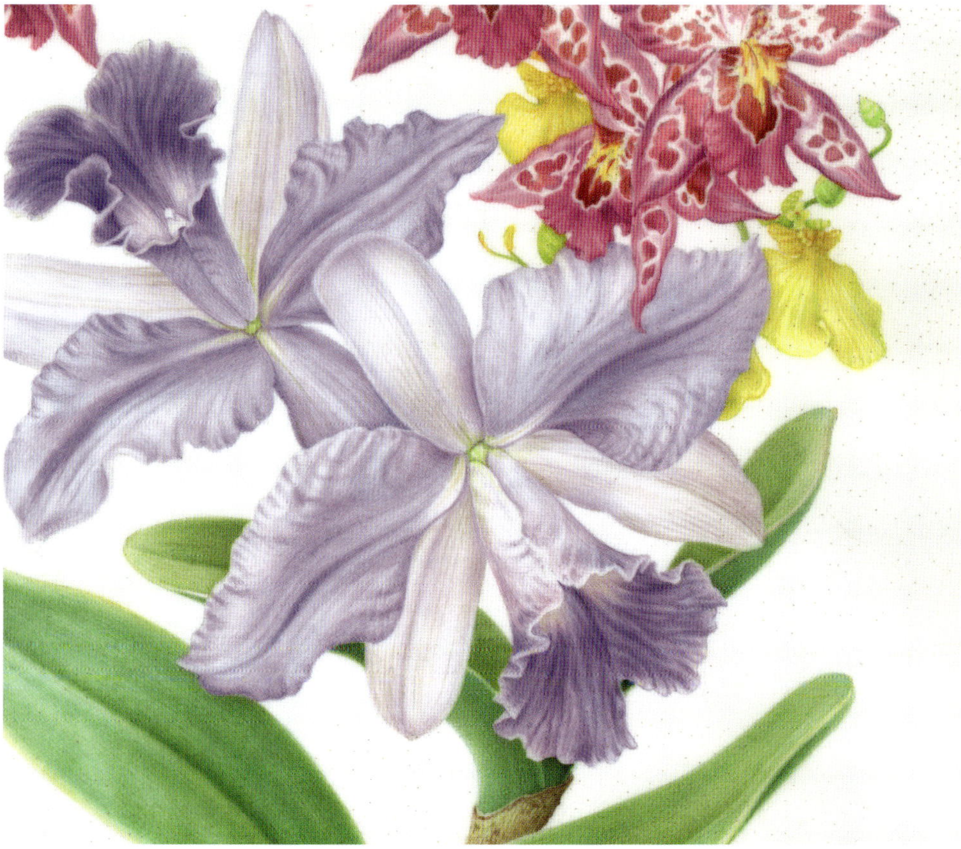

Drybrush

Once the values, form, veining, and ruffled edges are to your satisfaction, a tiny brush with the sharpest of points can be used to *drybrush*. When using this technique, minute details can be added and gradations further smoothed. Drybrush is important because it can give you a deep saturation of color and minute details.

Layering and drybrush takes many hours, but it can be meditative and relaxing. Don't feel as if it's a race. Just concentrate on what you're doing and little by little, the painting will take shape. Patience and practice can't be underestimated. When contours and form are evident, there are a range of values (dark, light, and various in between), colors are accurate, and details are added, the painting is complete

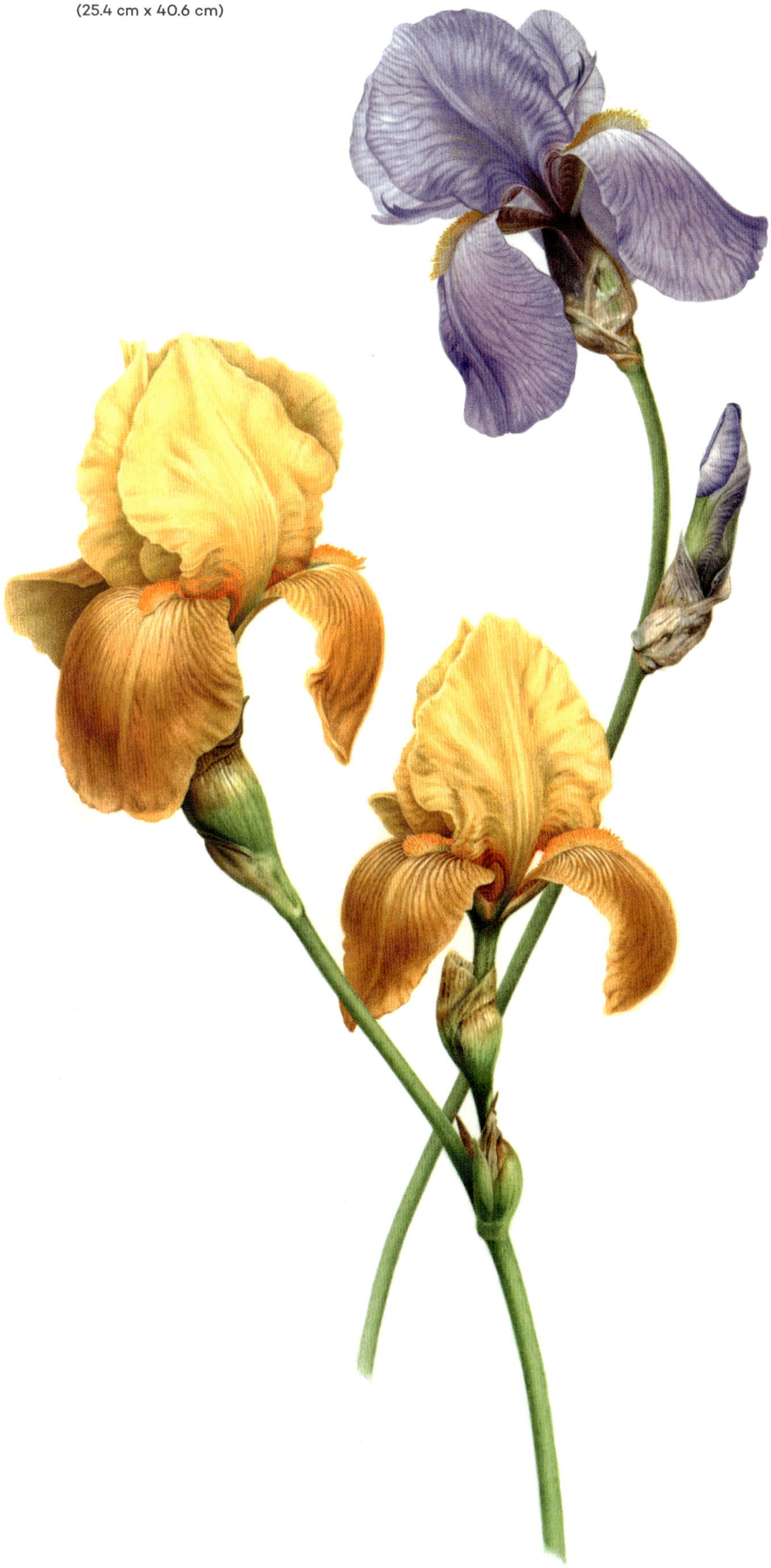

"German Iris" (*Iris germanica*)
watercolor on paper 10" x 16"
(25.4 cm x 40.6 cm)

Painting Petals: German Iris

Petals are often the showiest part of a botanical painting and so deserve special attention. I usually think about where the observer is going to take the most time looking at a painting and spend some extra time in this area getting accurate details, such as the petals, a visiting insect, or the shape of the center of the flower. When you're painting, think about the area where you might look as an observer and make sure you include a great deal of detail there.

The texture of your petals should have the right feel. If they are particularly thin and delicate, light washes may be appropriate.

Are you noticing the veining and contours of the petal? Is the petal fuzzy, smooth, bumpy, rippled, or velvety? The goal is to convey all the texture you see in your painting.

If petals are thick, the edges might have a harder line and maybe even some shadow. Edges that come toward the viewer the most should be sharper than receding edges. Similarly, leaves that recede may have less contrast than those in the foreground. In this way, you can play around with the atmospheric perspective. You might compare this to a landscape that has more clarity and definition in the foreground and less contrast in the background. The ochre petal in *German Iris* (at the right) can be a helpful reference to reproduce and practice technique.

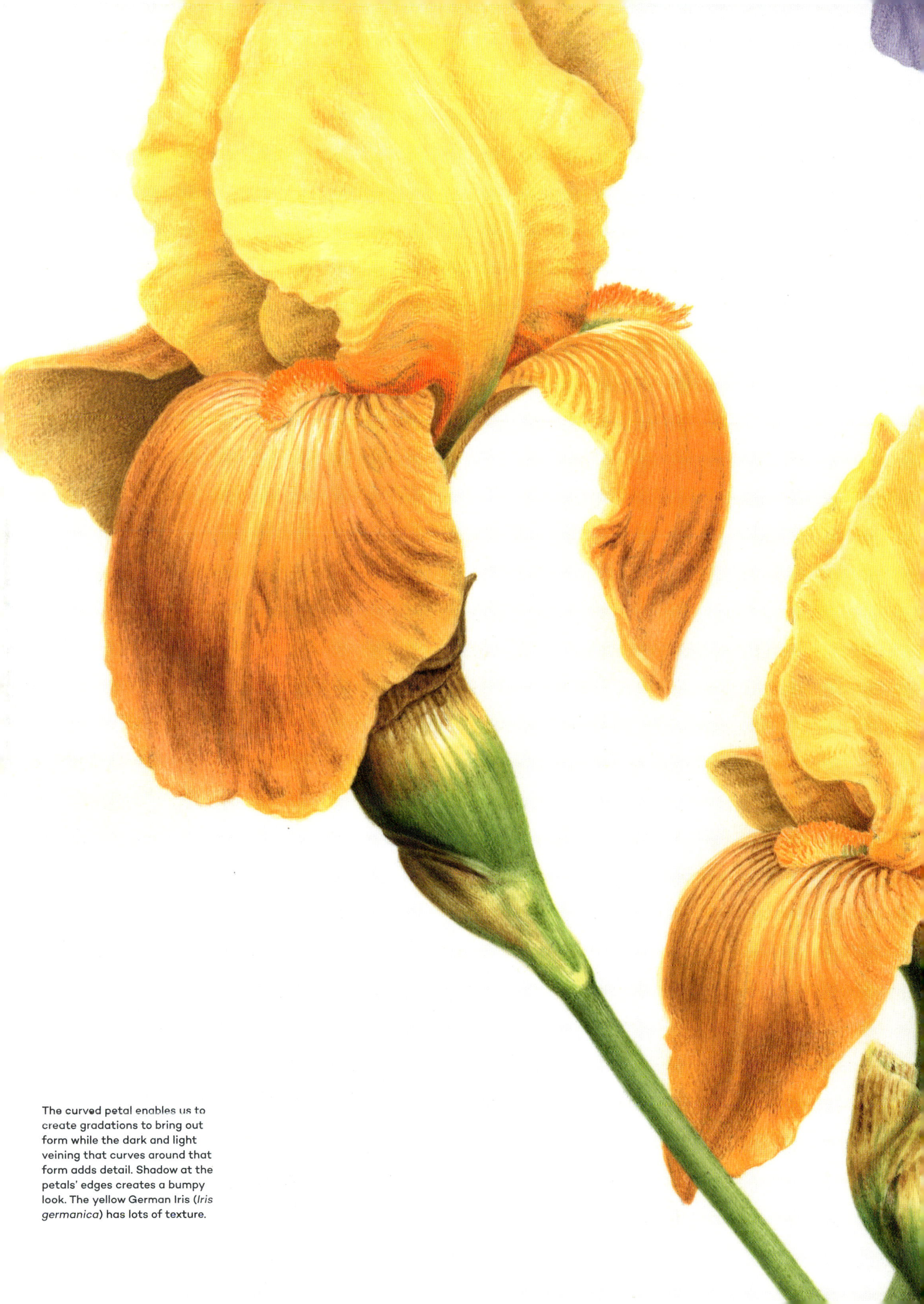

The curved petal enables us to create gradations to bring out form while the dark and light veining that curves around that form adds detail. Shadow at the petals' edges creates a bumpy look. The yellow German Iris (*Iris germanica*) has lots of texture.

Supplies

- 2B and 3H pencils
- Hot-pressed drawing paper
- Tracing paper (optional)
- Canson Hot Press Illustration Art Board
- No. 1 and No. 2 sable watercolor brushes
- Paper towel
- Scrap paper
- Water
- Paint palette
- Watercolor paints in the following colors: Cadmium Yellow Deep and Naples Yellow Deep
- Kneaded eraser
- Tombow MONO zero precision eraser
- Reducing glass (optional)

1. First, do some color matching by looking at your color charts and assess which colors are needed for your subject.

2. Transfer the iris petal to a Canson Hot Press Illustration Art Board and then apply a wash of Cadmium Yellow Deep to the entire surface. Note that the same color isn't usually applied as an overall wash. It's possible in this case because successive colors won't clash with but will instead deepen this beginning wash. Next, add Naples Yellow Deep to darker areas of the petal. Let the washes dry in between before adding the next.

3. Once the first few washes are in, use a kneaded eraser in a circular motion with gentle pressure to remove most of your pencil lines. You can use a Tombow MONO zero precision eraser to remove any stubborn lines.

4. Continue this layering to bring out the form of the petal while beginning to add darker veining. To build up the value, make many parallel lines in the same direction as the veining. A good quality brush will hold a lot of paint, and you can layer in this fashion for quite a while before needing to load more paint in your brush. As you near completion, hold the painting up to a mirror to see it in reverse. Looking at it in another way, you can often see things you would like to correct. You can also use a reducing glass or simply just look at the painting from a distance. When your petal has volume; dark, medium, and light value; and detail, it's complete.

1

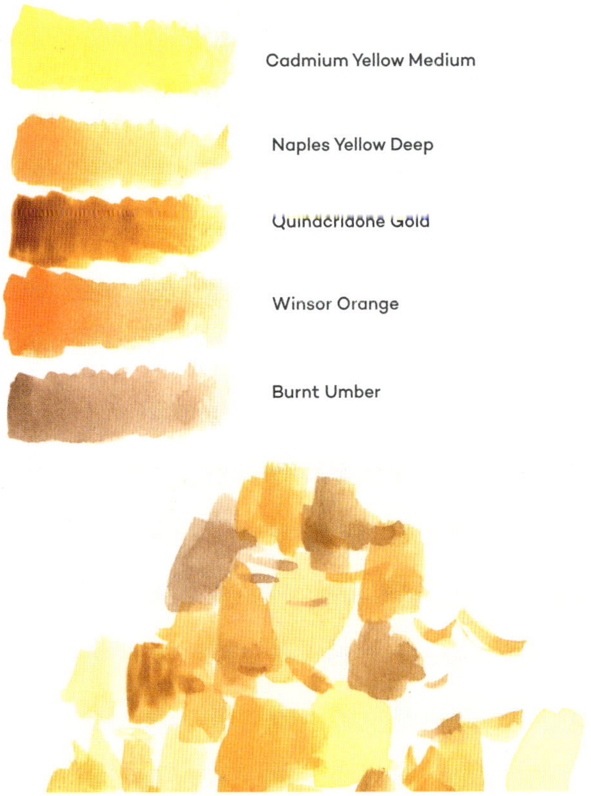
Cadmium Yellow Medium
Naples Yellow Deep
Quinacridone Gold
Winsor Orange
Burnt Umber

2

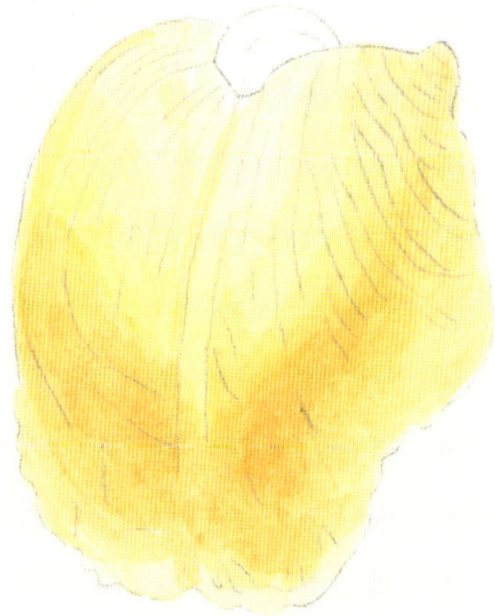

3

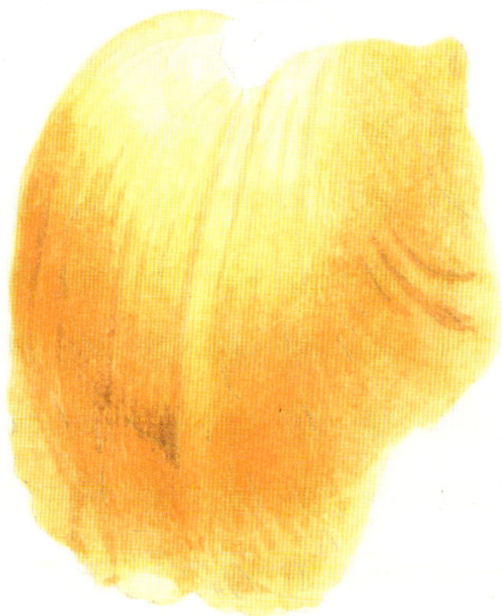

4

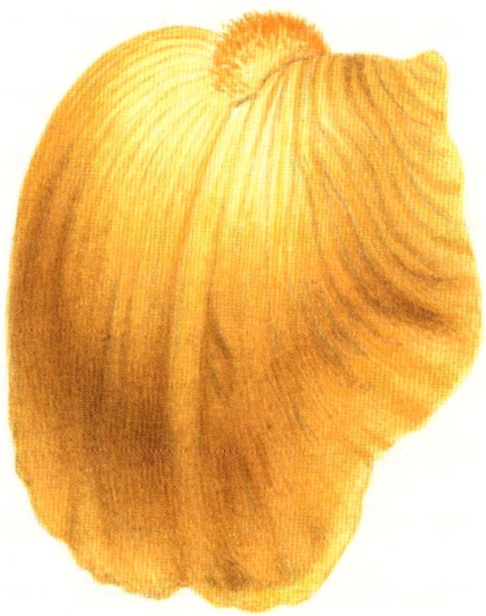

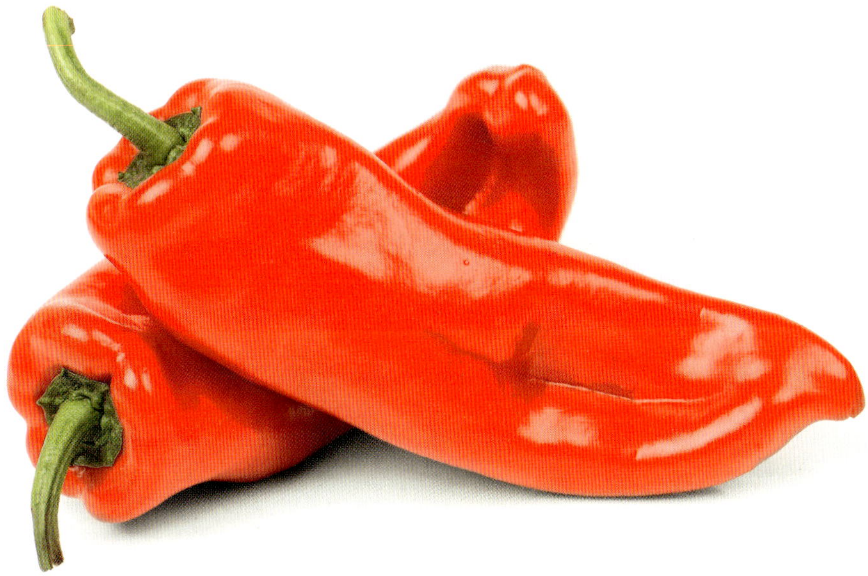

Red peppers have a smooth even tone and shiny looking highlights.

Red Pepper in Watercolor

This red pepper (*Capsicum annuum*) is a good way to practice simple areas of flat color and gradations because it only uses three shades of red. They are applied in separate areas and gradually blend together while layering.

Supplies

- 2H pencil
- Canson Hot Press Illustration Art Board
- No. 1 and No. 2 sable watercolor brushes
- Paper towel
- Scrap paper
- Water
- Paint palette
- Watercolor paints in the following colors: Scarlet Lake, Permanent Alizarin Crimson, Permanent Rose, Antique Seedling (Holbein), Sap Green, and Indigo

1. Draw the outline sketch on a Canson Hot Press Illustration Art Board.

2. Choose Scarlet Lake, Permanent Alizarin Crimson, Permanent Rose, Antique Seedling (Holbein), Sap Green, and Indigo to paint the red pepper.

3. Map the three distinct areas with Scarlet Lake, which is a true red; Permanent Rose, which is more pink; and Permanent Alizarin Crimson, which is darkest, for the shadows. Apply wide bands of color with vertical strokes. Leave the highlight free of paint to let the white of the paper show through.

4. Add additional layers of paint, keeping the same red, pink, and crimson areas.

1

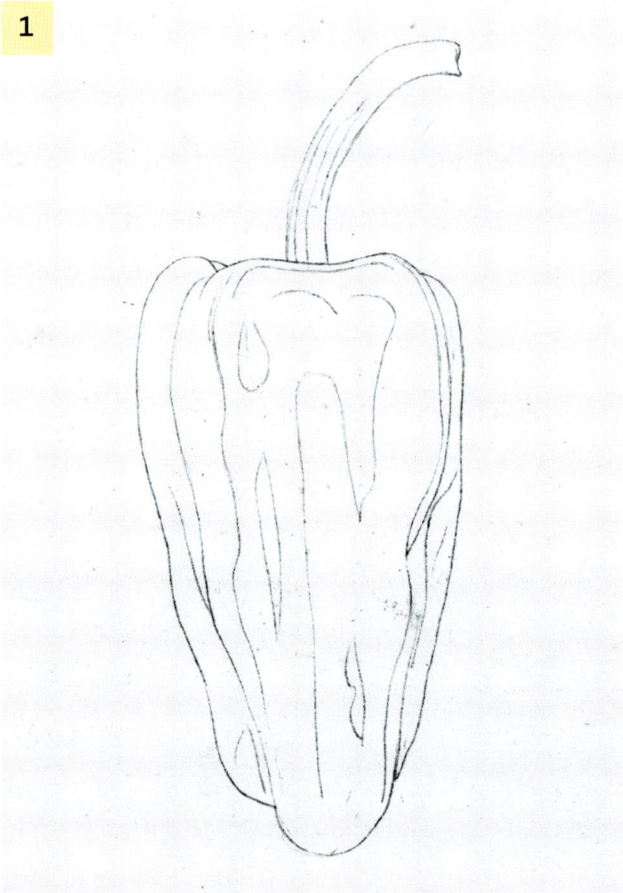

2

3

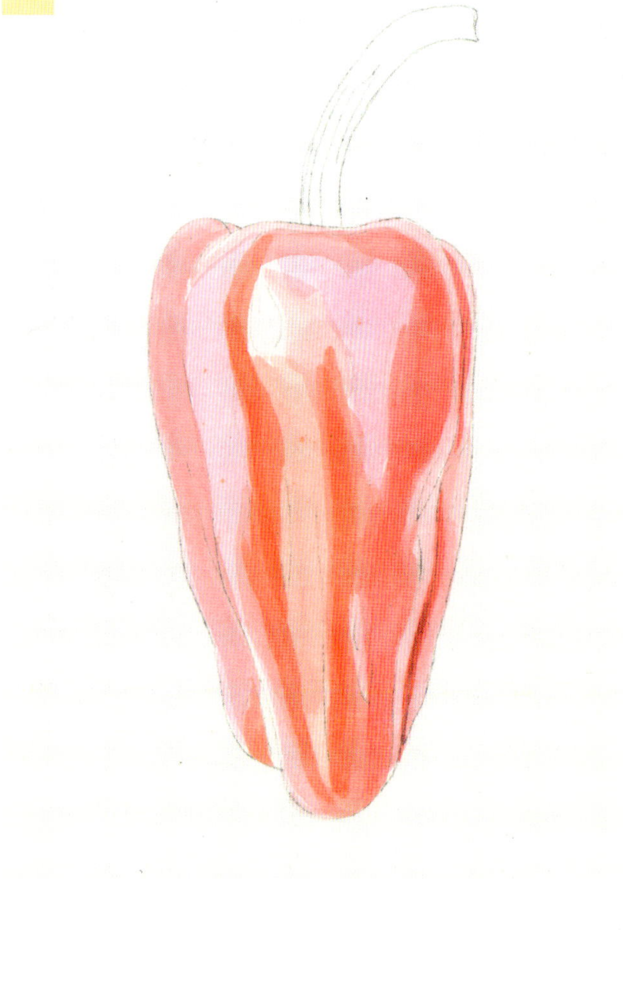

4

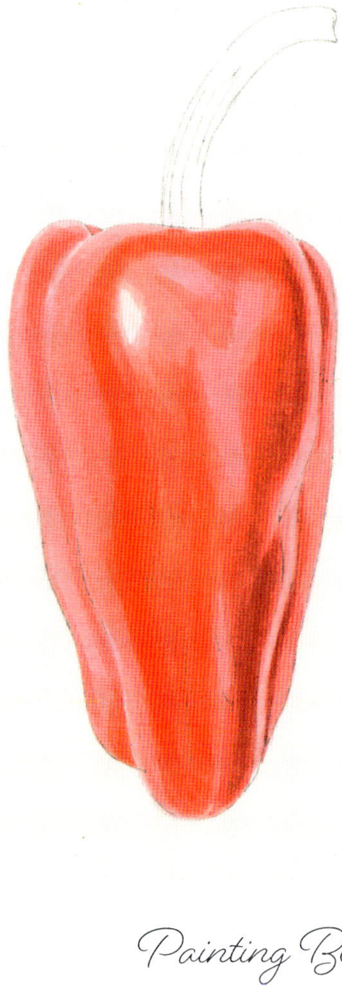

5

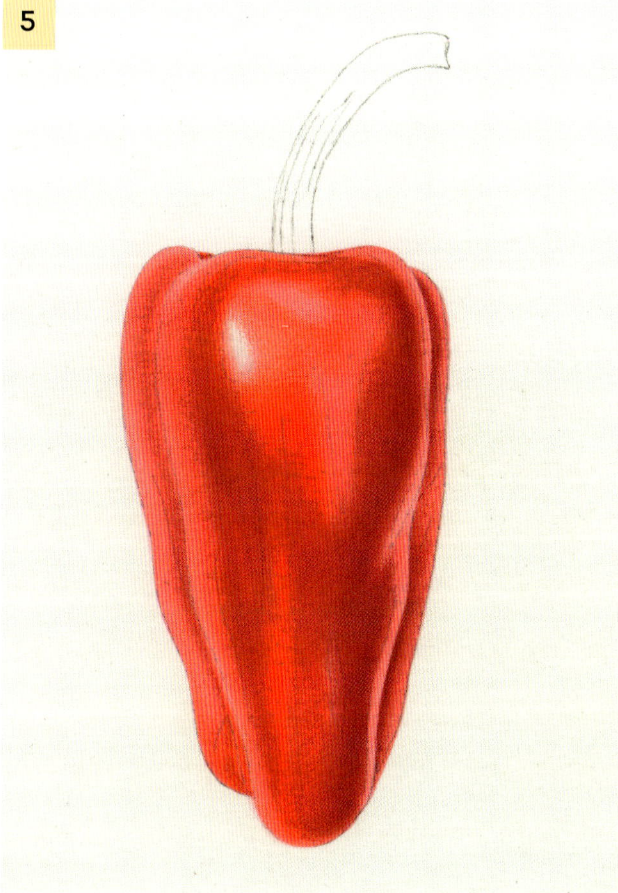

6

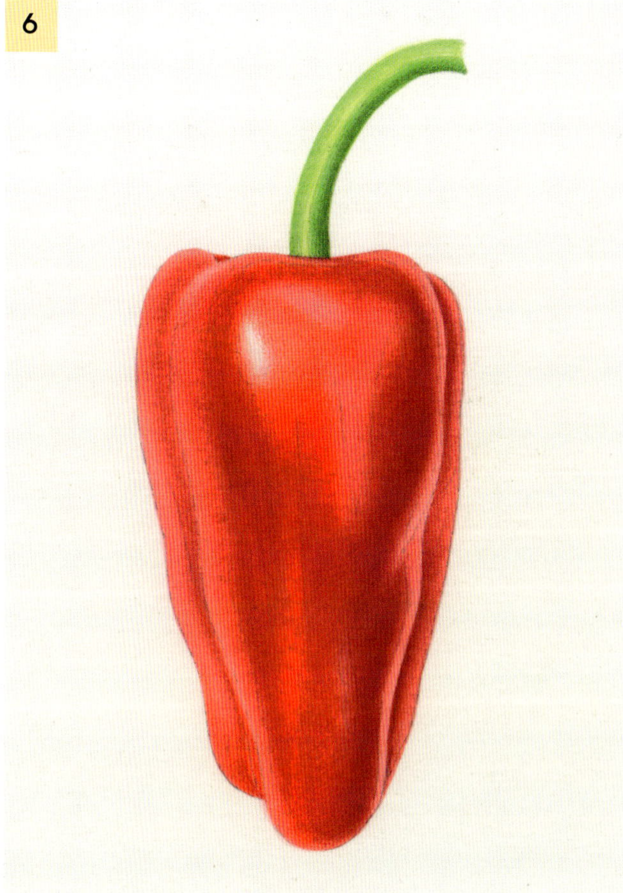

7

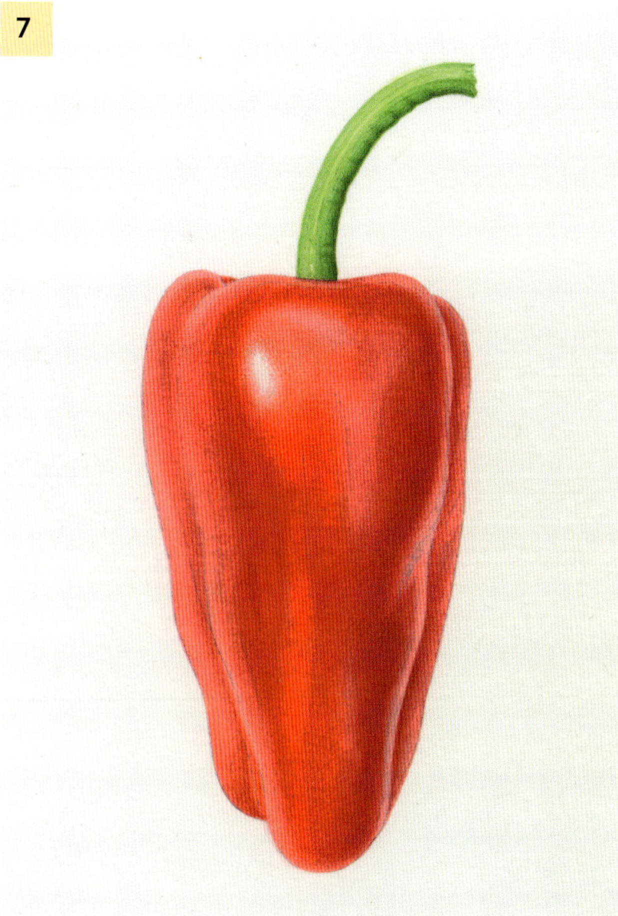

5. As you smooth out the colors with a No. 2 brush, they'll blend and overlap. The brush tickles the surface and the paint will dry as you draw with the point. Lift the paint around the edge of the whitest highlight (made only with the white of the paper) so there are no hard edges. Then, go back into these edges with barely any color in the brush to gently smooth the gradation. Darken the areas of reflected light at the pepper's sides with Permanent Alizarin Crimson, which is a red color that has more blue in it. The value of this reflected light should be dark enough that they look as if they're receding, which will help the pepper look rounded.

6. Add the Antique Seedling (Holbein) and Sap Green paints to the stem. At first, the gradations are done as though it's a cylinder shape.

7. Add the details to the stem.

"Beach Lane Pumpkin"
watercolor on paper
11" x 10" (27.9 cm x 25.4 cm)

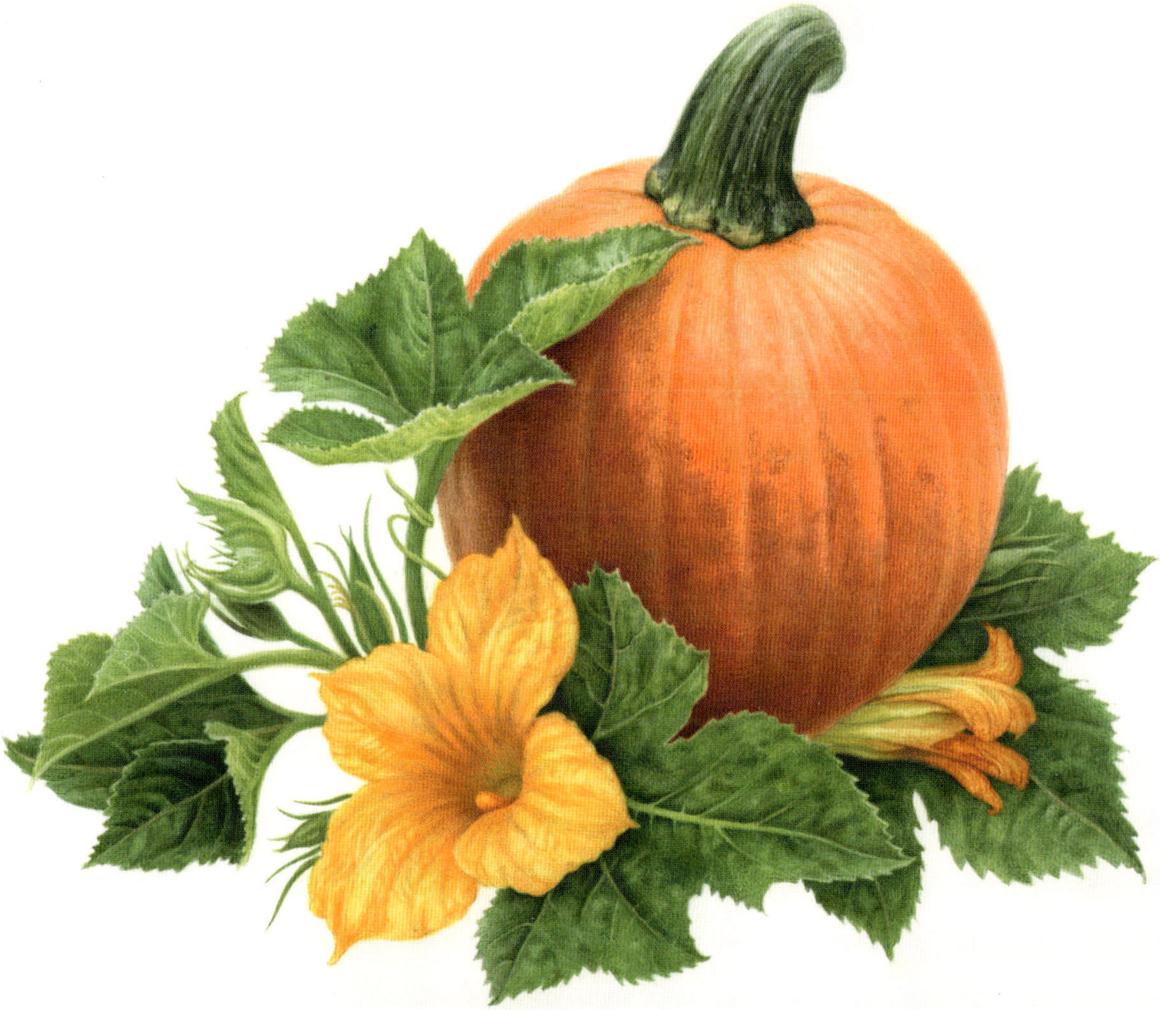

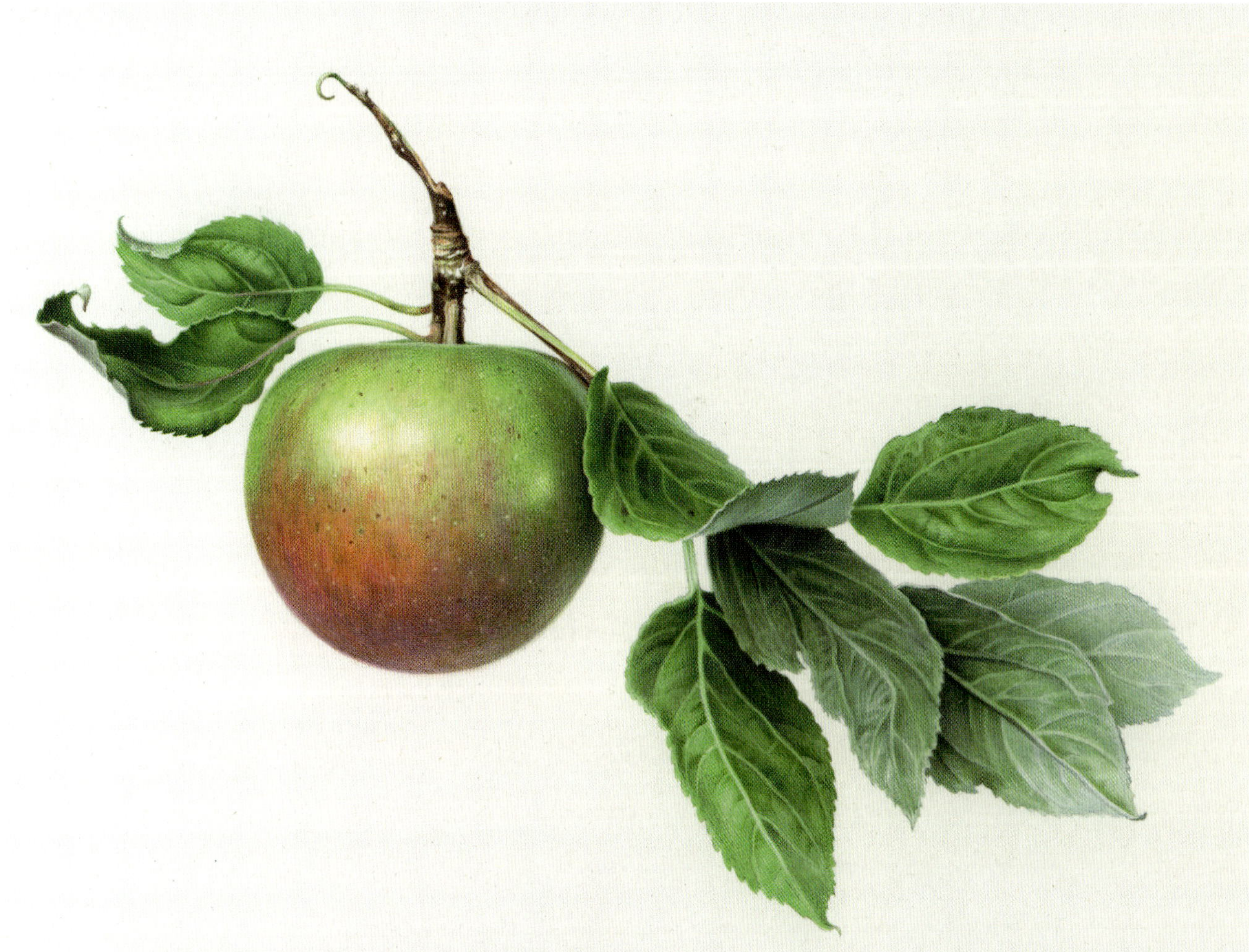

Green Apple. "Halsey Farm"
watercolor on paper
9.5" x 10.5" (24.1 cm x 26.7 cm)

PAINTING FRUITS AND BERRIES

Besides their shape and color, it's of utmost importance to capture the various textures seen in berries and fruits. Highlights may be very light and almost white on a shiny blackberry (genus *Rubus*) or more subdued on the dull surface of a banana (genus *Musa*). The rough texture on the outside of a pineapple (*Ananas comosus*) needs a different approach than the bloom on the skin of a plum (*Prunus domestica*). Really look at the texture of the fruit's surface and determine what is needed to convey that texture in your painting. The dull bloom on a plum often is a light blue color. Notice the irregularly shaped transition between the bloom and the dark purple of the plum. Some areas of bloom may be clearly defined, while others may fade away gradually.

Plum in Watercolor

A painting of fruit with bloom is both beautiful and challenging. Bloom is a natural waxy dusky blue protective coating on the surface of some fruit. Touching the bloom can remove it, so handle your specimen carefully. The plum's purple and red colors contrasting with the blue bloom make for an interesting image.

Supplies

- Kneaded eraser (optional)
- Water dropper
- Water
- 2H pencil
- Hot-pressed drawing paper
- Tracing paper (optional)
- Canson Hot Press Illustration Art Board
- No. 1 and No. 2 sable watercolor brushes
- Paper towel
- Scrap paper
- Paint palette
- Watercolor paints in the following colors: Cerulean Blue, Lapis Lazuli Genuine (Daniel Smith), Permanent Magenta, Indigo, Rose Madder Genuine, Naples Yellow, Sap Green, Indian Red, and Sepia
- Electric eraser (optional)

1

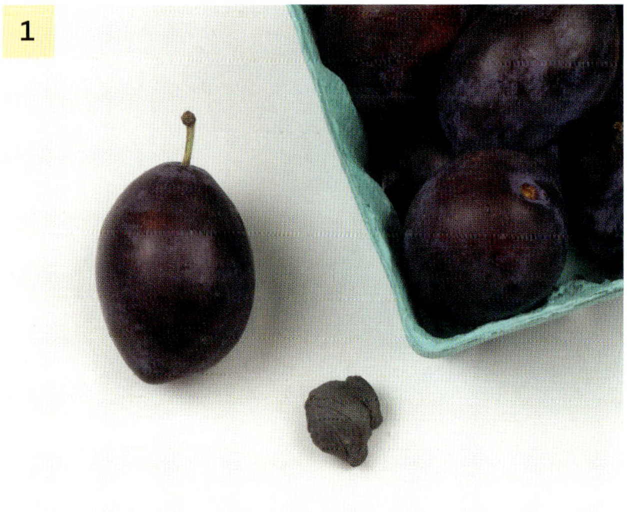

2

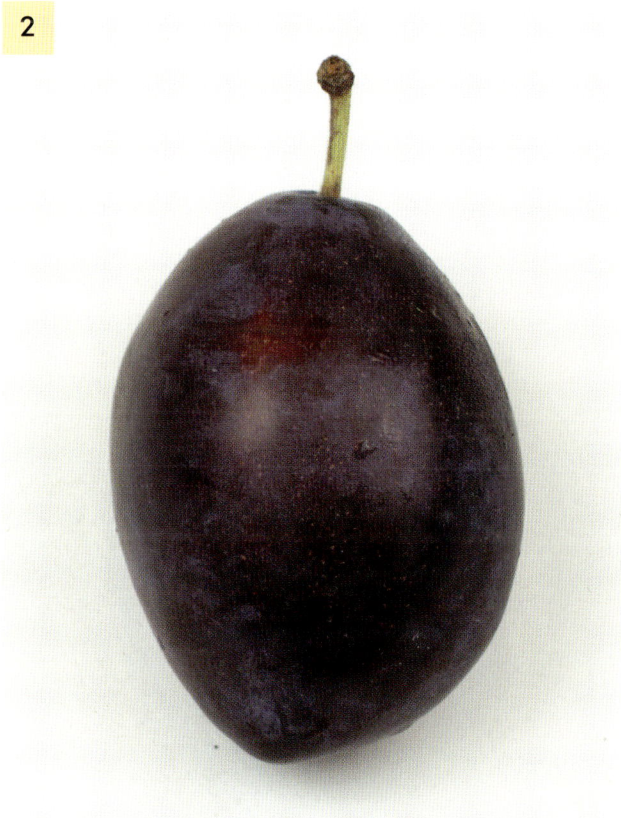

1. Wedge a couple of small pieces of kneaded eraser under the plum to hold it in place.

2. Add water drops to the plum. Water drops add realism to your subject. They can be fun to paint, but also a little tricky. Taking and using photographs for reference will be very helpful. I took photos both with and without water drops added to the plum's surface. The best way to add water drops is with a water dropper. You can place the water drops where you want them and control the size. Don't try to visualize what you think a water drop looks like! You'll have more success and your drops will be more realistic if you have good reference photos. The highlights on a small drop change a lot, and of course, the drops drip and move quickly on the fruit's surface, which would be very frustrating to replicate without a photo.

3. Look at your color chart and after studying the subject, make an educated guess as to what colors can be combined to accurately portray the subject. For this exercise, use Cerulean Blue, Lapis Lazuli Genuine (Daniel Smith), Permanent Magenta, Indigo, and Rose Madder Genuine.

4. Use a piece of the same type of paper to test your color mixes on.

5. Draw the plum with a 2H pencil on a Canson Hot Press Illustration Art Board. Include the details of the irregular contours of the bloom in your drawing. The reason this must be defined right from the beginning is that you don't want reds or purples going where that light blue bloom should go. Also indicate where the water drops are placed at this beginning sketch stage. When blocking in subtle colors, look at the color you've created and tested on your scrap paper before applying it to the painting. Sometimes, when the color looks right on the scrap paper, you may even be able to pick it up from there to use in the painting. Pencil lines are still visible under the light washes of paint but can be erased with an electric eraser when the paper is completely dry.

6. Build up layers of color with wide washes using the side of the brush. Use a relatively large brush (No. 2 or No. 3) and apply slight pressure, which will spread the hairs in the brush to cover more surface. Make sure to continue moving around the painting to allow the sections to dry. If the surface isn't dry, you'll end up removing the existing paint instead of adding to it. Another way to add and build up color is by making lines with a more condensed mix of paint. You can alternate making wide washes of color and then lines. In this way, you continually add pigment. In this stage of the painting, you can see the lines of paint going in various directions.

3

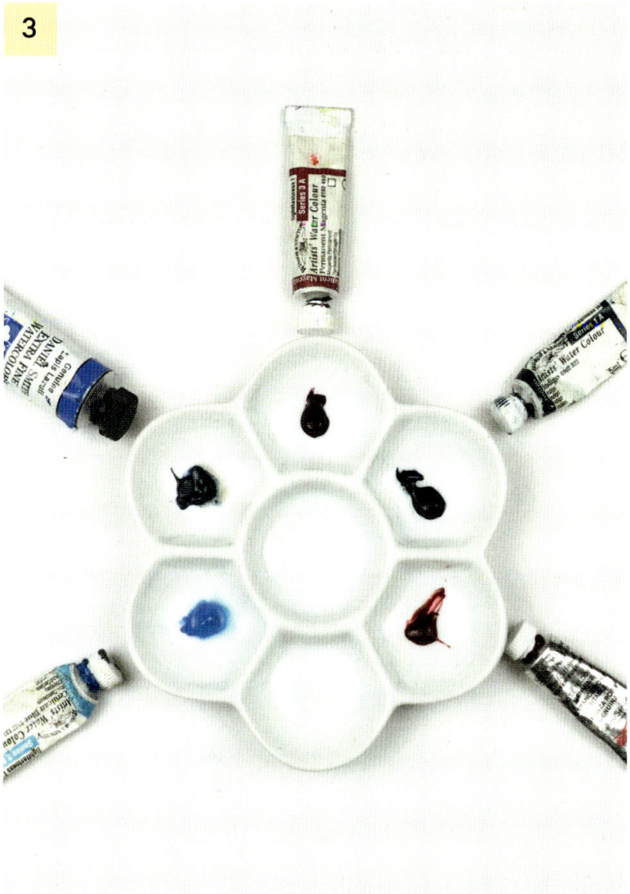

4

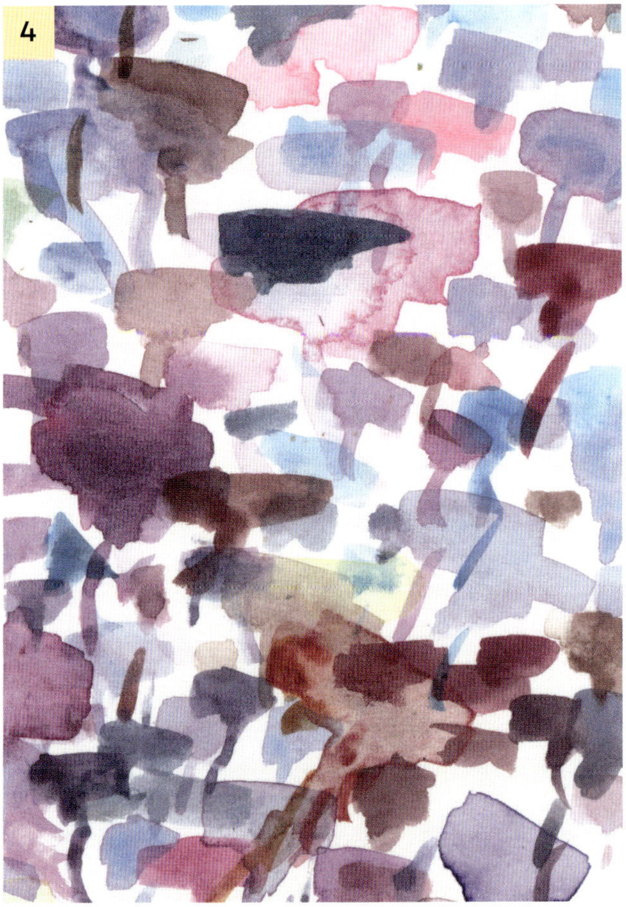

5

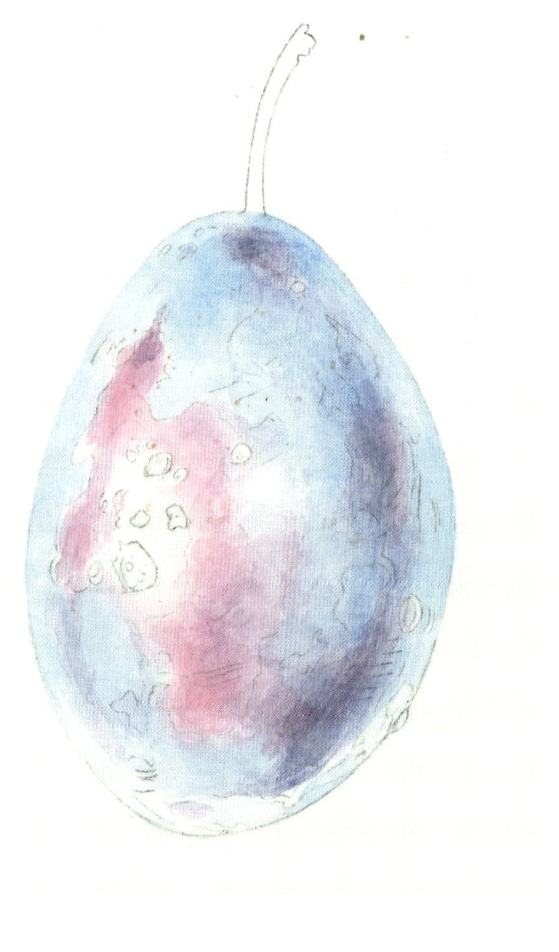

6

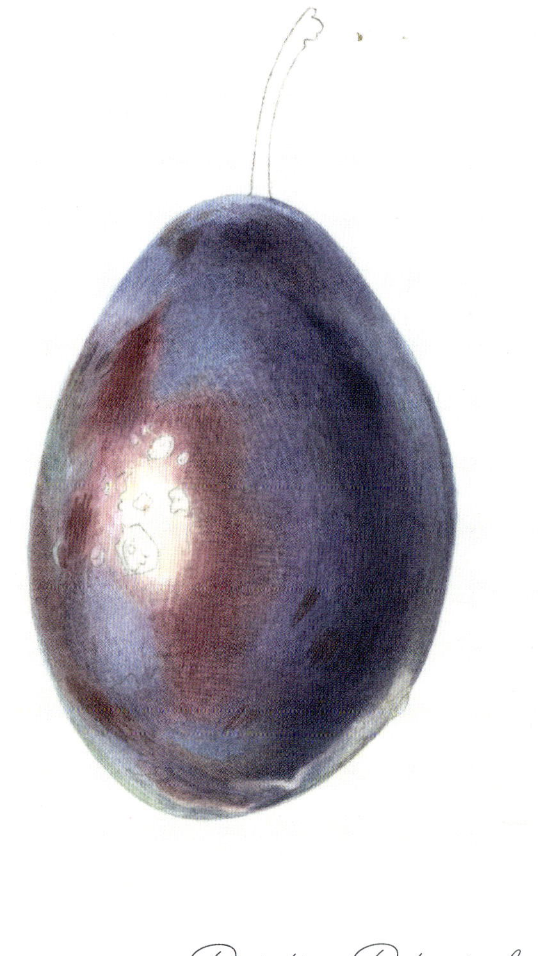

7. Once the values are almost to where you want them, you can switch to a smaller No. 2 brush. A good quality brush will have a very sharp point. Use the point at a more vertical angle to drybrush and fill in and even the gradations. Remember, this can take a long time. Begin to indicate the shadows that the drops create. Feel free to make adjustments to your colors as you go. For example, you may now see a yellow cast at edges of the plum, which was not something you noticed when choosing the paints on your palette. Imperfections and a mottling of the surface is also added at this stage. Draw small lines with the tip of the brush to create these shadowed areas. At this point, you haven't taken any paint away, you've only added it. Don't use any white paint; let the white of the paper show through instead.

8. Each of the water drops you paint will be of differing shapes and sizes. The highlights should be accurate to the curving round shape of the surface the drops are on. The drops at the sides of the plum have a light blue tone, while the drops where the plum's highlight is will have whiter highlights. These highlights will be more elongated at the sides and rounder at the front. Some drops will have more detail than others. A more detailed drop may have a dark shadow, whiter highlight, and mid tones. Others might have a dark shadow and a highlight that isn't very white. It all depends on how light falls over the surface of your subject and the water drops. Since the highlights were created by letting the white of the paper show through and not with white paint, if paint *does* flow into the highlight, you can use a clean, damp, small, and sharp brush to scrub out the small area. Then, quickly blot with a paper towel. This can be repeated until the highlight is light enough. As previously noted, photos will be immensely helpful as reference when painting water drops. It may seem crazy to go into such detail about painting tiny drops of water, but they can lend realism and that special something to your subject!

9. Paint the stem of the plum using Naples Yellow, Sap Green, Indian Red, and Sepia.

10. This plum has a lot going on for its small size. Reflected light on the right side, a dark gradated shadow, changing colors showing bloom, and water drops all add to the realism. The challenge is having everything come together in a balanced and cohesive way.

7

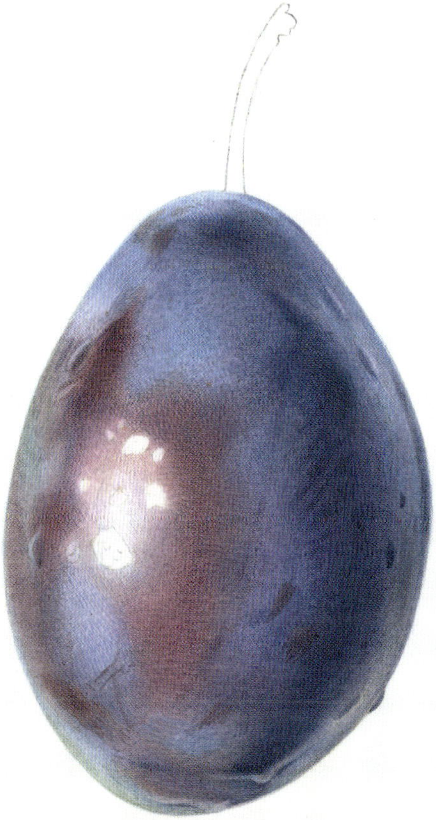

8

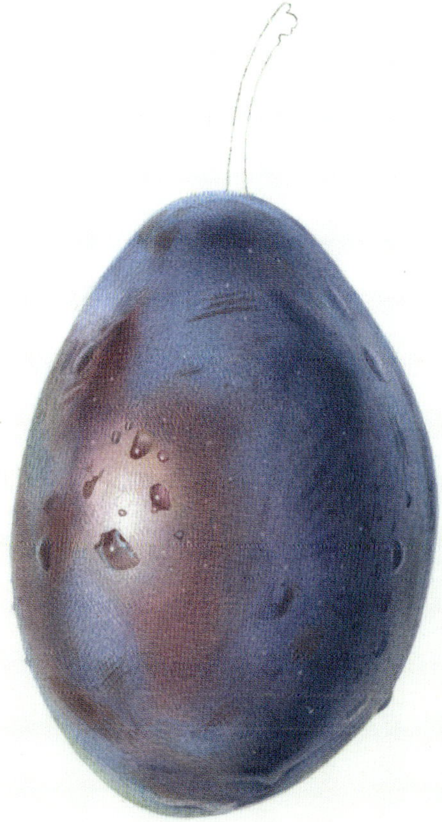

9

10

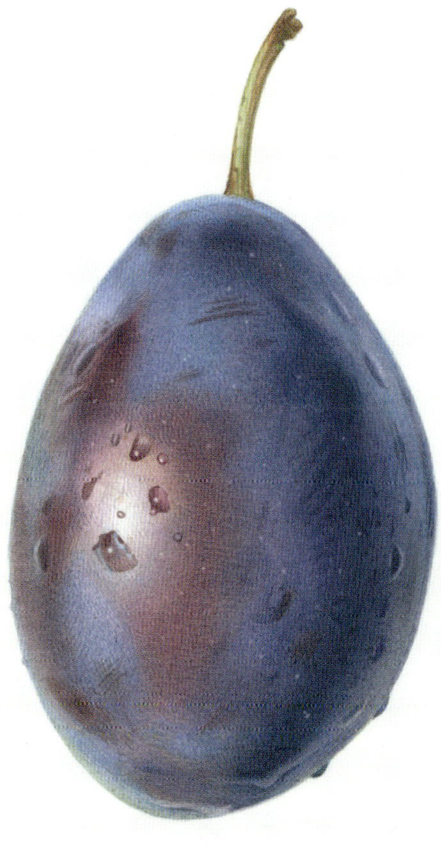

PAINTING STEMS AND BRANCHES

Stems and branches might easily be overlooked but once again they should always represent the subject accurately. Stems might be ribbed or hairy and branches gnarly or smooth.

Mixed Media Branch

Some subjects lend themselves to using more than one medium in a single piece of art. Often, graphite and watercolor are combined so that the subject is drawn with graphite, then an interesting or colorful element is highlighted in color with watercolor. Other times, a subject is painted with watercolor and elements of the composition that are in the background are drawn with graphite so that they appear to fade into the background. This creates an atmospheric perspective and gives depth to the piece. This branch has very little color except for the pale green lichen, so graphite is used for the woody branch and pale green watercolor for the lichen.

In this exercise, draw directly on the hot-pressed drawing paper without a preliminary sketch. This will give a spontaneous and irregular feel to the drawing much like the subject itself. Wiggly lines and an unsteady hand will work to your advantage with this imprecise subject.

The completed drawing will have detail, form, and a touch of color for interest.

Supplies

- HB, No. F, and 2H pencils
- Dividers or clear ruler
- Hot-pressed drawing paper
- Kneaded eraser
- No. 00 and No. 1 sable watercolor brushes
- Paper towel
- Scrap paper
- Paint palette
- Watercolor paints

1. To begin, determine the thickness and length of the branch. Note any predominant details like peeling bark or irregular edges.

2. Add texture and shadows from left to right. By working this way, you can note how the branch changes as you move along. Indicate where the darkest areas are and where there are little holes and irregularities.

3. Once the graphite areas are completed, create pale green lines to mimic the way the lichen grows. The fine curving hairs of lichen should look soft.

1

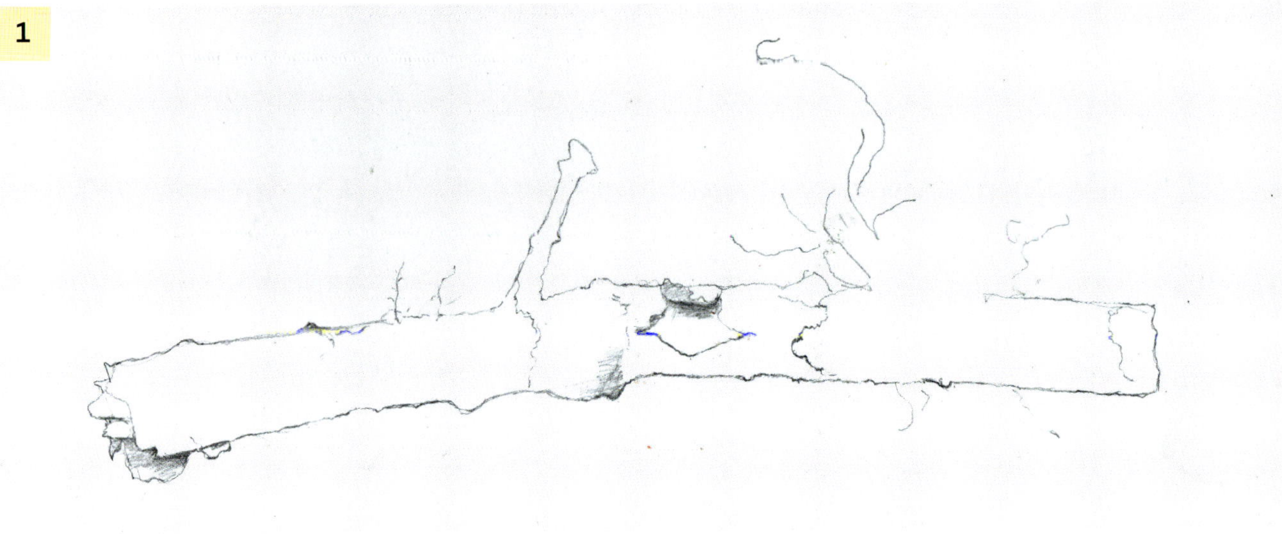

2

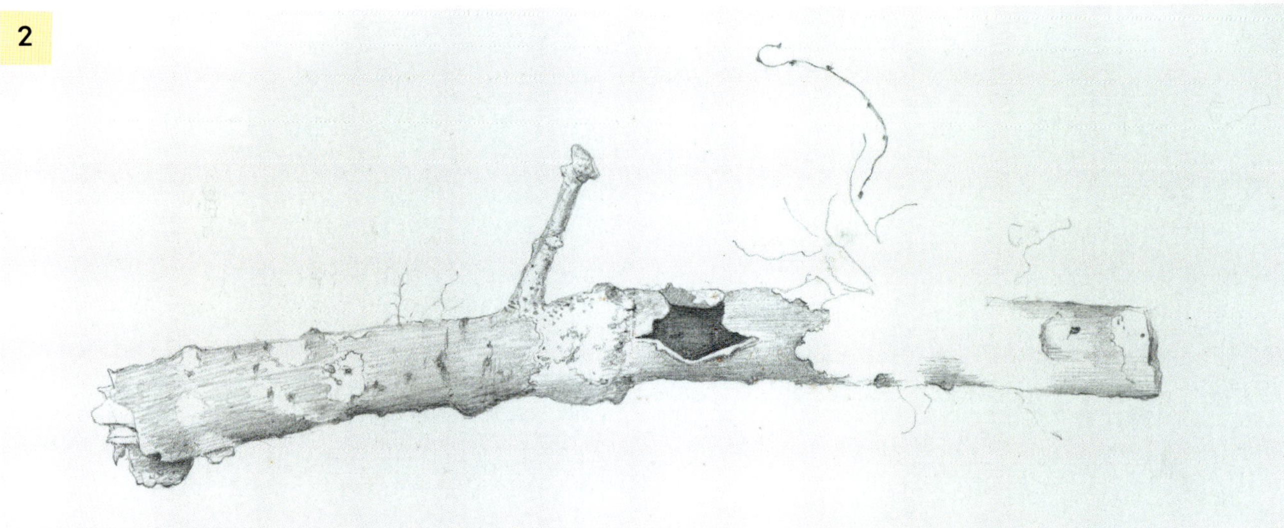

3

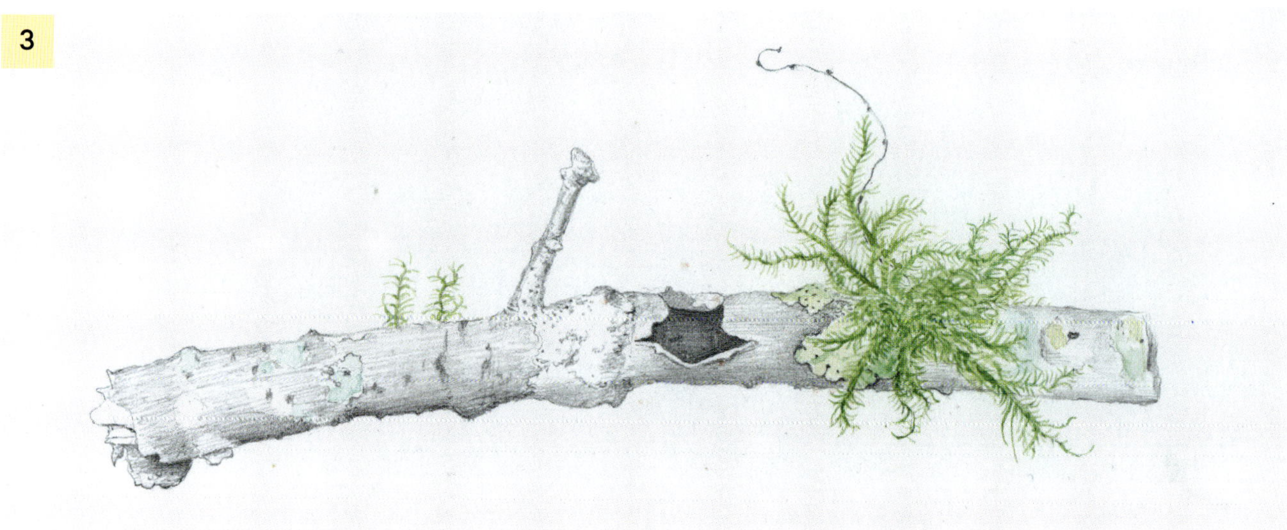

Final Thoughts

Paintings exhibited in major botanical exhibits are completed to the utmost exacting standards. Many aspects of the painting are considered, including scientific accuracy, composition, color, form, and detail. Works at this level take countless hours to complete and many hours of practice invested before that. If you ever have the chance to see one of these exhibits, please do! You'll be amazed by these artists from all over the world, all sharing the same love of painting botanicals.

Most artists, however, once they learn the basics, are also able to enjoy this relaxing and meditative practice of botanical painting. After reading through this book and completing the exercises, you'll have learned valuable tips and tricks while considering the composition, accuracy, and detail that will make your botanical artwork a success. With further practice, you'll find your work will become even more refined. Thank you for following along on this journey with me. I wish you a fulfilling practice of creating your own beautiful botanical works of art.

"Watercolor Anemones"
Ranunculaceae
watercolor on paper
9" x 12.5" (22.9 cm x 31.8 cm)

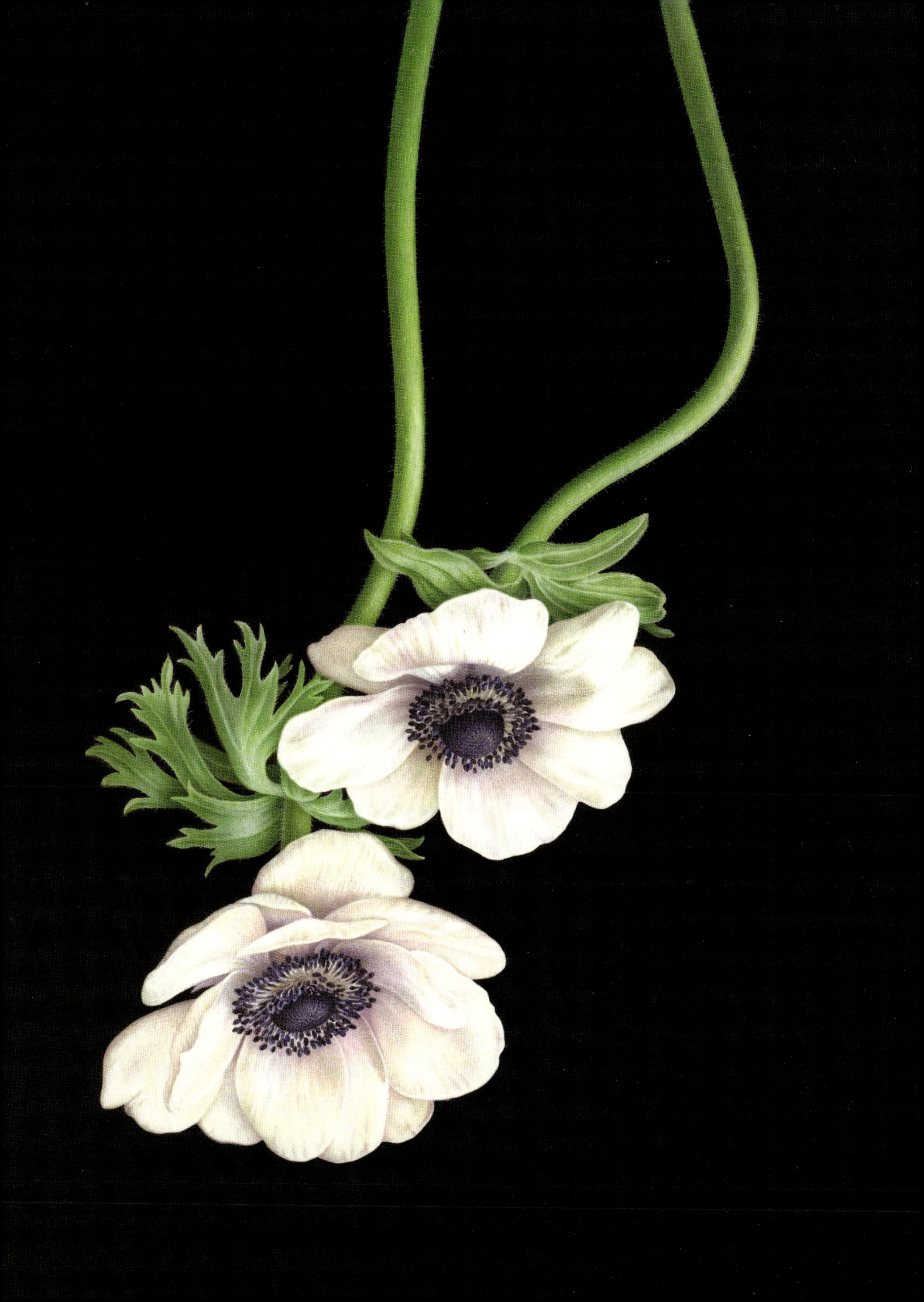

“Jim’s Peony”
watercolor on vellum
10” x 13” (25.4 cm x 30 cm)

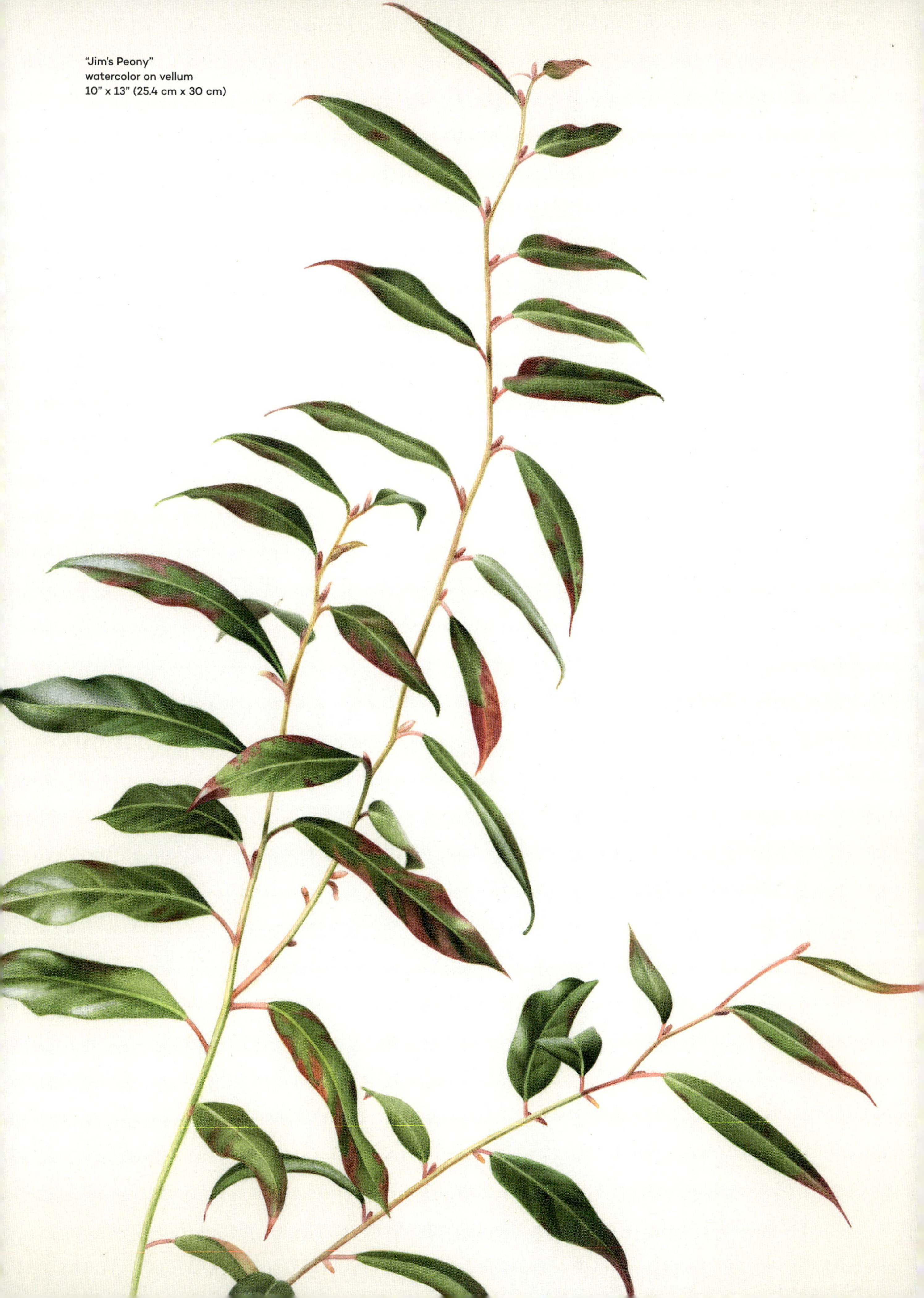

Resources

The materials and supplies I like to use, and have shown in this book, can be found at your local art or craft store as well as online.

Organizations and websites

American Society of Botanical Artists www.asba-art.org
Society of Botanical Artists www.soc-botanical-artists.org
Hunt Institute for Botanical Documentation www.huntbotanical.org
Guild of Natural Science Illustrators www.gnsi.org
Botanical Artist.com www.botanicalartists.com
Also see your local botanical Gardens website

Facebook groups

Botanical Art for Beginners
Botanical Artists
The Society of Botanical Artists (SBA)
American Society of Botanical Artists (ASBA)

Books

The Art of Botanical Painting by Margaret Stevens—in association with the Society of Botanical Artists, published by UK Collins

Botanical Sketchbook by Mary Ann Scott with Margaret Stevens, published by Smithsonian

Botanical Painting with Coloured Pencils by Ann Swan, published by UK Collins

The Joy of Botanical Drawing: A Step by Step Guide to Drawing and Painting Flowers, Leaves, Fruit and More by Wendy Hollander, published by Watson-Guptill

Rosie Sanders Flowers: A Celebration of Botanical Art by Rosie Sanders, published by Batsford

Billie Showell's Botanical Painting in Watercolor by Billie Showell, published by Search Press

Botanical Artistry Plants, projects & process by Julia Trickey, published by Two Rivers Press

The Modern Flower Painter: Creating Vibrant Botanical Portraits in Watercolor by Anna Mason, published by Search Press

Acknowledgments

I would like to acknowledge my wonderful art teachers. The beloved Mr. Travis who let students run wild in the art room, the enthusiastic booming voice of Bob Munford, and Marvin Mattelson who helped me to refine what the others started and coached me as an illustrator.

About the Author

Karen Kluglein began her career as an illustrator after graduating from the School of Visual Arts in 1980, with Dannon, Ragu, Pillsbury, Nabisco, *The Atlantic Monthly*, IBM, and Calvin Klein among her varied list of clients. After attending an American Society of Botanical Artists exhibit in the 1990s, Karen knew that her experience painting detailed food illustrations (such as berries and herbs) and her style were a great fit for the genre. In addition to teaching in-person workshops at the New York Botanical Garden and on eastern Long Island, and selling original art, prints, and instructional downloads and DVDs on her website, Karen also licenses her work, which can be seen on Celestial Seasonings packaging and on paper goods by Caspari Inc. Karen has won Best in Show and Best Painting in Show at the International Exhibition, and the Dianne Bouchier Award For Excellence in Botanical Art in 2010. She lives on Long Island, in East Hampton, New York. To see more of her work, visit botanical-paintings.com.

Index

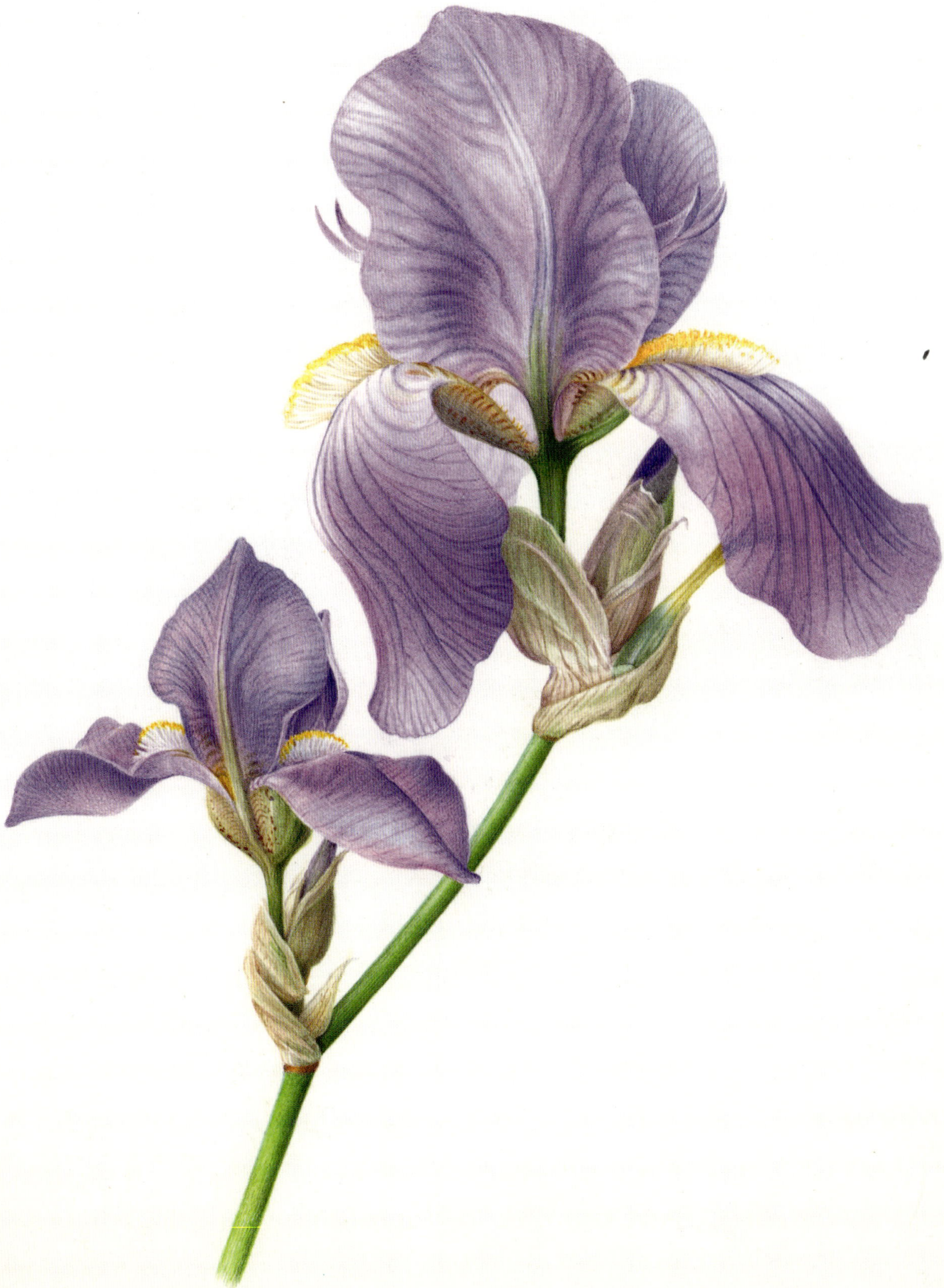

"Spring Iris" *Iris sibirica*
watercolor on paper
9" x 11" (22.9 cm x 27.9 cm)